Goethe's Lyric Cycles

UNIVERSITY OF NORTH CAROLINA
STUDIES IN THE GERMANIC LANGUAGES
AND LITERATURES

Initiated by RICHARD JENTE (1949–1952), established by F. E. COENEN (1952–1968)

SIEGFRIED MEWS, Editor

Publication Committee: Department of Gemanic Languages

For other volumes in the "Studies" see pages 190–191.

Send orders to: (U.S. and Canada)
The University of North Carolina Press, P. O. Box 2288
Chapel Hill, N.C. 27514
(All other countries) Feffer and Simons, Inc., 31 Union Square, New York, N.Y. 10003

NUMBER NINETY-THREE

UNIVERSITY
OF NORTH CAROLINA
STUDIES IN
THE GERMANIC LANGUAGES
AND LITERATURES

Studies in
Goethe's Lyric Cycles

by

MEREDITH LEE

CHAPEL HILL
THE UNIVERSITY OF NORTH CAROLINA PRESS
1978

PD
25
.N6
No. 93

© *University of North Carolina*
Studies in the Germanic Languages
and Literatures 1978

Library of Congress Cataloging in Publication

Lee, Meredith, 1945–
  Studies in Goethes's lyric cycles.

  (University of North Carolina studies in the Germanic
languages and literatures; no. 93 ISSN 0081–8593)
  Originally presented as the author's thesis, Yale.
  Bibliography: p. 171
   Includes index.
  1. Goethe, Johann Wolfgang von, 1749–1832–
Criticism and interpretation. I. Title. II. Series: North
Carolina. University. Studies in the Germanic
languages and literatures; no. 93.
PT1904.L4   1978   831'.6   78–57492
ISBN 0–8078–8093–0

  Manufactured in the U.S.A.

Contents

Acknowledgments

I would like to express my appreciation to Heinrich Henel, who supervised the preparation of this study as a dissertation for the Yale Graduate School. In his careful reading of my work he has combined critical judgment with insight and has been a constant source of inspiration. Professor Henel has learned much in his lifetime and shared freely with his students.

I would also like to thank Jeffrey Sammons, who encouraged and advised me in placing the manuscript with a publisher, and my colleagues Ruth Angress, Anton Kaes, Herbert Lehnert, and Thomas Saine, who read the manuscript in part or full and responded with helpful criticism.

To my typist Lisa Frieze and Laura Greulich, who prepared the index, my thanks for their patience and careful work.

Institutions as well as individuals deserve acknowledgment. The Fulbright Commission provided a year's grant to research this material in Göttingen 1972–73. I'm grateful to the University of California, Irvine, School of Humanities, for a generous grant towards the publication of this book.

M. LEE

Abbreviations

The following abbreviations are used in the text and the notes:

WA *Goethes Werke*. Herausgegeben im Auftrage der Großherzogin Sophie von Sachsen, Abt. I–IV (Weimar: Hermann Böhlaus Nachfolger, 1887–1919).

HA *Goethes Werke*. Hamburger Ausgabe in 14 Bänden (Hamburg: Christian Wegner Verlag, 1948 ff.).

Eckermann Johann Peter Eckermann, *Gespräche mit Goethe in den letzten Jahren seines Lebens*, ed. Heinrich Hubert Houben (Wiesbaden: F. A. Brockhaus, 1959).

Hecker *Goethe, Maximen und Reflexionen*, ed. Max Hecker, Schriften der Goethe-Gesellschaft, 21 (Weimar: Verlag der Goethe-Gesellschaft, 1907).

Zelter *Der Briefwechsel zwischen Goethe und Zelter*, 4 vols., ed. Max Hecker, (1913–1918; rpt. Bern: Herbert Lang, 1970).

I

Introduction

These studies in Goethe's lyric cycles are an inquiry into a selection of Goethe's poetry that represents forty years of his writing. The selection is based on a common structural characteristic—cyclical arrangement—and suggests that poems grouped as cycles constitute a unique literary form. As individual poems they are a diverse sampling of Goethe's middle and late lyric. Simple four-line stanzas as well as sonnets and elegies are represented. No single form dominates. Despite this diversity, however, the poems are in one essential aspect alike and distinguish themselves from all other poems that Goethe wrote. They have a dual character. They are most certainly individual poems, but simultaneously, each is also an integral part of a larger lyric composition.

At the time Goethe wrote the *Römische Elegien*, his first lyric cycle, and indeed throughout the eighteenth century, lyric poems were written and understood almost exclusively as single works. Critical discussions of the classical lyricists—Horace, Catullus, Ovid, Pindar—were focused entirely on individual odes, hymns, songs, without any apparent interest in the relationship of the collected poems to one another. Aesthetic treatises made no mention of complex lyric arrangements. Indeed, as a literary concept the word "cycle" was almost nonexistent; it first emerged in the early decades of the nineteenth century.

To speak, then, of Goethe's lyric cycles is to focus the discussion on a principle of lyric composition that is emerging at the turn of the nineteenth century,[1] that is as yet unnamed and relatively unnoticed in the critical discussions of the day, and that will not reach its zenith in popularity and critical acclaim until about a century later in the works of George, Rilke, and their contemporaries. It is also to speak of a poetic structural device that allows no rigorous definition, for the lyric cycle has never become a genre in its own right nor has it been confined to any single organizational model.

As lyric cycles, Goethe's poems are rooted in no single literary tradition. Their ancestry is diverse. To assume otherwise, that is, to assume a direct continuity between Goethe's cycles is both to misrepresent the works and to simplify the process by which the cycle emerges in these years as a conscious literary form. Goethe's earliest cycles were not conceived *primarily* as cycles. Rather, it is in his varied responses to a number of older traditions—to the Augustan love elegy, the Petrarchan sonnet, and the classic lyric poetry of Persia—that they have their beginnings. As Goethe experimented within these poetic traditions and adapted their varying forms to his writing, he created out of each a lyric cycle.

Goethe's lyric cycles are structurally diverse. To some extent this diversity reflects the assorted lyric traditions in which they have their origins. The cycles, however, are not bounded by these traditions. Instead, the lack of structural continuity indicates how little the lyric cycle, especially at the turn of the nineteenth century, can be regarded as a standard literary convention. Goethe himself never identifies these particular poems as lyric cycles. Nor does he even suggest that these groups are in some crucial way alike and open to comparison with one another.

There are, however, two factors which link these poems to one another and which can be said to justify this study. The first is historical. The term "lyric cycle" has in the years after Goethe's writing entered our critical vocabulary and secured a position among standard poetic terminology. Although its definition is often admittedly vague and its usage inconsistent, a degree of consensus has emerged about those texts to which the term is justly applied. Among these texts are a number of Goethe's poems. Second, although Goethe never explicitly identifies these poems with one another, they do distinguish themselves from all the other lyric poetry that he wrote by their organization into larger lyric groups. For Goethe this marks an expansion of his lyric forms beyond the boundaries and structural limitations of the single poem. These new lyric compositions do not, however, dissolve these boundaries. The poems do not simply by their presence in these lyric cycles cease to exist as poems, reduced as it were to the status of stanzas in a single large work. On the other hand, they no longer enjoy the complete autonomy of non-cyclical poems. They are a new mode of poetic organization and as such distinctive among Goethe's poetry.

This study has as its purpose the concrete illustration of what is meant by this "new mode of poetic organization," the lyric cycle. At the same time the history of the cycle will be reconsidered, a history whose accuracy depends on a clear understanding of the genesis and specific composition of each individual cyclical group. At the core of these studies are questions of a formal nature: the structure of the individual cycle, the peculiar relationship of the poems that comprise it to one another and to the whole, the particular interpretive problems presented to the reader. The reception of these cycles by Goethe's contemporaries, insofar as their formal organization drew any comment at all, and their relationship to other poetry being written during the same period will also be considered. Finally, the significance of Goethe's poems for the emergence of the lyric cycles as a recognized structural device in lyric poetry will be discussed in the concluding chapter.

It should be stated from the beginning that my intention is not to establish Goethe's poetry as the fountainhead of the numerous lyric cycles that followed in the nineteenth and twentieth centuries, nor to claim that his cycles stand as the aesthetic if not the chronological apex of this development. The intention is to clarify, through a critical analysis of these works, what forms and structures we are referring to when we talk about Goethe's lyric cycles. In this way a history of the lyric cycle can be suggested that avoids the simplification of previous studies, which have been too eager to trace the development of this poetic device with broad continuities and have failed to see the specific and curious aspects in the emergence of this mode of poetic organization at the turn of the nineteenth century.

The texts considered are the *Römische Elegien*, the *Sonette*, the *Chinesisch-deutsche Jahres- und Tageszeiten*, and a number of trilogies and smaller cycles, including the "Müllerin" ballads, the "Paria" trilogy, "Trilogie der Leidenschaft," the poems written in response to Howards "Wolkenlehre," *Wilhelm Tischbeins Idyllen*, and *Zu meinen Handzeichnungen*. Cyclical works that are not lyric poetry (such as *Vier Jahreszeiten* and *Venetianische Epigramme*)[2] as well as several general lyric collections, have been excluded. I do not intend the chosen texts as a canon, although I would assert that they are a strong sampling of those works by Goethe which have been appropriately and beneficially designated lyric cycles. I would also like to stress the word "studies" in the title of this work. No claim is made that the treatment of these works is in any sense exhaustive. Rather, the focus will be on specific critical issues that distinguish the cyclical poetry from Goethe's other non-cyclical lyric and mark the emergence of this structural device in Goethe's writing and in the works of his contemporaries.

Most apparent in its absence is the *West-östlicher Divan*. Two considerations led to its omission. The first is the size and complexity of the work. The *Divan* requires a separate study. The wealth of material it offers and the detailed study it demands are overwhelming and not manageable within the framework of the work I envisage. The second consideration was equally compelling. In the past two decades the *Divan* has attracted more critical attention than any other of Goethe's lyric poetry. While the *Divan* has long been a favorite for biographical probes, its recent critics have refocused the discussion and have dealt with the text almost exclusively as a lyric cycle. Many ideas for the present study sprang from these discussions—or rather, from a growing uneasiness about, and at times direct opposition to, some of their underlying assumptions. I found particularly limiting the tendency of certain critics to analyze the structure of cycles, in this case the *Divan*, almost exclusively in metaphors of organic growth. Thus, Carl Becker,[3] in one of the first articles to study the *Divan* specifically as a cycle, speaks of "Buch Suleika" as a "gewachsene," "organische," "lebendige" entity. Hans-Egon Hass[4] describes the *West-östlicher Divan* as "ein geistiges System höherer Art" with its unique "Lebensorganization" and "Organismusanalogen Bezugssystem."

The results of this approach to cyclic organization are twofold. First, it attributes an inferiority to lyric cycles that are not organized in a manner easily characterized by organic metaphor. Hass, for example, depreciates the artistic merit of both the *Römische Elegien* and the *Sonette* because they lack the *Divan*'s "Lebenssystem."[5] Second, it limits the formal analysis of cyclical structures to a single conceptual model that unnecessarily prejudices the inquiry. It posits an ideal relationship among the poems (i.e., organic wholeness) and then argues that the poems in the cycle display a coherence that achieves this ideal. Thus, the structural analysis becomes a search for a specific kind of unity instead of an investigation of the complex and highly diverse possibilities of cyclical organization. Recent studies of the *Divan* have raised similar objections to these analyses of cyclical structure and have advanced alternative approaches to the formal organization of the poems. The two most important of these are Friedrich Burkhardt's dissertation, "Über die Anordnung der Gedichte in Goethes West-östlichem Divan" (Mainz, 1965) and Edith Ihekweazu's *Goethes West-östlicher Divan. Untersuchungen zur Struktur des lyrischen Zyklus* (Hamburg, 1971).

There is no explicit study of Goethe's lyric cycles. They have been discussed in Helen Mustard's history of the cycle in German literature[6] and in Elisabeth Reitmeyer's *Studien zum Problem der Gedichtsammlung*.[7] Both are inadequate. Mustard devotes less than twenty pages to Goethe's poems in her survey and omits half of his cycles without explanation. The book is primarily a descriptive catalog and offers scattered observations on the structure of the works. Goethe's cycles do not mesh neatly with the conceptual framework of the study nor with its organization, which is primarily chronological. Consequently, the analysis is superficial if not misleading. As a history of the lyric cycle Mustard's book relies too heavily on broad generalizations and suggests a continuity among Goethe's cycles that is nonexistent. Reitmeyer is interested in the formal organization of the editions of poetry prepared by Goethe for publication. She subordinates her discussion of the lyric cycle to Fritz Strich's contrasting definitions of classical and romantic form and is as a consequence obscurely distant from the texts.[8]

Goethe's lyric cycles, in their diversity and poetic excellence, allow a unique introduction to the lyric cycle as a mode of poetic organization that acquired both name and new significance at the turn of the nineteenth century. In this study I share my skepticism about fixed notions of the cycle and its structure, my curiosity about the specific genesis and composition of each of Goethe's cyclical groups, and my appreciation for the varied designs he employed and the poems that he joined together in his lyric cycles.

II

The *Römische Elegien*

Goethe never called his *Römische Elegien* a cycle. In his correspondence during the months he worked on these poems they are referred to most often as "die Erotica,"[1] but on two occasions also as "Späße": "Späße im Antikern Styl" (WA IV, 9, 111), "Fragmenten Art erotischer Späße" (WA IV, 9, 147). The completed collection is called "ein Büchlein"[2] in letters to Karl August, Knebel, and Göschen, the poems themselves simply "meine Elegien."[3]

The absence of the direct designation "Zyklus" for these poems is not surprising. At the time Goethe finished the *Römische Elegien*, and five years later as he corresponded with Schiller about their publication in the *Horen*, "Zyklus" was a fairly new Graeco-Latin loan word in the German language with no specific application to lyric poetry.[4] After 1800, and until his death in 1832, in the years when "Zyklus" acquired a more active literary meaning, Goethe rarely discussed these poems. They belonged to a closed chapter of his personal life, a completed phase in his poetic development, and quietly assumed their assigned place in his collected works between the *Balladen* and the longer elegies of the middle Weimar years.

At least since 1846, however, discussions of the *Römische Elegien* have not hesitated to call these poems a cycle.[5] Since Gundolf[6] no commentary to Goethe's lyrics fails to join the *Römische Elegien*, *Sonette*, and *West-östlicher Divan* under the rubric of the lyric cycle and to herald in the *Elegien* the advent of this new lyric mode in Goethe's writing. The result is a suggestion of kinship among these poetic groups that is more apparent than real and an obscuring of the real origin of the poems in question. The *Römische Elegien* did not begin as a cycle; they began as *erotica*.

On 31 October 1788 Goethe ended a letter to Fritz Jacobi with: "Hier ein Erotikon" (WA IV, 9, 46). On 16 November 1788 he closed a greeting to Karl August with the same words (WA IV, 9, 57). These are the first references in his correspondence to a new poetic occupation, a new "genre" (WA IV, 9, 111) as he later called these poems in elegiac distichs, whose writing was to extend through the rigorous months in which *Torquato Tasso* was being completed and on into the second trip to Italy and Goethe's arrival in Venice. There, eighteen months after having sent his first *eroticon* ("Süße Sorgen")[7] to Karl August, he wrote once more to his prince: "Ich fürchte meine Elegien haben ihre höchste Summe erreicht und das Büchlein möchte geschlossen seyn" (WA IV, 9, 186). On the same day he reported to Herder: "Meine Elegien sind wohl zu Ende; es ist gleichsam keine Spur dieser Ader mehr in mir." And to both letters he added the almost identical statement: "Dagegen bring' ich Euch ein Buch Epigrammen mit" (WA IV, 9, 198).

"Erotica," "Späße," "Elegien," "Epigramme"—these names are not without significance for an understanding of the origin of the *Römische Elegien*. "Erotica" is by far the most frequent of these and the most unusual. "Süße Sorgen" is an *eroticon*; an elegy by Propertius that Knebel had just translated is an *eroticon*; and, finally, all the unnamed distich poems that Goethe was writing are *erotica*. After 3 April 1790, when Goethe made a clear distinction between the two new books he intended to bring fromVenice, one of elegies and one of epigrams, the designation *erotica* was abandoned. The title of the collected poems was changed from "Erotica Romana"to "Elegien, Rom 1788." What are the *erotica*? They are for Goethe a genre, a specific mode of poetry. Formally, they are a resumption of his experiments with the hexameter and pentameter lines, a return to the distichs first cultivated from 1781 to 1784 in Weimar. In content they are a blend of motifs, some gleaned from the intensified classical studies that followed Goethe's return from Rome, others highly personal. The erotic content is stylized, and a literary distance is achieved through classical forms carefully chosen and maintained. The numerous *erotica* do not appear to be the product of any preconceived and deliberately executed poetic scheme. Quite to the contrary, they would seem to belong to the poetry that Goethe was able to write rather spontaneously and effortlessly. In almost all of his references to these poems as he is writing them, there is an air of relaxation and ease about their composition— not only in his naming them "Späße" (using the word in the sense of its Italian equivalent with overtones of light amusement) but also in the deliberate playful puzzling with Karl August about their content and the undisguised well-being and pleasurable sensuality he associated with them.[8] In clearest contrast is the labored attention required by *Tasso* in these months. "Tasso wächst wie ein Orangebaum sehr langsam" he wrote in February, 1789 (WA IV, 9, 86), and several months later asserted: "An Tasso muß ich nun es koste was es wolle" (WA IV, 9, 111). How different in tone is the offhanded closing remark in this same letter: "Indessen ist ein Nagelneues Erotikon angelangt." In the "Jahresplan" for 1789–90 *Tasso* took top position on the list; the *erotica* were much less urgent (WA III, 2, 323). Finally, on 2

August 1789, *Tasso* was completed, and on 10 August Goethe wrote
to Herder: "Nun sind wir frey von aller Leidenschafft solch eine
konsequente Composition zu unternehmen. Die Fragmenten Art erotischer Späße behagt mir besser. Es sind wieder einige gearbeitet
worden" (WA IV, 9, 147).

This is one of the very few direct statements from Goethe regarding
the actual composition of the *Römische Elegien*. He considers them, at
least in contrast to the rigorous demands of his final revisions of the
Tasso manuscript, to be a far less exacting task. The extreme caution
and control, the intensively honed lines necessary to sustain the
tightly structured drama are not demanded by the elegies.

Goethe's comment suggests that, at this stage in his writing of the
poems, he saw no need to associate them with a principle of "konsequente Composition." Rather, they are for him lyric bits and pieces
about erotic subjects and done in a playful manner. His use of the
word "Fragment" to describe them need not suggest an incomplete-
ness for the individual elegies, but most certainly it indicates a certain
degree of discontinuity among them.

Unfortunately Goethe said little more about the composition and
organization of these poems in the intervening seven months that
preceded his announcement in April, 1790, that his writing of elegies
had come to an end. On 1 January 1791 he wrote to Knebel, his
closest collaborator in this poetic venture, simply that both the book
of elegies and the book of epigrams, the *Venetianische Epigramme*, had
been "gefaltet und gelegt" (WA IV, 9, 239).

This silence regarding the genesis of the *Römische Elegien*, a genesis
all the more interesting because the completed poems demonstrate a
mode of lyric composition more highly sophisticated and complex
than any of Goethe's previous poetry is regrettable but not atypical.
Even in the years of correspondence with Schiller, Goethe hesitated
to talk much about his poetic writing. At least in part this silence was
rooted in a fear that premature discussion of unfinished poems might
interfere with the creative process—a process which always remained
for him somewhat of a mystery and one to be respected.[9] In the
months that mark the genesis of the *Römische Elegien* this silence was
intensified by the lack of a confidant matching Schiller's critical perception and enthusiasm for theoretical musings.

Knebel would have been the most likely candidate for this role.
Herder and Karl August were absent from the court a good deal
during this time. Wieland was in Weimar, and we know that Goethe
discussed the poems on more than one occasion with him. Frau von
Stein maintained a distance from Goethe and did not allow their
former relationship to resume, despite his repeated begging. With

Knebel, more than any other, Goethe actively shared his poetic schemes. Their correspondence reveals an intense occupation at this time with problems of metric form. They offered one another mutual encouragement in their experiments with classical metrics. They met frequently, exchanging visits in Jena and Weimar. What is lacking in the letter between Knebel and Goethe, however, as in all the other correspondence of these months, is any direct documentation of the process by which the *erotica* were conceived and written, and later developed into the "Büchlein" that Goethe announced in April of 1790.

The scattered references that Goethe makes to the *erotica* in his correspondence, even after they have been gleaned for every possible detail, are too sparse to support an argument on the composition of the elegies. Only a few of the poems in the cycle can be dated,[10] too few even to speculate on their order of composition, except to assert, not surprisingly, that they were not written in the same order in which they now appear. It goes without saying that questions of aesthetic relevance about the development of specific motifs and metaphors, the preparation of the first and last poems in the collection, the trimming of material which ultimately proved extraneous to the cycle are almost totally beyond documentation. To what extent the cycle became in the course of its composition a self-generating process, at what stage some overriding conceptual framework for the organization of the poems emerged, if indeed such a conscious framework had a significant role in the genesis of individual poems, cannot be known.

That so much concerning the composition of the *Römische Elegien* must be relegated to the realm of speculation is unfortunate for several reasons, not the least of which is the novelty of the poems. Not only are they Goethe's first lyric cycle, but also, as Goethe perceived them, a new genre in his writing. Furthermore, they are a departure from the contemporary understanding of the Latin love elegy as it was being promoted both directly and indirectly by those scholars, translators, and poets at the end of the eighteenth century who were absorbed in furthering the knowledge of Latin lyric poetry, and specifically, the poems of Tibullus, Catullus, and Propertius.

It is no secret that Goethe's *Römische Elegien* are consciously in the tradition of the Latin love elegy, that the fifth elegy places him deliberately in the company of "Amors Triumvirn." Even if we did not have the supporting knowledge of Knebel's concern with Propertius in these months, and a draft for a summarizing table of his poetic works that Goethe prepared in 1823 for Louis Bonaparte, former King of the Netherlands, in which the poems are described as "*Elegies*

Romaines dans le gout de Properçe,"[11] the literary ancestry of the
Römische Elegien would be unmistakable.

It is too easily forgotten, however, that in 1788 a poet's decision to
write in the tradition of the Latin love elegy, and specifically, as
Goethe claims, in the style and manner of Propertius, did not inevitably mean that he would compose a number of poems to be joined
together into a larger poetic work, the lyric cycle we recognize today
in the *Römische Elegien*. It is obvious only in retrospect, and to a
critical taste accustomed to multi-member poetic groupings, that an
adaptation of Propertius's lyric mode should reflect this aspect of his
craftsmanship. It was not obvious in Goethe's day. It would in fact be
out of character with the lyric taste of the time and the attitude dis-
played towards the classical elegists to expect in a modern re-creation
of Propertius's poetry anything other than single poems.

This assertion deserves elaboration. A closer look at the contemporary appreciation of the classical elegists is necessary to mark Goethe's
poems as the significant departure from convention that they are. In
the eighteenth century the works of Catullus, Tibullus, and Propertius were all accessible in standard editions. Translations were also
beginning to appear. As the writings of these Latin poets found ad-
mirers and imitators among German-speaking writers, in every case
it was the individual poem, the single elegy and ode, that was the
focus of attention.

For example, it was considered entirely appropriate, indeed it was
the norm, for translations of poems to appear individually in the
various literary journals of the day. The translations were undertaken
piecemeal and published singly. Representative is the selection published in the *Berlinische Monatsschrift* of 1788, the year in which Goethe
began the *Römische Elegien*:

April	An den Aristius Fuscus.	Horace I, 22
May	An Phyllis.	Horace IV, 11
June	Daphne.	Ovid Met. I, 5
July	An die Lesbia.	Catullus VII
September	Klagelied an den Vergil.	Horace I, 24
October	Wider einen schmähsüchtigen Richter seiner Schriften.	Martial VI, 64
December	Verwünschung eines Knob- lauchgerichtes.	Horace V, 3

Also published during this year were two small clusters of Martial
epigrams (in the February and March issues) and a selection of four
epigrams from the *Greek Anthology* (in the July issue).

It was not surprising, therefore, that the poets writing at this time
in conscious imitation of these Latin models also chose to restrict

themselves to single and often rather short poems. One need only to think of Klopstock's and Ramler's odes, the wealth of variations of the anacreontic on the theme of Lesbia's sparrow, and the first rather hesitant experiments in German with the classical distich. Indeed, Goethe's "Der Besuch," 1788, his first adaptation of a poem by Propertius (I, 3) should be mentioned. As an integrated series of poems, the *Römische Elegien* are an anomaly among these responses to the poetry of the Roman world.[12]

It is also interesting in this context to note that Knebel, who more than any other person actively shared Goethe's appreciation at this time for the Latin love elegy, apparently saw no need to publish the poems of Propertius in completely intact books. Inspired by Goethe's successfully completed *Römische Elegien*, Knebel polished his selected translations of Propertius and submitted them for publication in Schiller's *Horen* in 1795. Like his contemporaries he was concerned exclusively with the individual poem.

His completed translation of Propertius's poems was published in 1798. Although in its format it retains the four book division of the original, the translations are again but a selection from Propertius's elegies. The elegies he offered were chosen, in his words, for being "die auserlesensten, schwersten und besten,"[13] the "vorzüglichsten"[14] from Propertius's poems. The classical sense of proportion and wholeness that Goethe expresses at this stage in his aesthetic writings is echoed in Knebel's introduction to his translation, where he praises Propertius's poems for "die ausgewählte schöne Form und die richtige Übereinstimmung der Theile zum Ganzen."[15] But Knebel finds this wholeness only in the individual poems, not in their interrelationship or their integration into a lyric whole.

Knebel is not atypical. No critical commentary of the time regarded Propertius's elegies as a lyric cycle, even very loosely conceived. Although the standard editions of the eighteenth century presented the works of the Latin elegists as lyric collections—Propertius's elegies duly divided into four books and each elegy numbered appropriately—critical notes to these editions dealt with each poem independently. Indeed, the commentary proceeded for the most part line by line through the poems, noting textual variants in the manuscripts, clarifying syntactical difficulties, and elaborating on mythological and literary allusions.

Most of the translations retained these scholarly notes, augmenting the philological commentary with interpretive observations. Even in notes written some thirty to forty years after Goethe's *Römische Elegien* no attention is paid to Propertius's elegies as a lyric cycle. It was not until 1838, when the cycle had been established as a literary form

in the German-speaking world, that the discussion of Propertius began to show an interest in his work as a lyric collection. The introduction of Wilhelm Adolf Boguslaw Hertzberg's edition *Sextus Aurelius
Propertius. Elegien im Versmaß der Urschrift* refers to a group of very
early poems which Propertius adapted from Callimachus as a cycle
and claims that fragments of this cycle are to be found in the fourth
book of the elegies.[16] Hertzberg also shows a great deal of interest in
the broader structure of the four books, speculating on chronology,
apparent gaps in the text, and distinctive stylistic traits; and he re-
gards Book I of the elegies as "ein geschlossenes Ganze."[17] Thus the
adaptation of the designation "Zyklus" for Propertius's elegies parallels the acceptance of the term in relation to Goethe's *Römische Elegien*.

Not only was there no talk of cycles in 1788, but also there was a
lack of any extraordinary enthusiasm for Propertius. It is noteworthy
that he is not represented in the 1788 selections in the *Berlinische
Monatsschrift*. Propertius was the last of the Roman elegists to become
available in German translation and to be popularized by conscious
imitation. Because of his abundant and at times obscure mythological
allusions and syntactical complexity he was considered a difficult
author, far less suitable for Latin instruction than his contemporaries.[18] Translations of his works were delayed by these same difficulties. Propertius I, 3, "Die schlafende Cynthia," was the first of his
elegies to appear in German, published in 1710 in Menke-Philander's
"Galante Gedichte."[19] For the most part, however, Propertius was
neglected until the 1770s and the 1780s, the decades that saw an
unprecedented enthusiasm for the lyric poetry of the Greek and Roman world and the possibilities of its assimilation into the German
language. The first translation of his poetry into distichs was not
made until 1783 and then only as a six poem appendix to a translation
of Tibullus.[20] Propertius was not completely translated until 1830.[21]

This is the literary context in which the *Römische Elegien* appeared.
They are unanticipated by the poetry of Goethe's day, and, although
Goethe's reading of the Latin love elegy at this time is well documented,[22] they were unanticipated within his own poetry as well.
Only "Der Besuch" provides an earlier indication of growing interest
in Propertius. This is a minimal claim, however, for little more than a
slight thematic appropriation links this poem to the works of the
Roman elegist. It has limited significance for the writing of the *Römische Elegien*.

While it is not unlikely that the *erotica* were begun with little awareness of the sophisticated lyric composition they were to become, we
must admit, finally, our inability to describe with any greater speci-
ficity the conception and genesis of the cycle. Goethe said little about

the actual transformation of his "Fragmenten Art erotischer Späße" into the twenty-member cycle published in 1795 in Schiller's *Horen*.

But a few words do remain to be said about the writing of the *Römische Elegien* before turning to the poems themselves; for, in 1795, when they appeared in Schiller's *Horen*, they did not appear as the collection of twenty-two poems Goethe originally intended. (It is interesting to note that the first book of Propertius, *Liber I*, like Goethe's "Büchlein," contained twenty-two elegies.) What interfered and altered the composition of the cycle had little to do with improving the poetic quality of the collection. Rather, it was a question of sexual explicitness that was at issue. Two poems, originally numbered 2 and 16 in the cycle of twenty-two elegies, were removed at Schiller's suggestion. When Goethe sent the manuscript for consideration for the *Horen*, Schiller marked passages in a number of poems[23] which he considered to be in questionable taste and which for that reason should be deleted from the cycle. Apparently, Schiller intended that the elegies themselves remain in the collection—only the questionable lines were to be removed.[24] Goethe, however, responded: "Mit den Elegien wird nicht viel zu thun seyn, als daß man die 2te und die 16te wegläßt: denn ihr zerstümmeltes Ansehn wird auffallend seyn, wenn man statt der anstößigen Stellen nicht etwas currenteres hinein restaurirte, wozu ich mich aber ganz und gar ungeschickt fühle" (WA IV, 10, 256). The problem was that the poems were too explicit in their depiction of sexual delight and danger. If the poems were to be accepted by the better circles of German society, indiscreet details, such as the celebration in the loudly creaking bed and the recognition of venereal disease, had to be removed.[25] Apparently, Goethe felt that the cycle could sooner do without the poems than the poems without their offensive lines. He dropped both the second and the sixteenth, and rearranged the order of the first four elegies to amend the loss of narrative continuity.

This was not the first time that the content of the *Elegien* had hindered their publication. Similar considerations had prevented them from being published in 1790. Both Herder and Karl August dissuaded Goethe at that time from releasing the poems (WA IV, 9, 239).[26] There had been enough tension in Weimar already due to Goethe's mésalliance with Christiane Vulpius. There was no need for him to flaunt his new pleasures in such a public way.

Thus appropriately trimmed, the *Elegien* appeared in the sixth issue of Schiller's *Horen* in 1795. This is the text, with only minor variation, that Goethe standardized in subsequent editions of his *Werke*.[27] There exists a *Reinschrift* of the cycle, identified as H[50], that predates the *Horen* publication.[28] In it the second and the sixteenth elegies have already been removed, the opening elegies rearranged, but the original numeration of the poems retained. The second poem (at that time still numbered IV) exists in two versions. A limited number of variants indicate Goethe's polishing of the manuscript.

What does it mean finally to call these poems a cycle? There are twenty *Römische Elegien*. They are all distich poems, but they are not all alike. They are individual in length, structure, tone, and content. In answering this question it will be as important to stress the distinctive variations among the poems as it will be to determine their final coherence. It is, in fact, one of the particular characteristics of the cycle's organization that diversity, thematic range, and contrasts in emotional intensity and setting prevail. This variety is not, however, unbounded. Certain *erotica* that Goethe wrote between 1788 and 1790, most specifically "Süße Sorgen," his first *eroticon*, and two elegies introducing the god Priapus and his message of fertility were not admitted to the collection.[29] The *Römische Elegien* are a conscious selection of poems; they are intended to be a coherent unity.

To speak of the *Römische Elegien* as a cycle, to examine both the structural diversity and the bonds that join together the individual poems is not, as it may seem, a backing away from the critical issues already raised. At the beginning of this chapter it was argued that Goethe's *Elegien* are a departure from the conventional response to the Latin love elegy in the eighteenth century. In order to emphasize the significance of Goethe's innovation in these poems, it was necessary to demonstrate how little they were heir to any established mode of poetic organization. But this point having been made, it remains to clarify what consequence the poetry of the Latin love elegists does hold for the structure of the *Römische Elegien*. It is by no means slight. In form as well as content the *Römische Elegien* are inextricably bound to the literary tradition in which they are rooted. A study of these poems in terms of a cycle entails an investigation of their relationship to the Latin love elegy.

The positivist critics[30] intended a definitive description of this relationship in the catalog of borrowed metaphor and motif, direct translation, and oblique allusion they prepared for the poems. It is doubtful whether a single classical reference remains in the *Römische Elegien* which has not been noted and identified by them. In their eagerness for learned reference they reduced the text of the *Elegien* to a clever pastiche of Greek and Latin sources.

This is not what is meant in this study by the relationship of the *Römische Elegien* to the Latin love elegy. The matter is far more complex. To be sure the poems do visibly employ the formal and stylistic conventions of the Latin love elegy. They are written in distich couplets, ostensibly by a poet-lover in a Roman setting. The language of Propertius and his contemporaries is echoed in the selected motif and metaphor used to characterize the lovers and their affection, in the abundance of apostrophe and rhetorical posing, and in the learned references to the works of Horace and Ovid. But it would be difficult to reconcile the image of the clever and raging Cynthia, who is the object of Propertius's passion and the source of his despair, with the model of constancy and fidelity celebrated in Goethe's *Elegien*. The love the poems celebrate is the antithesis of the torment that the Roman poet's devotion brings to him. His city is rife with social and political obstacles to his pursuit of pleasure. The Rome of the *Römische Elegien* is the protective enclosure within which the love is nourished.

The *Römische Elegien* are far more than a discreet imitation of the Latin love elegy. That the poetry of Propertius, Tibullus, and Catullus is visible within them is intentional. That the poems are completely Goethe's own is essential to their meaning. For it is the bold claim fundamental to these poems that the Latin love elegy is not a literary relic. When, in Elegy V, the poet asserts himself as heir to the night-time favor Amor afforded the Roman Triumvirate in centuries past, he is not only placing himself and his poetry firmly within the tradition of the Latin love elegy, but he is also making of this tradition a modern reality. He is asserting that the Roman world tended by Amor need no longer be regarded as a splendid anachronism. There is a Roman world of the present. It is accessible, it is creative, it is the world of the Latin love elegy, and it is realized within the *Römische Elegien*.

It is for this reason that an understanding of the relationship of the *Römische Elegien* to the Latin love elegy is so fundamental to an interpretation of the cycle. Like so many of the poems that Goethe wrote, the *Römische Elegien* are, finally, poems about poetry itself. They are about themselves as a renewal of the Latin love elegy, clarifying what makes this particular mode of poetry possible, celebrating the promise of its re-creation. The poems are about Rome, the setting of the Roman elegy. They are about the fusion of the lover and the poet that characterizes the genre. Finally, they are about poetic form, the shaping of experience, the interplay of this distinctively Roman life and its art. The renewal of the Latin love elegy is formally and thematically the organizing principle for this cycle of poems; it is both conscious theme and actualized reality. It is not apparent from the beginning of the cycle, however, that this is what the poems will accomplish. How this becomes clear and how they do accomplish this must now occupy our attention.

In the *Maximen und Reflexionen* Goethe wrote of symbolic language: "Die Symbolik verwandelt die Erscheinung in Idee, die Idee in ein

Bild, und so, daß die Idee im Bild immer unendlich wirksam und unerreichbar bleibt und, selbst in allen Sprachen ausgesprochen, doch unaussprechlich bleibe."[31] Goethe's struggle to find adequate representation for a reality that finally defies articulation is the foundation of his poetry. The poem, "die Idee im Bild," is this representation. According to Goethe, the *Idee* is inextricably bound to the physical world, underlying all nature, and yet it is inaccessible in any pure form. In poetic language, in the poetic image itself, it is made visible, "die Idee im Bild." It is the poem that is the clearest possible image of a reality that is both wholly immediate and essentially enigmatic. Consequently, what a poem is about cannot be adequately reproduced in descriptive language. It remains ineffable, "und selbst in allen Sprachen ausgesprochen, doch unaussprechlich."

Many of Goethe's poems, and especially his later works, are implicitly about themselves as poetry, about the poetic process of making visible the *Idee* they incorporate. Consequently, it is his later poetry that is most often linked with Goethe's discussion of symbolic language. It is a mistake to assume, however, that only in Goethe's later poetry are poetic language and its images employed in a symbolic sense. Werner Keller in his book *Goethes dichterische Bildlichkeit* argues persuasively that a symbolic mode informs Goethe's poetic practice throughout his life.[32] Perhaps less thematically focused in his earlier works, certainly unarticulated in any theoretical sense (indeed, Goethe's poetic theory never receives the systematic treatment he affords his biological pursuits, or even the critical attention granted problems relating to epic and drama),[33] symbolic language is nevertheless the essence of Goethe's poetry. It is in the metaphor of the "Schleier" that Keller locates this fundamental poetic function, calling this image of transparent concealment "das Urbild in dem alle Bildlichkeit der Dichtung gründet."[34] Goethe wrote in Paragraph 219 of the *Farbenlehre*: "Man bedenket niemals genug, daß eine Sprache eigentlich nur symbolisch, nur bildlich sei und die Gegenstände niemals unmittelbar, sondern nur im Widerschein ausdrücke."

To illustrate Goethe's concept of the poem as "die Idee im Bild" we will consider "Herbstgefühl," also entitled "Im Herbst 1775," a poem written many years before the *Römische Elegien*:

> Fetter grüne, du Laub,
> Das Rebengeländer,
> Hier mein Fenster herauf.
> Gedrängter quillet,
> Zwillingsbeeren, und reifet

Schneller und glänzend voller.
Euch brütet der Mutter Sonne
Scheideblick, euch umsäuselt
Des holden Himmels
Fruchtende Fülle.
Euch kühlt des Monds
Freundlicher Zauberhauch,
Und euch betauen, ach,
Aus diesen Augen
Der ewig belebenden Liebe
Voll schwellende Tränen.

The poem takes as its theme the all-encompassing process of maturation that characterizes the fall landscape, but it is far from being simply a nature description in sixteen lines. The poet himself is intimately part of what is being presented, and it is his relationship to the world about him and the specific manner of his participation in this fall of ripening fullness that is the poem's subject. To bring this world to fruition is the urgent imperative that begins the poem. This is finally done through the poet himself. A union, realized between him and the autumnal world outside his window, completes the process of maturation. The poem actualizes the union, supported by a careful integration of syntax and imagery, and becomes the realized image, the *Bild*, of the fullness and maturity that is the essence of autumn and of Goethe's particular autumn in the year 1775.

To assert that a similar process of poetic actualization is fundamental to the *Römische Elegien* may seem at first to be a curious claim, for it would be difficult to find a lyric composition in greater contrast to "Herbstgefühl." The poem is brief and its sixteen lines are tightly organized. Parallel syntactical structures complement the progression of imagery and make possible the union between the poet and the autumnal world he addresses. In contrast, the *Elegien* appear ranging and unfocused. There is an absence of the internal conflict that Goethe so often employs to organize his poems, and little tension to move the poems forward towards a resolution. Consequently, the *Römische Elegien* seem in many ways atypical of Goethe's poetry. Nevertheless, fundamental to the *Elegien* is a use of poetic language that is not only familiar to other poems by Goethe, but their essence. As in "Herbstgefühl," there is in the *Römische Elegien* the attempt to make visible the reality of a world that defies direct description. The Rome of the *Römische Elegien* is like the autumnal landscape of "Herbstgefühl." It is the meaning of the poet's participation in this Roman setting that is finally the meaning of the poems themselves.

The crucial difference is one of intention. We must turn at this point once more to the relationship of the *Römische Elegien* to the Latin love elegy, for in a very real sense, it is Goethe's desire to deal in the *Römische Elegien* with this established poetic tradition that distinguishes them so completely from "Herbstgefühl" and the numerous lyric poems that appear to be more typical of Goethe's lyric mode.

Let us take Rome as our starting point. It is the setting of the elegies, the locus of the poems' meaning, and, although urban in its definition, it is, like the autumnal setting of "Herbstgefühl," a landscape whose full meaning must be realized in the course of the poems. But there is a difference. Unlike the natural setting evoked in "Herbstgefühl," a world of growth and maturation, a world not yet complete, but to be completed within the poem, the Rome of the *Römische Elegien* is a world already come of age, a place of established physical definition and clarified perimeters. The poet cannot creatively participate in this urban landscape in the same manner as the poet of "Herbstgefühl." Although in a window-framed world apart from the ripening fruit he addressed, he brought together within himself the processes of growth that simultaneously matured the fruit and organized the poem, and in doing so, united himself with the earth he helped bring to fruition.

The poet of the *Römische Elegien*, in contrast, cannot stand apart and call the city to fulfillment within himself. Rather he must present himself to the city. He arrives at its gates, enters its walls and calls to its stones, palaces, and streets to accept him, to respond to his pleas for admittance. The Rome of the *Römische Elegien* is anterior to the poet. He must come to it, submit himself to its foreordained pattern, and only then discover the secret of its existence and participate in the life it offers.

In the *Römische Elegien* the idea of participating in a literary tradition is taken very seriously and really quite literally. Goethe, in writing his *Elegien* with a conscious eye and ear towards the conventions of the poetry of Propertius, Catullus, and Tibullus, crafted poems that can be said to participate in this tradition of classical poetry. Within the poems there is another poet, who in the fiction of the cycle (and this is very much within the conventions of the Latin love elegy), has written the elegies we are reading. He, too, participates in the tradition of the Latin love elegy, and it is his participation in this tradition that is the immediate and tangible content of the cycle. It is also, of course, symbolic, a *Bild*, in Goethe's sense of the word.

The Rome of the *Römische Elegien* is a Rome that has been known to poets of the past. It is new to the poet-wanderer who arrives at its gates in the opening elegy. What is means to be in Rome is the question fundamental to the cycle. In the first elegy it is posed. The poems that follow provide the answer.

But the answer doesn't come at once. Goethe deliberately casts his poet-wanderer as an observer in the first elegy. He listens, peers at the city, the cautious and proper outsider examining with detachment. The question of Rome's essence is posed at the close of the first poem. No single poem provides an answer. No single experience is totally adequate to the poet-wanderer's understanding of the Rome he is seeking in the first elegy. Only in time, in a series of experiences and encounters, will he perceive and be able to give expression to the essence of Rome itself.

With extreme skill the first of the elegies introduces this design. The opening elegy of the cycle records the entrance of the poet into Rome. It is an elegy of expectation and one organized by the naming of three specific experiences within Rome that the poet anticipates. Each experience is presented as a means through which the city might be opened and be made accessible to the new arrival. For despite his physical presence within the walls of the city, the persona of the *Römische Elegien* finds himself an outsider, one who has not yet been accepted into the Rome he is seeking. Two tensions prevail, the first spatial, the second temporal. The first, as it is developed in three successive images, suggests that the object of the poet's quest is interior, hidden, a secret to be revealed within the innermost reaches of the city, both intimate and immanent to its existence. There is a "Genius," an indwelling spirit within the mute stones and streets to speak to him. There is a "holdes Geschöpf" to be reached behind the now undifferentiated windows. There is a temple, "Amors Tempel," to receive the initiate into its secret rites. The monuments to Rome's historic greatness that are now visible to the poet and define the urban landscape within which he wanders are not the Rome he is seeking. There is more and it will be made visible. The second tension, the temporal, accompanies each of these three images and asserts with complete certainty that in time, and indeed, soon, the city will be opened: the silence will be broken, the beloved will be revealed, the temple of love will receive its initiate. The key word is "noch" and it occurs in lines 4, 7 and 9:

> "nur mir schweiget noch alles so still . . . "
> "Ahn' ich die Wege noch nicht . . . "
> "Noch betracht' ich Kirch' und Palast . . . "

The poet's conviction that there is more to Rome than meets his present ears and eyes is the assertion fundamental to this first elegy.

It is a well-conceived introduction to the cycle of poems, for it immediately marks the city itself as the focus of inquiry—that which is to be revealed in the poems and made known—and at the same time, it indicates that Rome, as it is deemed desirable and attainable, is not simply a geographical designation. The physical Rome has been attained. Now the essence of Rome must be realized.

The first elegy concludes with a succinct epigrammatic formula:

Eine Welt zwar bist du, O Rom; doch ohne die Liebe
    Wäre die Welt nicht die Welt, wäre denn Rom auch nicht Rom.
                                                        (I,13–14)

The lines are both clever and functional. They unmistakably echo an old formulaic description of the city transmitted in the fifth century by Bishop Sidonius Apollinaris. It is uncertain whether Goethe knew the *versus reciprocus*: "Roma tibi subito motibus ibit Amor."[35] The a priori identity it establishes was, however, common knowledge and a standard descriptive equation: Roma–orbis–Amor. Goethe is not simply engaging in verbal play when he concludes the first elegy with this ancient formula. Like so many of the succinct statements that conclude his poems, these lines present a distilled restatement of the idea that has organized the verse: Rome is a world, and a world within which the poet has arrived, but the real Rome, Rome in its true identity, is only made accessible through love.

There are multiple examples in Goethe's lyric poetry of similar formulas at the end of poems:

Und doch, welch Glück, geliebt zu werden!
Und lieben, Götter, welch ein Glück.
                                        (Willkommen und Abschied)

Die Veränderung, ach, wie groß!
Liebe, Liebe, laß mich los!
                                        (Neue Liebe, Neues Leben)

Glück ohne Ruh
Liebe, bist du.
                                                    (Rastlose Liebe)

It is not at all surprising in the *Römische Elegien* to find Goethe once more attributing to love the organizing and creative function in his poetic world.

Yet, I would like to suggest that for all its epigrammatic conclusiveness and the familiarity of this poetic structure, the final distich in Elegy I of the *Römische Elegien* is unusual. It does not simply conclude a poem. It begins a cycle.

The three images that are used to depict the poet's soon to be realized accomodation into the imperial city and that effectively structure the first elegy are not explicitly linked within the poem. The suggestion is that these three images give varying expression to the same inner dimension of the city, that each is part of the same unrevealed life of the Rome that is now hidden from the newly arrived wanderer. They seem to be parallel. Goethe associates them most skillfully through a consistent development of the temporal and spatial tensions cited previously and by the precise allotment of two distichs for each image. The elegy progresses from "Genius" to "Geschöpf" to "Amors Tempel." But examined closely, this is a very curious progression. Within the economy of six distichs the elegy has moved from the opposition of the poet and the *genius loci* to a fusion of initiate and temple. The walls of the eternal city in line 3 ("in deinen heiligen Mauern,/Ewige Roma"), a descriptive commonplace, have become, literally, the holy walls of Amor's temple in line 12. How this transformation is to be accomplished is not articulated. We are told in the third and fourth distichs, in the second of the three images, that there is a woman in a window and that there are pathways to reach her, pathways that lead behind the walls of the first image and into the inner realm of Rome. The concluding distich affirms this sequence of images in a most abstract manner: Love is the essence of Rome. It both poses, and provides a partial answer to, the question fundamental not only to this elegy but to the entire cycle: what is this Rome the poet seeks and how can it be attained?

What distinguishes this closing formula from those that are used to conclude Goethe's other lyric poems is that, when all is said and done, the poem remains without a conclusion. Not that a reader senses that a few verses have been forgotten, or that the elegy was ended just one distich too soon. Formally, the poem is complete. The epigram has effected a strong closure. Rather, it is the failure of the poem to achieve any kind of resolution, to translate the abstract potential of Rome into a realized setting. The concluding formula does not give expression to what has taken place before it in the poem. In this first elegy anticipation is all. This is of course intentional. For this reason the first elegy, and particularly the use of the closing distich, begins the cycle so effectively. It doesn't conclude anything. It has presented three future possibilities for the poet's participation in the eternal city. It has posited and proclaimed the identity of Amor and Roma as the essence of the poetic world taking shape in these poems. But it is all unrealized; the identity of Amor and Roma has no substance. In the poems that follow the meaning of this identity must be made visible. That is the task the first elegy has set for the cycle.

How is this done? In good part, by means of metaphor. Our discussion of the cycle will begin here. More basic than verbal links, syntactical parallels, linear continuity, it is the metaphors, the modification and elaboration of core images, that give meaning to the Roma–Amor identity and, consequently, determine the development of the cycle.

It is very difficult to describe adequately the function of these metaphors, for they quickly defy the role of figurative ornament, an addendum as it were to the main purpose of the gathered poems, and become the vehicle by which the meaning of the poems is most fully realized. I have argued earlier that Goethe's poetry is an attempt to make visible by means of concrete and tangible image that essentially intangible and ineffable reality of nature and of man's existence that gives the world life and form. I have argued as well that this is the fundamental issue in the *Römische Elegien*. It is the meaning of Rome, the world that the poet has come to in the first elegy that is at issue. What does it mean to gain entrance to a world defined by the synonymity of Roma and Amor? Goethe does not answer the question directly. Instead he provides us with a series of poems, each revealing and yet concealing the secret of the identity he has posited. The poems are individual, discontinuous, but the metaphors recur, as do key phrases and turns of speech.

It is not enough to identify the various metaphors in the poems. They do not function in a simple one-to-one equation. For example, to note the consistent use of fire and flame and to equate these images with ardor and passion is only to begin to understand the use of these specific metaphors in these elegies. Indeed, fire is an image fundamental to the cycle and, indeed, it is used to express the love of the poet for his beloved. It is hardly a new image, either to Goethe's poetry or to the lyric convention that Goethe employs here.[36] Two observations are essential. First, rather than speak of individual metaphors, it is more helpful to note image clusters in these elegies. Consider the reference to Amor's temple in the first elegy. It belongs to a series of images that express the religious dimension of the Roman experience. These include the motifs of offering, service, the altar, incense, as well as the figure of the initiate. Other complexes that suggest themselves immediately include the various images of asylum-enclosure, the expansion of the North-South dichotomy in terms both temporal and existential, the statues and the motif of ancient art, the heroic and the harvest. Although, and this brings us to our second point, these image complexes can be separated and cataloged for descriptive purposes, any attempt to do so is necessarily misleading. In the first elegy the fire that "versengend erquickt" and "Amors Tempel" are introduced as completely distinct metaphors.

There is no association. In the course of the cycle, however, with deftness and skill, the two are brought together.

No image in this cycle of poems remains unmodified. Rather, in each new appearance of a metaphor Goethe expands its field of association. The images, in the course of the cycle, steadily acquire new meaning and become increasingly interrelated. The differentiated images of fire and the temple in the first elegy ultimately encompass the literary and heroic past of the city, its aesthetic potential, as well as the daily experiences of the lovers. The metaphors are not intended to function in abstract reference. They record that which is tangible and immediate to the poet's experience in Rome. At the same time they create, in the fullness of their association, the final meaning of the identity posited in the first elegy, the equation Amor–orbis–Roma.

The Rome that the poet seeks is a unified world, and the metaphors employed in the cycle function as the gathering place where the meaning of this unity is revealed. One of the associative links the poems create might be described as: flame–hearth–enclosure–embrace–bed–altar–festival–light–flame. But this is only one. The network of images is expansive. Its links are sometimes quite explicit equations, at other times slight verbal ties. Once into the cycle the reader cannot trace any single strand of association without neglect of significant alternatives. This becomes, in a very basic usage of the word, the context for the individual poem. Context derives from a word meaning "to weave": patterns, continuities, various threads that run through a single poem and then a series, forming a kind of fabric, a display of old and new design. The fire of passion, anticipation and protective enclosure, the festival, the altar of Amor, the beloved as a statue, the statues as lovers, the workshop that is a Pantheon, a love that creates poetry and a poetry that creates a world of love—these designs are made visible.

It is necessary at this point to select one of the core image clusters of the cycle and demonstrate this process. It is a difficult task, for the associative patterning quickly opens the entire cycle to discussion and makes focused analysis seem tedious and petty. In the first five elegies the metaphor of fire is recurrent:

I. . . . das holde Geschöpf, das mich versengend erquickt

II. [Sie] Teilt die Flammen, die sie in seinem Busen entzündet

III. Dringen die andern ins Mark, zünden behende das Blut

V. Und es durchglühet ihr Hauch mir bis ins Tiefste die Brust.
    Amor schüret die Lamp' indes und denket der Zeiten,
      Da er den nämlichen Dienst seinen Triumvirn getan.

It is immediately apparent that in none of these elegies is the metaphor of fire extensively developed. Only once is it suggested by a noun (II). More often the verbs carry and extend the associations of enflamed passion (I, II, III), renewal (I), and inspiration (V). In Elegy III it is a mere verbal tie that recalls the "entzünden" of Elegy II, a repetition that is not only deliberate, I would submit, but also frequent in the cycle. The flame that Amor guards in Elegy V has no direct link as yet to the fire the beloved has ignited in the poet. But in the course of the cycle he is revealed as a guardian of far more than a single lamp. Host and protector, he is himself the source of passion and inspiration.

In Elegy VI the flame is explicitly used as a metaphor and developed at some length to give expression to the rebounding strength of the lovers' relationship. There has been a quarrel:

Dunkel brennt das Feuer nur augenblicklich und dampfet,
    Wenn das Wasser die Glut stürzend und jählings verhüllt;
Aber sie reinigt sich schnell, verjagt die trübenden Dämpfe,
    Neuer und mächtiger dringt leuchtende Flamme hinauf.
(VI, 31–34) [37]

Nouns dominate: "das Feuer," "die Glut," "die Flamme." Here for the first time in the cycle the image of fire is equated directly with the established love of the two lovers. The metaphor has marked the intensification of their relationship. Here, also, a second and closely related complex of images is introduced. Water and its association of "dunkel," "trüb," "verhüllt," and "Dampf" are directly opposed to the strong, bright flame.

This opposition becomes important in Elegy VII, for although there is no metaphor of flame or fire, there is once more the direct opposition of opaqueness ("trübe") and the light. Two distichs are allotted to each metaphor complex. The poet's past, the gray North, desperation, heaviness, and deep introspection are joined in the one, and the present, the South, light, contour, and color in the other. Fire is now part of the growing complex of metaphors that give direct expression to the unbounded happiness the poet celebrates in this elegy.

In Elegy IX the flame is the dominant image. Its field of association can only be sketched. The fire in the hearth, the hearth of protective enclosure and asylum, opens the elegy. It is the source of the poet's joy, for in the flames he reads the promise of the beloved's visit. The flame is, of course, the poet's love as well, and the beloved has the gift of rekindling its brightness. The flame is creative, and its quickening will transform the warmed night into a festival. Furthermore, the flame in the hearth is itself used as a metaphor to describe the poet's sexual delight. The beloved's ability to rekindle it in the morning is a metaphor for her skill in arousing his flagging passion. It is said that Amor has granted her this gift. This is important. The fire is finally explicitly of Amor's making. It has become quite literally the fire of love and at the same time in the sequence of elegies this fire has also been revealed as the source of the poet's creativity, the source of his joy, and an attribute of the city of Rome that the poet now carries within himself. It should be mentioned that by this point in the cycle other images that are employed in Elegy IX have also acquired a strong field of association, particularly "das Fest" and "Freude." Goethe once commented in reference to classical painting that art at its highest level achieves "eine Symbolik, die zugleich sinnliche Darstellung ist" (WA I, 49[1], 191). The fires of love are a visible part of the Roman setting.

After Elegy IX it is primarily the multiple associations that have been established that continue to recall the primary metaphor of the flame. In Elegy X, for example, the poet exhorts: "Freue dich also, Lebend'ger, der lieberwärmeten Stätte" (X, 5); it is a conscious recollection of Elegy IX:

> Dann flammen Reisng und Scheite,
> Und die erwärmete Nacht wird uns ein glänzendes Fest.
>
> (IX, 5–6)

Light, form, and festival emerge in the elegies that follow as the dominant images, but none of these can be used without recalling in part the inspiring flame, the warming hearth, and the quickening joy.

What does this demonstrate? The fact that this process can be repeated with the images of enclosure-asylum, temple-initiate, festival of love and religious celebration, as well as with various less expansive motifs becomes significant when the thematic consequence of this metaphoric intertwining is realized. The bed that is Amor's altar (XIII), the beloved who is the entrance to the holy temple (in the original 16, now Nachlaß II), the workshop as a Pantheon (XI), and the two lovers as an assembled congregation (XII) share a single purpose. That purpose is one of creation. The cycle is so structured that out of the interaction of myth and festival, the nights spent with the beloved and the days in anticipation, the awareness of historical and poetic analogies to this experience, there arises in particular detail the meaning of life in this Roman setting that the poet has achieved. Rome is made visible. At the same time the more the poems probe the meaning of Rome for the poet, the more closely he himself becomes a part of the setting. He is transformed from observer to initiate. The new life he is being initiated into is also a new mode of creativity.

Ultimately, to be in Rome is to realize this creative potential. But this is not yet clear. We must turn our attention once more to the cycle itself.

Amor contends in the central Elegy XIII that it was he who all along made the Rome of historical and poetic fame possible. It is not surprising that this is the only elegy of the cycle that Goethe ever published separately. It, more than any other, presents explicitly the direct equation Amor–Roma in its full asethetic implication:

> Du betrachtest mit Staunen die Trümmern alter Gebäude
> Und durchwandelst mit Sinn diesen geheiligten Raum.
> Du verehrest noch mehr die werten Reste des Bildens
> Einziger Künstler, die stets ich in der Werkstatt besucht.
> Diese Gestalten, ich formte sie selbst!
>
> (XIII, 9–13)

This boastful claim is not unprepared in the cycle. Amor has previously been revealed as princely host in this Roman setting (II), founder of the city (III), protector of its poets (V), and source of its erotic delights (IX). The poet's well-being has been directly related to his gifts. In Elegy XIII, however, the full meaning of this design becomes apparent. Amor announces that the Rome that he made possible in classical times remains a possibility in the present:

> War das Antike doch neu, da jene Glücklichen lebten!
> Lebe glücklich, und so lebe die Vorzeit in dir!
>
> (XIII, 21–22)

Amor's invitation to the poet, now made explicit in this elegy, is to share in the re-creation of his Rome in the present day. It is offered boldly. Amor presents himself to the poet as the benevolent headmaster in a school whose excellence remains undiminished by the years. There is the promise that under his tutelage the lessons of that school can be mastered to great delight and profit. There is also the implicit threat that apart from his instruction all creative endeavors are in vain:

> Stoff zum Liede, wo nimmst du ihn her? Ich muß dir ihn geben,
> Und den höheren Stil lehret die Liebe dich nur.
>
> (XIII, 23–24)

What Amor fails to mention, and the reasons for the poet's angry charge of deception in the opening distich of the elegy, is that Amor's power to inspire creativity, when fully realized, necessarily leaves the poet incapable of writing verse:

Nun, verräterisch hält er sein Wort, gibt Stoff zu Gesängen,
Ach! und raubt mir die Zeit, Kraft und Besinnung zugleich.
                                                    (XIII, 27–28)

There is a tension between the immediacy of inspiration and the reflective moments necessary to composition that is central to the elegy. On the most explicit level it is carried by the image of the poet unable to pause long enough in his lovemaking to gather thoughts and energy to create his poems, or left so exhausted by this process of inspiration that he is unable to summon the strength for his writing. The irony of his plight is evident. That it does not seem particularly tragic is due to the poet's obvious enjoyment of the inspiration he receives despite the frustration it brings. The tension, however, is a serious one and one not completely resolved in the poem.

It is clear that nothing in the Rome that the poet has sought out and that is being revealed in the elegies exists apart from the creative power of love. This is Amor's proud boast and one the poet does not refute. It is also clear that as the poet is transformed from observer to initiate in this Roman setting he makes this creative power increasingly his own. He shares in the re-creation of Amor's Rome in the present day. The *Römische Elegien* themselves are the demonstration of his success. But what the central Elegy XIII also makes clear is that this is not accomplished simply by sensuous abandonment to the erotic delights Amor offers. Writing, poetic creation, requires "Besinnung" as well as inspiration, and the greater the moment of inspiration, the more difficult this process of reflective contemplation becomes. The two are not strictly speaking antithetical (in no way will a neglect of Amor's inspiration improve the poet's writing), but rather are joined in a creative tension that is the source of the elegies. Elegy XIII, therefore, can only conclude in the reaffirmation of this tension and not its resolution. Accordingly, the poem ends as the beloved awakens and Amor's power makes itself felt anew. But just as significant, the elegies continue after XIII, attesting to the poet's accomodation to his plight, and his continued participation in the re-creation of Amor's Rome.

Throughout the cycle and in various ways, the re-creation of Amor's Rome, the making of it a present reality, has been taking place. Three elegies, III, XII, and XV, demonstrate three ways in which the poet has accomplished this.

In Elegy III the poet is attempting to reassure his beloved that her rapid surrender to his desires ought not be considered improper. It is an example of how Goethe expands a single experience of the two lovers to encompass the erotic, poetic and historical dimension of this

Roman world and finally to re-create it. The poet recounts to his
mistress a number of tales from Greek and Latin mythology of a love
as rash and impulsive as their own:

> In der heroischen Zeit, da Götter und Göttinnen liebten,
>   Folgte Begierde dem Blick, folgte Genuß der Begier.
>   (III, 7–8)

The sequence "Blick-Begierde-Genuß" originates with Ovid and is
taken from the story of Mars and Rhea Silvia, the same story that
Goethe uses to close the elegy:

> Silvia Vestalis . . .
> sacra lavaturas mane petebat aquas . . .
> Mars videt hanc visamque cupit potiturque cupita . . .
> somnus abit, iacet ipsa gravis. iam scilicet intra
> viscera Romanae conditor urbis erat.
>   (*Fastes* III, 11, 21, 23–24)

Goethe's final distichs read:

> Rhea Silvia wandelt, die fürstliche Jungfrau, der Tiber
>   Wasser zu schöpfen, hinab, und sie ergreifet der Gott.
> So erzeugte die Söhne sich Mars!—Die Zwillinge tränket
>   Eine Wölfin, und Rom nennt sich die Fürstin der Welt.
>   (III, 15–18)[38]

He follows the Latin sequence closely, but as these distichs stand
within the poet's speech to his beloved they are not simply the final
example in a series of poetic defenses of a rash and impulsive love.
Instead, they reveal that this pattern of enflamed desire and quick
erotic fulfillment is not only permissible but desirable, for it first enabled the foundation of the city of Rome. In their own strong desire
and its fulfillment the two lovers have reenacted a scene from the
ancient heroic times. They have re-created the city's beginnings in
their own beginning together.

Elegy III is simultaneously a re-creation of the poetry of two of the
city's finest poets, Ovid and Propertius. The meaning of Ovid's tale
of Mars and Rhea Silvia has been brought to life once more and his
verse renewed in the poet's address to his beloved. In his series of
mythological examples that buttress his argument for quick surrender,
the poet marks his kinship with Propertius. A poem in the tradition
of the Latin love elegy celebrates the swift consummation of the poet's
desire.

In quite a different manner Elegy XII also designates the lovers as
renewers of the past. The sound of harvesters returning from the

fields presents an opportunity for an extended description of an ancient mystery, a rite of fertility retold and resynthesized from the legends of Demeter and Jasion. These ancient celebrations have been forgotten, the poet tells his beloved. He invites her to join him in re-creating them:

> Laß uns beide das Fest im stillen freudig begehen!
> Sind zwei Liebende doch sich ein versammeltes Volk.

(XII, 7–8)

The metaphors of festival, light, initiation, and the sacred night have been introduced by this point in the cycle, and the elegy continues to expand their network of association. The promise from the first elegy that the poet himself will be an initiate into Amor's temple is recalled. The moment of revelation arrives, the secret is revealed, but not without considerable irony. Goethe's contempt for the Greek mysteries and their priests is visible as the poet describes the unfolding of the Eleusinian rites and the fearful anticipation of the trembling neophyte with mock solemnity. After considerable hocus-pocus the awesome secret is revealed:

> Erst nach mancherlei Proben und Prüfungen ward ihm enthüllet,
> Was der geheiligte Kreis seltsam in Bildern verbarg.
> Und was war das Geheimnis, als daß Demeter, die große,
> Sich gefällig einmal auch einem Helden bequemt . . .

(XII, 21–24)

The secret, so carefully guarded in sacred images, is no more than the story of a goddess yielding to a mortal. Even the trembling neophyte catches the point, gestures to his beloved and follows the clear directive to swift and pleasurable fulfillment. The poet, likewise an initiate, but also as much a rogue as Amor in the elegy that follows (XIII), has spun a tale as elaborate as the Eleusinian rites to capture his beloved's imagination. It only remains for him to complete the story in a similar gesture of invitation. Together he and his beloved will re-create the proper conclusion to the story just told and celebrate the Roman harvest. The only thing consigned to the past is the useless mystification by the ancient priests. In the present moment the lovers eagerly re-create the festival's climax.

Finally, in Elegy XV in a delightful encounter between the poet and his beloved in a Roman tavern, the past, and this time predominately a literary past, is recreated with far less mysterious an air. The poet playfully puns on an exchange recorded between Hadrian and the poet Florus in which each declared his distaste for the rigors of the other's occupation. The North–South dichotomy resurfaces briefly in this quick interchange. The poet's taste for the South and its taverns is not explained in metaphors of Northern bleakness and introspection, however. His preference is readily understood. The beloved is present. Strongly visual, the scene records the brief communication between the lovers as they sit at separate tables, speech hindered by the presence of family and friends. Signs written in wine spilled on the table are exchanged to set the pending rendezvous. It is a scene familiar to Ovid, now reenacted by the modern Roman lovers.[39] The poet, powered by the creative pattern established by this point in the cycle, the pattern of seeing and desiring, exhorts the sun to wind his way swiftly towards the west. Self-consciously a new Horace, just as he began the elegy a self-styled compatriot of Florus, he creates a hymnic address in praise of the city to while away the hours.

It is Amor's claim in Elegy XIII that it was he who created Rome, he who creates the modern experiences of love within it. He made the art of the classical world possible. He can renew this art in the present. In each of the three elegies we have just discussed this renewal is taking place. They are not the only examples. In truth, the entire cycle is tribute to his creative power, to the renewal of the Latin love elegy he has made possible.

Yet, each of the twenty elegies is individual. They display great variety in setting, structure, use of metaphor, and thematic focus. In some elegies, as in poems VIII and IX, a single image (the berry, the flame) is at the center of the poem. Others move by citing a catalog of examples (III, XI). Metaphors and motifs effect their network of association by means of constant modification and elaboration; settings shift; narrative elements are present and create shorter fictions within the fiction of the cycle as a whole. The continuity of the poems is not, strictly speaking, logical. There is considerable variation in the structure of single poems, and the independence of the individual works is frequently underscored by a very strong closure in the final distich of an elegy.[40]

This asymmetry is purposeful. Goethe did not compose twenty homogeneous elegies to be linked in a tidy narrative continuity. He intended to give expression to the meaning of Rome by creating a symbolic setting synonymous with the love that created it. And he sought to do this by means of a sequence of individual images, or *Bilder*, each making visible the meaning of the city through a poet giving form to and being formed by his experiences within it.

The twenty poems of the *Römische Elegien* do not create an unbroken narrative. There are gaps between the poems in the cycle. Time moves unevenly. Productive tensions, both sequential and non-linear, lend a coherence to the collection that only underscores the independence of the single elegy. Allusions to the literary and mythological past of the city are frequent but diverse, and patterns once established are recalled in creative variation. Elegy XI provides an example. It stands in particular relationship to Elegies III, V, XII, and XIII. The setting is the artist's workroom, a veritable Pantheon filled with assorted statues of the gods. In the gazing and glancing ascribed to them they become almost human in their interaction. (In contrast, the poet's beloved is twice explicitly viewed as a piece of sculpture, in Elegies V and XIII.) Throughout the *Römische Elegien* there is an immediacy ascribed to the process of seeing. It invariably incites to creative action. The final distichs of Elegy XI provide no exception:

Aber nach Bacchus, dem weichen, dem träumenden, hebet Cythere
Blicke der süßen Begier, selbst in dem Marmor noch feucht.

(XI, 9–10)

"Blicke—Begier—." The sequence is familiar. It recalls the third Elegy:

In der heroischen Zeit, da Götter und Göttinnen liebten,
Folgte Begierde dem Blick, folgte Genuß der Begier.

(III, 7–8)

But where is the "Genuß?"

Seiner Umarmung gedenket sie gern und scheinet zu fragen:
Sollte der herrliche Sohn uns an der Seite nicht stehen?

(XI, 11–12)

The implication is clear. The space between Elegies XI and XIII will not go unused. Once our attention has been diverted and we are occupied by the returning harvesters of Elegy XII, Priapus can take his place in this Pantheon. This creative potential is the essence of Rome. It is realized in the imagination of the reader.

The invitation to the reader to grasp the allusion, to complete the suggested patterns and in this way to participate in the realization of the poet's work is fundamental to the composition of the *Römische Elegien*. Killy has called attention to this feature in his article "Mythologie und Lakonismus"[41] and cites a passage in a letter Goethe wrote to Eichstädt on 15 September 1804, where Goethe describes this process:

Jeder Dichter baut sein Werk aus Elementen zusammen, die freylich der Eine organischer zu verflechten vermag, als der Andere, doch kommt es auch viel auf den Beschauer an, von welcher Maxime dieser ausgeht. Ist er zur Trennung geneigt, so zerstört er mehr oder weniger die Einheit, welche der Künstler zu erringen strebt; mag er lieber verbinden, so hilft er dem Künstler nach und vollendet gleichsam dessen Absicht. (WA IV, 17, 196)

Killy's particular use of this principle in his interpretation of Elegies I, III, and IV is, however, troubling. It illustrates that this creative imperative can also lead astray. In an attempt to deal in a sensitive manner with the rich interplay of imagery, literary allusion, and mythology in the poems, he has failed to recognize the boundaries set for the interpretive imagination by the poems themselves.

Killy asserts that the passages cited from classical sources in the *Römische Elegien*, the mythological examples used, and the imagery found in the poems are not to be taken merely at face value. To understand each poem in its "wahren poetischen Sinne"⁴² the reader must recall the complete story to which the mythological reference alludes, the total context of the quotation cited. His interpretation of Elegy III, which we have already mentioned with its distinctive "Blick-Begierde-Genuß" sequence, illustrates his point.

Killy justifies his approach to the poem on the basis of a specific understanding of poetic structure in the cycle: "Der Lakonismus ist eine von Goethe geliebte, stilbestimmende Redeweise, ohne die es kein poetisches, vor allem kein lyrisches Sprechen gäbe. Er beruht auf der sinnfälligen Abbreviatur komplexer Verhältnisse, welche die verschiedensten Formen anzunehmen vermag."⁴³ His claim is general in its formulation and encompasses, by Killy's own definition, all symbolic language. Specifically he writes of the mythological references in Elegy III: "Ihr *bedeutender* Charakter wird erst sichtbar, wenn man sich durch die anspielende Verrätselung locken läßt und (den Spielregeln folgend) die Lakonismen aufzulösen trachtet, wobei man sich von hier unübertrefflich Gesagte und Geschaute zurückgewiesen sieht."⁴⁴

It is Goethe's intention, according to Killy, that the reader not be lulled by the apparent idyllic quality of the mythological relationships the third elegy records. Rather, in Killy's reading of the elegy, the tragic dominates. He insists that the poem implicitly recalls the fateful consequence of each of the impulsive acts cited. The reader is expected to supply each fateful conclusion. Venus and Anchises (III, 9–10) brought forth Aeneas, it is true, but Anchises met a fate of drought and blindness as a consequence. The passion of Hero and Leander (III, 13–14) led to their death. Aurora's awakening of Endymion (III, 11–12) would have cost him his sleep of eternal youth. (Here Killy is hedging, for Goethe's point is that Luna did not tarry in her kiss, and thus prevented this loss.) Killy reads Elegy III as a radical qualification of its own moment of happy fulfillment, for unavoidably Amor is accompanied by a dreadful fate. "Sie zeigt, daß die Elegie keine Idylle ist und nimmt dem *Nun bin ich endlich geborgen!* (II, 1) die Sicherheit."⁴⁵

Despite Killy's assertion that there are rules to be followed in the decoding game he plays, his laconic principle apparently allows an almost unrestricted uncovering and incorporation of association. In Elegy III, however, there is, quite in contrast to that which Killy perceives, a deliberate exclusion of tragic action from the *Römische Elegien*. While Goethe followed the conventions of the Latin love elegy, he resolutely excluded one of its characteristics. Disasters such as social strife, passionate but unfulfilled desire, slander, war, separation, and sorrow are not found in Goethe's poems. The strife lies behind the poet, outside the walls of Rome. Potential threats to the security of the lovers are unrealized. They do arise, recorded first in Elegy VI, and later in a series of shorter poems (XIV–XVIII), but they are deliberately and quickly defused. Elegy VI marks the first quarrel between the lovers, but it is a quarrel that is based on misunderstanding and false accusation and works ultimately only to intensify their devotion to one another. Indeed, the quarrel is a successful means to depict an increase in affection and ardor that would otherwise be difficult to portray after the unqualified happiness and joy Elegy V expresses. Similarly, the threats in the later poems (XIV–XVIII) are more apparent than real. Some are taken from the tradition of the Latin love elegy, as is the distrust and resentful jealousy of VI, and contrast all the more explicitly for their absence of malice. Others are Goethe's own invention. In either case there is a pervasive air of well-being and satisfaction, even in the face of growing impatience and long, expectant hours awaiting the beloved's arrival.

Likewise, the lovers bring no harm to those about them. In the invitation to celebrate the harvest festival by participating in the mystery as it is revealed to the initiate, the poet assures his beloved that they, unlike Demeter, do not neglect higher duties in the fulfillment of their love:

> Verstehst du nun, Geliebte, den Wink?
> Jene buschige Myrte beschattet ein heiliges Plätzchen!
> Unsre Zufriedenheit bringt keine Gefährde der Welt.
>
> (XII, 32–34)

(Characteristically, in the following poem, the central Elegy XIII, the pursuit of love proves, in playful paradox, a distraction to the poet, but there is no danger. The love that distracts is also the love that is the essential source of the poet's happiness and of his poetry as well.)

Goethe has created an idyll out of the world of the Latin love elegy.[46] This is not to claim that he has endowed the poet's Roman experience with a promise of permanence. No utopian fiction is recorded. The poet is neither hero nor permanent guest of the gods, although he willingly assumes both disguises. Nor has time been abolished by the lovers' happiness. Quite to the contrary, it constantly reasserts itself within the cycle, bringing with it the poetic benefits of anticipation and recollection. The Roman world also carries with it its own termination; the idyll is not unbounded. But its end is not tragic. We are not invited to probe endlessly behind the scenes to discover the "true meaning" of the mythological events and literary allusions presented in the poems. Goethe's fiction is selective, and the images of Rome he offers are a disclosure that is more than adequate to the realization of its meaning.

This meaning cannot be abstractly derived from any one poem. It is part of all of them, the verbal context that is created and that in turn enhances the lyric statement of each individual elegy. Although it is true that not all the poems of this cycle are of equal significance and that a number of the elegies have rightly been accorded a disproportionate amount of critical attention, there is no single turning point in the cycle's structure, no single high point in the poet's love.

The poems of the *Römische Elegien* are largely discontinuous in their narrative content. Not only do we recall Goethe's reference to them as "Fragmenten Art erotischer Späße" during their writing, but also the ease, albeit with regret, with which he elected to omit the second and the sixteenth poems after Schiller became uneasy over their content. It should not be forgotten that he never reinserted them into the cycle, although Schiller suggested this at the time. Goethe is not telling a story. If he were, every member of the cycle would be indispensable to the narrative advancement. As it is, narrative continuity is of only slight importance. Rather, Goethe is evoking a world, making Rome visible.

This is not to deny, however, that the cycle displays a purposeful linear organization. The poems are not placed randomly, although I would suggest that within bounds their sequence could be altered without adverse effect. It is important to realize that not all lyric groupings achieve their coherence in the same way. There are lyric cycles where even the slightest realignment of the poems would be unthinkable.[47]

The poet of the *Römische Elegien* is a wanderer, but it is not his journey, as one might anticipate, that determines the placement of the poems in the cycle. Nor, once the poet has found asylum in Rome (Elegy II), is there a clear narrative sequence to order events. A few thematic considerations do affect the arrangement of the elegies. The poet is not presented as writing poetry until he has experienced the full happiness of Rome, the love of his beloved. There is a pattern of recollection that begins in Elegy IV and continues through V, VII, VIII, and XI. Often cued by explicit phrases such as "ich denke der

Zeit," the recollection allows an incorporation of personal or historical memory into the texture of the cycle. Not until after the proclamation of Amor's creative power in Elegy XIII and the poet's struggle for
rest and reflective strength, however, is the time recalled also a time
experienced within the cycle (XVII). Thus a passage of time is indicated
that complements the frequent exhortations within the elegies that
time move swiftly to bring the lovers together. There is no pattern to
the sequence of setting as it shifts from bedchamber to workshop,
cafe, vineyard, and Roman hilltop. No ongoing dialog links individual
elegies.

Where does one find meaningful order? There is no single principle
to be discerned. The temptation to try to define one is great. In one of
the few essays on the *Römische Elegien* as a cycle Gerhard Kaiser[48]
proposes a model. He identifies the idyllic quality of the Rome experience as the creative achievement of the poet-wanderer and explains
the productive tension between the temporal sentimental stance of
the poet-lover and the timelessness of the idyll he attains, thereby
elucidating much of the thematic structure of the cycle. No other
study has dealt so successfully with the organizing motifs that inform
the progression of the poems and has related so lucidly their various
strands. In his discussion of linear organization, however, his analysis proves reductive. He writes:

Und so stellt sich in der Folge der Elegien zwar kein Ablauf in der Zeit dar,
aber eine durchgehende Auseinandersetzung mit den großen Phänomenen
Zeit und Tod. Diese Auseinandersetzung ist so wesentlich, daß sie das innere
Baugesetz des Zyklus bestimmt und die zwanzig Elegien des Zyklus zu vier
Fünfergruppen anordnet.[49]

He identifies these four groups as follows:

I–V   Zeit des Wandrers und Zeitlosigkeit der Idylle
VI–X   Vergänglichkeit und Tod als Hintergrund
XI–XV   Sieg der Liebenden über die Zeit
XVI–XX   Vollbesitz des idyllischen Zustands

Time does pass in the elegies, within the poems as well as between
poems, although Kaiser is right in not stressing this chronology. Far
more troubling is, however, his selection of one thematic tension in
the cycle as a basis for an encompassing schematic summary of its
structure. Not only does it imply a thematic coherence that does not
take seriously enough the discontinuity of the poems and the variety
of thematic and verbal elements that relate them to one another, but it
also implies that a symmetrical composition ought to and can be
discerned here and that its identification is a useful step in a critical
interpretation of the poems.[50]

Symmetry is not fundamental to the cycle's organization. Rather, carefully planned contrasts set off individual poems. Verbal and thematic links relate otherwise disparate elegies. A number of sequences suggest themselves. Two of these (VIII–XII and XIV–XVIII), both cutting across the boundaries of Kaiser's groupings, illustrate how Goethe is able by means of careful selection and placement of poems both to augment the meaning of the individual elegy and to sustain a sense of coherence for the cycle as a whole.

The poet's rapture in Elegy VII, his metaphorical transport to the halls of the gods, and his heroic pose find an abrupt end as Jupiter interrupts the reverie to put down this mortal he suspects of presumptuous behavior. The elegy begins with the opposition of the poet's northern past and his southern present. His delight with his new surroundings, its light, contour and color, assumes hymnic proportion, and the poet in bold metaphor compares his presence in Rome to that of a hero being received by the gods. A longing to dwell forever in these blissful environs is scarcely stated, however, when Jupiter, on guard against mortal trespassers, interrupts the metaphorical flight. The god, revealed as singularly literal-minded in his duty, totally misapprehends the poet's metaphor. With a feigned humility to disguise his roguish response, the poet politely corrects the god: "Vergib mir: der hohe/ Kapitolinische Berg ist dir ein zweiter Olymp." The poet's presumption in correcting the literal-mindedness of the god is quite as great as the presumption Jupiter first suspected— a desire to be received in the immortal halls of the gods as a chosen hero. While the poet willingly accepts his own mortality, he expresses the desire once more to pass the rest of his days in Rome and to enter Orkus through the gateway it provides.

It is a powerful elegy and presents a very real problem to the organization of the cycle. What can effectively follow such a forceful piece? The solution found, a solution used again after Elegy XIII, is a series of shorter poems, contrasting emotionally and thematically with the antecedent elegy. The great emotional and spatial distance covered in Elegy VII is answered by images of security, enclosure, and earthbound reality in VIII–XII. In Elegy VII the poet was at the center of the poem, his ecstatic experiences revealing Rome in its heroic splendor. In Elegy VIII it is the beloved, tones of intimacy, and images of slow, patient maturity that prevail. The metaphor of ripening fruit in Elegy VIII and the warmth of the fall fire in IX evoke without direct statement the autumnal setting that is central to the harvest rites of Elegy XII. Only in Elegy X, after the protective intimacy of the poet's love for his beloved has been reestablished, is the death motif reintroduced. Now no longer coupled with a sense of loss, it becomes a playful admonition to enjoy the love-warmed night and the beloved's presence.

In addition there is a recurring verbal motif that binds these poems. It begins in Elegy VII and continues through XII:

VII   O wie fühl' ich in Rom mich so froh!
IX   Diesen Abend erfreut sie mich mehr
X   Freue dich also, Lebend'ger
XI   Der Künstler freuet sich seiner/ Werkstatt
XII   Laß uns beide das Fest im stillen freudig begehen!

Security and joy are constant, but each poem gives individual expression to its realization. The effect is cumulative; no one elegy defines the poet's happiness. The sequence is not exclusive, and the five poems that form it are clearly linked in other ways to the rich thematic and metaphoric development of the cycle, as our earlier discussions of elegies IX, XI, and XII have demonstrated. Additional poems could be inserted without loss of continuity, but not just any poem would do. Those that are part of the second sequence (XIV–XVIII), for example, would be jarringly out of place. They, unlike the poems between Elegies VII and XIII, are fraught with signs of frustration and danger.

After Elegy XIII the problem of an appropriate and effective continuation of the cycle once again arises. The closing line, "Ewig nun hält sie dich fest," is conclusive. Goethe's solution is to turn once more to contrast in tone, setting, and theme. In the shortest poem in the cycle the images of permanence and fulfillment that end Elegy XIII are given a playfully ironic turn. The lament of the poet in Elegy XIII was that Amor provided no time for him to write his verse:

Nun, verräterisch hält er sein Wort, gibt Stoff zu Gesängen,
Ach! und raubt mir die Zeit, Kraft und Besinnung zugleich.
(XIII, 27–28)

In the elegies that follow time is plentiful, but it is a time apart from the beloved. These elegies are the record of waiting and frustration, miscalculated rendezvous and joyful anticipation of final reunion. Repeatedly the poet's imaginative powers are called upon to hasten the beloved's return. In Elegy XIV, with a light tone of self-irony the impatient lover tries to artificially induce nightfall by closing the house and lighting his lamps. In Elegy XV the poet exhorts the sun to a speedy departure, but does not forget in wise precaution to ask the Fates to slow the thread of his own life. The Muses, called to his aid in passing the hours, successfully mitigate the frustration of time's slow motion:

So, ihr lieben Musen, betrogt ihr wieder die Länge
Dieser Weile, die mich von der Geliebten getrennt.
(XV, 49–50)

Furthermore, Amor's promise has been kept, for out of this fusion of
recollection and anticipation arise the poet's songs.

The sequence of poems XIV–XVIII records a number of possible
threats to the lovers' security. Intended rendezvous are made difficult
by guardians, neighbors, scarecrows in the vineyards and barking
dogs next door. Each threat is given a playful turn and proven harm-
less, but the separation of the two lovers remains the central motif.
Not until Elegy XVIII is their happy reunion once more the content of
the poems. The participation of this elegy in the sequence is assured
as it continues the catalog of possible threats to the lovers' happiness.
No longer so playful, the thinly veiled danger of venereal disease is
introduced, but it is its absence, not its presence, that is recorded.
The reunion of the two lovers is no new high point in the cycle.
Rather it is a reaffirmation of the happiness they enjoy, the security of
their mutual love. Their happiness is expressed in images of mutuality:

XVIII,   Darum macht Faustine mein Glück; sie teilet das Lager
9–10   Gerne mit mir, und bewahrt Treue dem Treuen genau.

XVIII,   Welche Seligkeit ist's! wir wechseln sichere Küsse,
13–14   Atem und Leben getrost saugen und flößen wir ein.

XVIII,   So erfreuen wir uns der langen Nächte, wir lauschen,
15–16   Busen an Busen gedrängt, Stürmen und Regen und Guß.

All possible hindrances have given way to fulfillment, and Goethe has
prepared his way to end the cycle. This he does through an ironic turn,
for it is the very fullness of the lovers' relationship, their unqualified
love, and not some external threat, that signals the end of their security
and the end of the poems. This conclusion is not arbitrary. It has been
prepared throughout the cycle. The sequence of poems that follow
Elegy XIII provide the specific motifs.

It is difficult to end a series of poems that, by thematic intention,
have no explicit conflict to resolve. The lovers' repeatedly demonstrated happiness removes a great deal of poetically productive tension from the cycle. In the individual elegies this problem is frequently
solved by an abrupt return and reaffirmation of the present moment
in the final lines of the poem, a stress on the immediacy of the experience the lovers share.

IV   Doch stille, die Zeit ist vorüber.
Und umwunden bin ich, römische Flechten, von euch.

XII   Verstehst du nun, Geliebte, den Wink?
XIII   Ewig nun hält sie dich fest.
XV   Lebet wohl! Nun eil' ich . . .
XVI   Nun, des Alten Wunsch ist erfüllt . . .
XVII   Jetzo, hör' ich ihn bellen . . .

In the final two elegies in the cycle a similar pattern can be observed. It is the fullness of the present moment that marks the conclusion of the cycle. In Elegy XIX, the penultimate poem in the cycle, Amor, patron and perpetuator of the Roman idyll, is locked in an ongoing feud with Fama, goddess of good name and reputation. The story concludes with a description of the unfortunate consequence this feud holds for the mortals favored by these jealous divinities. The poet knows at first hand of their strife:

> Und so geht es auch mir: schon leid' ich ein wenig; die Göttin,
>   Eifersüchtig, sie forscht meinem Geheimnisse nach.
>   (XIX, 67–68)

In Elegy XX the story of Midas is told and the terrible burden the knowledge of his extended ears proved for his servant. The unfortunate man, unable to contain the awful secret, tried to bury it in the ground. Reeds shot forth and revealed the truth to the winds of the earth. In a rhetorical turn to magnify his own plight the poet concludes:

> Schwerer wird es nun mir, ein schönes Geheimnis zu wahren,
>   Ach, den Lippen entquillt Fülle des Herzens so leicht!
>   (XX, 15–16)

The motif of the secret is first introduced in Elegy XII. Its revelation marks the high point of the rite of initiation the elegy records and the realization of the temple-initiate relationship that the opening elegy proclaimed. It is not explicitly recalled until Elegy XVII, when a barking dog threatens to reveal the secret of the lovers' nighttime association. Metaphors of secrecy and asylum repeatedly characterize the Rome the poet has sought; they characterize as well the love Amor has made possible in this Roman setting. Five times the word "Geheimnis" is used in Elegy XX. It opens the elegy and closes it. It marks the culmination of the cycle and of the lovers' happiness. In the final poem in the cycle the fulfillment of the word "Geheimnis" is disclosed.

In a reenactment of the story of Midas's servant, the poet seeks a repository for the secret he can no longer contain—the secret of the love he has found in Rome. Friends, both male and female, are considered and rejected. Their response is untrustworthy. The grove and echoing rocks are also rejected. Young romance and its landscape of solitude is not the poet's milieu. Finally, a worthy hiding place is named. The lovers' secret, their happiness, is entrusted to the elegiac distich, to the hexameter and pentameter lines of the Latin love elegy. Poetic form is discreet, but it is never a permanent silence. It conceals, but it also reveals the secrets entrusted to it. Although not explicitly stated, Goethe has made of his twenty *Römische Elegien* quite literally an "offenbares Geheimnis." In the closing distichs a harmonious protective nature is evoked that simultaneously shrouds the secret association of the two lovers and nurtures the poetry of their love. Nowhere else in the cycle is alliteration as important to the poet's expression as in these closing lines:

> Zaudre, Luna, sie kommt! damit sie der Nachbar nicht sehe;
> Rausche, Lüftchen, im Laub! niemand vernehme den Tritt.
> Und ihr, wachset und blüht, geliebte Lieder, und wieget
> Euch im leisesten Hauch lauer und liebender Luft.
>
> (XX, 27–30)

The poetry of Roman happiness will blossom. The image of fulfillment, of fruition, like the earlier metaphor of the overflowing heart, marks the end of the *Römische Elegien*; the revelation of the lovers' secret is not a tragic event, but the final consummation of a fulfilled love.

In a very literal sense the *Römische Elegien* themselves, the twenty poems that we have read, are both the revealed secret of the lovers' happiness and the consummation of the poet's experience in Rome. In the first elegy the poet admonished the stones of the city to speak, to reveal the secret they had hidden from his sight. In the final elegy it is clear that they have spoken—they have spoken through him. The poet has realized Amor's admonition in Elegy XIII: "Lebe glücklich, und so lebe die Vorzeit in dir!" The entire cycle is the record of this creative happiness.

Knebel wrote to Goethe in 1798 to thank him for his positive response to the translations of Propertius that he had completed: "Daß Du meinen Properz so freundlich aufgenommen hast, danke ich Dir sehr. Ich wollte Du hättest mir nur was von dem geschickt, was er Dir eingegeben hat. . . . Du hast den Geist *zu bilden*; doch sind Deine Bildungen in andrer Ansicht als die Properzischen, wenn ich nicht irre; obgleich in Manier und Behandlung oft so ähnlich."[51] Knebel is perceptive. The *Römische Elegien* are not a simple imitation of the poetry of Propertius. They are modern. It is essential to their meaning that they are the creation of a poet not native to the Roman setting of the Latin love elegy. The process of making the meaning of this setting visible informs the structure of the entire cycle. It is the task of an outsider, and the task of a poet. The completed elegies are bold testimony to the poet's successful re-creation of this classical past.

Indeed, among Goethe's contemporaries were those who found the testimony far too bold. The shocking moral character of the elegies was the chief objection raised by the critics of the poems.[52] The most perceptive of Goethe's contemporaries were, however, enthusiastic. Schiller named Goethe "der deutsche Properz."[53] Friedrich Schlegel celebrated him as a "Wiederhersteller der alten Elegie."[54] August Wilhelm Schlegel, in the first critical review of the *Römische Elegien* to be published, recognized the cycle as a unique response to the tradition of the Latin love elegy: "Die Elegien im sechsten Stück [der *Horen*] sind eine merkwürdige, neue, in der Geschichte der Deutschen, ja man darf sagen, der neuern Poesie überhaupt einzige Erscheinung."[55] Attempting to clarify more specifically the distinctive quality of the poetry Schlegel continues:

Und das ist es eben, was an diesen Elegien bezaubert, was sie von den zahlreichen und zum Theil sehr geschickten Nachahmungen der alten Elegiendichter in lateinischer Sprache wesentlich unterscheidet: sie sind originell und dennoch ächt antik. Der Genius, der in ihnen waltet, begrüßt die Alten mit freyer Huldigung; weit entfernt, von ihnen entlehnen zu wollen, bietet er eigene Gaben dar, und bereichert die römische Poesie durch deutsche Gedichte.[56]

Propertius had not even appeared in a distich translation until 1783. (At the time Schlegel was writing Knebel's poems were still unpublished.) A mere decade later there is German poetry of high quality to set beside the works of the classical elegists. Schlegel's enthusiasm is well-founded.

In the first round of critical response to the *Römische Elegien*, no one showed any particular interest in the structure of the twenty poems as a coherent lyric group. Undoubtedly the fact that the poems were a collection of elegies and in this way more closely resembled the books of Catullus, Tibullus, and Propertius contributed in part to the repeated claim made by the Schlegels that Goethe, in these poems, introduced the elegy in its true form to Germany.

Several years later in his *Berliner Vorlesungen* August Wilhelm Schlegel continued the praise he accorded the *Römische Elegien* when they first appeared and extended his analysis to include observations on stylistic variation within the cycle: "Der Ton ist meistens muntrer, als man ihn selbst bey den alten Elegikern gewohnt ist: das wahre zur Elegie gehörige Verhältniß zwischen Bewegung und Ruhe, musikalischer Stimmung und Contemplation findet sich demungeachtet."[57]

Friedrich Schlegel, on the other hand, revised his opinion of the poems. Unlike Goethe's shorter lyric poems, which he asserted would be appreciated for centuries to come, the *Römische Elegien* together with the longer elegies of the middle Weimar years, the *Venetianische Epigramme*, and numerous distich collections would finally be forgotten as necessary metric exercises of interest only to literary historians. Friedrich Schlegel proposed that the entire corpus of distich poetry, including the *Römische Elegien*, be revised and combined into one long didactic poem: "Wir glauben, man müsse alle diese Elegieen und Epigramme nicht als einzelne Gedichte ein jedes für sich, sondern sie alle als ein zusammenhängendes Ganzes betrachten, dem nur die letzte Einheit und Verknüpfung fehlt, um wirklich und in der Tat *Ein Werk* zu sein. . . . "[58] As they now stand the *Römische Elegien* are unsatisfactory: "In den *Römische Elegien* finden wir dagegen weit mehr Unebenheiten and Disharmonisches. Das Geheimnissvolle, die Phantasie aber, fehlt in allen."[59] We can be grateful that Friedrich Schlegel was already out of favor in Weimar and that his suggestions had no influence.

Goethe did not write a second collection of poems like the *Römische Elegien*. He continued to write distich couplets and completed a number of epigrammatic collections in the decade that followed—not only the *Venetianische Epigramme*, which were published the following year in Schiller's *Musenalmanach*, but also *Vier Jahreszeiten*, *Weissagungen des Bakis*, and the *Xenien*. He also continued to write elegies, although none within the tradition of the Latin love elegy he so successfully renewed in the *Römische Elegien*.

It appears that no author of note followed Goethe's lead in the restoration of the Latin love elegy. In Schiller's *Musenalmanach* of 1798 a series of four elegies appeared, entitled simply *Elegien*. Like the *Römische Elegien* they are in the tradition of the Latin love elegy. Set in a modern Rome of political and social turmoil that greatly disturb the "Oheim," uncle of the poet's beloved, the poems describe how the two lovers are otherwise occupied. Nighttime pleasure, the harvest festival, and homage to the gods of love and revelry are the content of the four elegies. Several distichs unmistakably recall the *Römische Elegien*:

II   Wenn sie traulich des Abends in meinem Arme sich wieget,
       Vor uns ein knisterndes Licht flammt mit verglimmendem Docht.

IV   Dunkle Lauben lebt wohl, wo oft in süßer Umarmung
       Luna und Hesper uns fand, wo uns Aurora geweckt,
       Reizende Hügel lebt wohl und Dank dir Amor und Bacchus;
       Freundliche Demeter du, bleibet uns gnädig und hold.
       Diesen kleinen Altar hab ich mit Nine errichtet,
       Und wir weihten ihn Euch, Freude bringende Drey!

The poet is Heinrich Keller, designated simply K. in the *Musenalmanach*, a Zurich sculptor living in Rome. His manuscript, sent by Jakob Horner to Schiller for publication, demanded extensive revision, both due to metric flaws and over-explicit erotic content. Fifty-three of the fifty-seven distichs were altered and sixteen simply deleted.[60] That the passage in the second elegy is so like the *Römische Elegien* is, finally, more Schiller's doing than Keller's. He revised the original hexameter which read: "Wenn nach mühlichem Tag winket die freudige Nacht."[61] Indeed, there is evidence that Keller had not seen Goethe's *Römische Elegien* until he had completed the first two elegies.[62] But his imagery in the third and fourth elegies, including the lines cited above from the final poem, which is essentially Keller's own text, attest to his later awareness of Goethe's work. Schiller made minimal changes in the third elegy to distance it from Goethe's text.[63] Keller wrote a second collection of four elegies that were never published.[64] His *Elegien* are enjoyable enough, but decidedly lightweight in contrast to the *Römische Elegien*. They drew mixed comment and no imitators.[65]

Although there were other poetic responses to the *Römische Elegien*, Keller's *Elegien* are the only example I have found of a collection of poems in the tradition of the Latin love elegy. For example, in 1797 the eighth volume of Schiller's *Horen* included a single elegy of fifteen distich couplets entitled "An Eulalia. Bei der Übersendung von Göthe's Elegien." The poet, Karl Gustav von Brinkmann, is a minor figure and the elegy is his single contribution to the *Horen*.[66] The title as well as the final line suggest the kinship between this poem and the *Römische Elegien*:

Ihr nur bringe den Kranz—O! daß Sie dem Zauber erläge
    Der holdseligen nur, die mich versengt und entzückt.

(In its original version in the *Horen* Goethe's first elegy read:

O! wer flüstert mir zu, an welchem Fenster erblick ich
    Einst das holde Geschöpf, das mich versengt und erquickt?)

Finally, one must also not forget the direct incentive the publication of the *Römische Elegien* provided Knebel for the completion of his Propertius translation.[67]

One must conclude, however, that the *Römische Elegien* made no immediate contribution to the emergence of the lyric cycle as a conscious poetic structural device at the turn of the nineteenth century. The lyric cycle was taking on its structural definition elsewhere. As we turn now to Goethe's *Sonette* we come nearer its early beginnings.

III

The *Sonette*

As was the case with the *Römische Elegien*, Goethe never referred to his *Sonette* as a cycle. He mentioned the poems infrequently in his correspondence and journals, and when he did, he usually called them simply "meine Sonette." In a draft for the *Tag- und Jahreshefte*, however, one of the few direct statements he made on the poems and perhaps the most often quoted, he designated the seventeen sonnets a "Sammlung": "denn die kleine Sammlung Sonette, deren Gefühl ich immer gern bei mir erneuere, und an denen auch andere gern Theil genommen, schreibt sich aus jener Zeit her" (WA I, 36, 392). At the time Goethe wrote his sonnets, most sonnet collections, and indeed most collections of lyric poetry, were called "Sammlungen." This term encompassed a range of organizational possibilities. It was used to describe anthologies as well as sonnet sequences with a specific conceptual or formal design. As the standard descriptive term used at this time, "Sammlung" neither guaranteed nor denied the possibility that the poems in question might reveal a more elaborate structural relationship.[1] August Wilhelm Schlegel, for example, consistently referred to Petrarch's *Canzoniere* as a "Sammlung," both in 1796[2] when he argued that the poems lacked the necessary coherence to be regarded as an aesthetic whole and in 1803[3] when he proclaimed the collection a true and perfectly conceived lyric novel.

Goethe was not partial to new and popularized poetic schemes, as his prolonged resistance to the sonnet form testifies, and he avoided fashionable titles as well. It was often the simple generic name that he favored for his works: "Elegien," "Episteln," "Sonette," "Novelle," "Märchen." Using the generic name he was able to present each of these works as an exemplary model of the genre he had chosen. The process granted him a great deal of freedom in the conception and execution of his works. In this way he was not bound by the traditional rules of the genre, but rather set up a new genre whose rules he established by presenting the canonical work. In this decade of sonnet proliferation, the simple title "Sonette" and the collective appellation "Sammlung" acknowledged the literary tradition without a prescription of either content or composition for the work. Goethe's *Sonette* are the product of this artistic license.

45

When in December of 1807 Goethe was moved by the social sonneteering of the Frommann circle in Jena to join in the "sonnet madness" he had mildly condemned in previous years, he was fully aware that sonnet sequences enjoyed not only a long tradition but modern revival. The organization of sonnets into poetic sequences is almost as old as the sonnet itself. Over five hundred years before Goethe wrote his *Sonette*, Italian masters of this new lyric form were experimenting to find effective ways to join single sonnets together. In the beginning they chose a simple design. The thirteenth-century poet Folgore da San Gemignano cataloged a lifetime of worldly pleasures in twelve sonnets, one for each month of the year. He later completed a second collection of poems, one written for each day of the week.[4] His compatriot Fazio degli Ubreti composed a seven-member sonnet series in which each of the seven poems was devoted to one of the seven deadly sins.[5] As it became standard practice to collect sonnets (as well as canzoni and madrigals) in large number and to arrange them in poetic sequence, the patterns became more diverse. Some collections were organized by theme alone. Others began to experiment with interlocking rhymes. Eventually the repetition of entire lines was not uncommon and the elaborately conceived "corona dei sonetti," the fifteen-member sequence with its crowning "sonetto magistrale" was realized.[6]

It was Petrarch's *Canzoniere*[7] that assured the continuing popularity of sonnet collections even after interest in the intricate design of the "corona dei sonetti" waned in the eighteenth century. Petrarch's book of 366 poems—predominantly sonnets, but also *canzoni, sestine, ballate,* and *madrigali*—had already reached 167 editions in the sixteenth century.[8] In the last decade of that century the Petrarchan sonnet was introduced to England by Sir Thomas Wyatt and the Earl of Surrey, and it soon flourished. Countless sonnet sequences were written by the Elizabethan poets eager to display and develop Renaissance forms.[9] In the same century in France the group of the Pléiade and their leader Ronsard assured the permanent influence of Petrarch not only in the literature of their own country, but in Holland and Germany as well.

Despite this growing enthusiasm for the sonnet—it eventually became one of the most popular lyric forms in seventeenth-century Germany—sonnet sequences never were the fashion in Germany they had been in Elizabethan England.[10] The poetics of the Baroque were exclusively preoccupied with the definition of the sonnet form itself, and primarily the problems of meter and rhyme. With the advent of the eighteenth century and the lack of interest in the sonnet that characterized the literary life of France and England as well as Germany, sonnet sequences disappeared without a trace.[11]

When they were finally revived near the end of the eighteenth century it was Petrarch's *Canzoniere* that provided the model. Interest in Petrarch and his poems had been quickening for over a generation. The Halberstadt poets had responded to Meinhard's *Versuche über den Charakter und die Werke der besten italiänischen Dichter* (Braunschweig, 1763–74) with several lyric collections. Gleim's *Petrarchische Gedichte* (1764) and Klamer Schmidt's *Phantasien nach Petrarcas Manier* (1772) are perhaps the best known. Interest in Petrarch did not mean immediate recovery of the sonnet, however. Meinhard continued the eighteenth-century condemnation of the sonnet form and neither Gleim nor Klamer Schmidt included any sonnets in their two Petrarchan collections.[12] Although Blankenburg credits Johannes Westermann for the earliest return of the sonnet to German literature in 1765, he sharply criticizes the fourteen volumes of his *Allerneueste Sonette* (1765–89) by noting that "eine immer schlechter als die andere ist."[13] They were ignored. Single and at times awkward attempts followed in the 1770s. The poets included Klamer Schmidt, Friedrich Schmitt, and Ludwig August Unzer; the sonnets were published in lyric collections and in scattered literary journals.[14] New editions stimulated interest: the *Rime* appeared in Dresden in 1774 and the *Antologia Italiana* in Weimar in 1776. The approaching Petrarchan revival was being clearly signaled, but it was not until the appearance of Gottfried August Bürger's *Gedichte* in 1789 that the return of the sonnet to German literature was assured.

Bürger's *Gedichte* contained sonnets, and not just scattered poems, but sonnets in a sequence that chronicled his love for Molly and his grief at her death. Although these poems were not separated in any way from the other "Lyrische Gedichte" of his collection and each bore a separate title, a coherent sequence was suggested by the thematic organization. The poems were so arranged that two loosely connected groups were described, not unlike the two-part division that had been made explicit in the *Canzoniere* since the sixteenth century by the titles "In vita di Madonna Laura" and "In morte di Madonna Laura." Other lyric forms were occasionally interspersed in this sequence of love poetry, but the sonnet dominated.

There was hardly a *Musenalmanach* in the following years that did not offer at least a few sonnets to its readers.[15] As the sonnet continued to grow in popularity (the sonnet would soon be described as the romantic epigram)[16] the sonnet cycle became a standard setting. Yet it is not Gottfried August Bürger, but rather his student in Göttingen,

August Wilhelm Schlegel, who can claim the final credit for establishing the sonnet cycle in German literature. Obsessed by form, Schlegel lent the German sonnet formal excellence.[17] His sonnet sequences were widely read.

Schlegel had sent Goethe his first collection of lyric poems, *Gedichte*, in March of 1800 after its publication. In the collection sonnets are well represented, appearing both in sequence and as individual poems. Four sonnet sequences are included:

Geistliche Gemählde	11 sonnets
Die italiänischen Dichter	6 sonnets
Gemählde	3 sonnets
Cervantes	6 sonnets

Unlike Bürger's sonnets, these poems are clearly organized into distinct groups. Each sequence is titled, and each individual sonnet has a heading and a Roman numeral. All the sequences—we may call them cycles if we wish, although Schlegel does not do so—are organized by a very simple principle. One sonnet describes one painting, or one Italian poet, or one work by Cervantes. The cycle as a whole is a descriptive catalog, and its structural principle is additive. There is very little that relates individual sonnets to one another beyond this formal unity. (The coherence of the *Geistliche Gemählde* is augmented by the arrangement of the sonnets according to Biblical chronology.) For Schlegel the poems were distinguished by the dignity of their content. In anticipation of their publication he wrote to Goethe: "Sie werden sehen, daß ich die Sonette ganz auf Italiänische Weise zu bilden gesucht,—ich wollte ihnen dadurch mehr Größe geben, da man sonst bey uns im Sonette bloß auf das Weiche und Liebliche gegangen ist."[18]

Far more personal and clearly beyond the simple formal design of the sonnet cycles in the *Gedichte* is a group of poems which Schlegel published the following year in the *Musenalmanach auf das Jahr 1802*. The nine poems of the *Todten-Opfer für Augusta Böhmer* (the first and the eighth are not sonnets) were written by Schlegel after the sudden death of his step-daughter in the summer of 1800. Unlike the sonnet portraits of the *Gedichte*, in which the poet is scarcely visible and the individual work of art (or in the case of *Die italiänischen Dichter*, the individual artist) is presented with descriptive clarity, in the *Todten-Opfer* the poet himself is at the center of the poems. It is his grief and the search for a personal accomodation with the reality of untimely death that organizes the sonnets. Unexpected and tragic, the death of Augusta has challenged his belief in an ordered and purposeful universe (so Schlegel relates in the opening poem, "Sinnesänderung"), and the sonnets that follow chart the return to his step-daughter's grave and the attainment of solace. The earthly paradise and its spring-time promise only sharpen his awareness of death's pervasive power. With explicit reference to the *Hymnen an die Nacht*, but in verse that fails to attain the lyric force of Novalis's hymnic vision, the poet turns to the realm of night, of dream, and of poetic lament for comfort. Goethe specifically mentioned rereading the *Todten-Opfer* in December of 1807 (WA III, 3, 305). Although many of Schlegel's sonnets were models of formal excellence, his writing often lacked personal reso-nance. The poems written at Augusta's death are exceptional. They demonstrate that the sonnet, and specifically the sonnet in sequence, can give expression to the most tragic of personal experiences. Goe-the's rereading of these poems at the time he began his own cycle of sonnets, coupled with the sonnets of Zacharias Werner, which Goethe later praised precisely for the quality of tragic intensity (WA I, 36, 392), undoubtedly influenced his decision to attempt not just scattered sonnets for social amusement during the convivial Jena evenings, but a sequence of poems of personal import, namely the sonnet cycle he completed the following year and published in the *Werke* in 1815.

It should be noted, at least in passing, that other lyric forms as well as sonnets had begun by this time to be published in cyclical groups. The *Musenalmanach auf das Jahr 1802* is distinguished by no fewer than six lyric cycles in addition to Schlegel's *Todten-Opfer*. They are:

Tieck	*Lebens-Elemente*	8	poems
Schütze	*Die Tänzer*	15	poems
Tieck	*Der Besuch*	4	poems
Schlegel, Fr.	*Abendröthe*	21	poems
Novalis	*Geistliche Lieder*	7	poems
Schlegel, Fr.	*Hymnen*	3	sonnets

While none of these has direct significance for the study of Goethe's *Sonette*, they indicate a new and growing interest in multi-member lyric composition. The young Romantic poets were its enthusiastic promoters.[19]

No higher premium was attached to sonnets written in sequence than to those published singly, and no one structural model deter-mined how groups of sonnets ought to be organized. As Goethe joined in the sonnet writing that, to his own surprise and delight, had captured his poetic imagination during the month's stay in Jena, he was free to devise his own mode of composition.

As with the *Römische Elegien*, Goethe's letters and journal entries provide little insight into the specific conception of the *Sonette* as a cycle. They were begun in December of 1807. Goethe had been in

Jena since 11 November; on 2 December Zacharias Werner arrived, and to Goethe's delight the exuberant poet provided stimulating company. Repeatedly, Goethe's letters assert his pleasure at Werner's presence and the hours shared discussing his lyric and dramatic works:

Meinen hiesigen Aufenthalt macht mir Werner sehr interessant. Es ist ein sehr genialischer Mann, der einem Neigung abgewinnt, wodurch man denn in seine Productionen, die uns andern erst einigermaßen wiederstehen, nach und nach eingeleitet wird. Übrigens treiben wir allerley wunderliche Dinge und thun wir gewöhnlich mehr als wir sollten, nur gerade das nicht was wir sollten. (WA IV, 19, 470)

Again a few days later: "Es ist mir hier sehr wundersam gegangen, besonders hat die Gegenwart des Thalssohnes eine ganz eigne Epoche gemacht. Ich habe mancherley gethan, nur gerade das nicht was ich mir vorgenommen hatte" (WA IV, 19, 473).[20] In four letters Goethe repeats that he is happy doing what he never intended to be doing with his time in Jena: "Ich hatte mir manches zu arbeiten vorgesetzt, daraus nichts geworden ist und manches gethan woran ich nicht gedacht hatte; d.h. also ganz eigentlich das Leben leben" (WA IV, 19, 477). Goethe's major poetic project in these weeks was to be the writing of *Pandora*. The sonnets are a diversion and, when they begin to take the upper hand, an unexpected pleasure.

Goethe had written few lyric poems of any note for several years, his best creative efforts being absorbed instead by the *Farbenlehre* and related optical experiments. Additionally, the fall in Weimar had been constricting and unproductive. Hankamer's description of Goethe's illness and sense of a deep and irreversible loss in the years following Schiller's death locates this period of poetic stagnation within a crisis of great personal and social dimension.[21]

The sonnets mark a new beginning. Everything that Goethe has written about them indicates that he greeted their composition with confidence and the expectation of returned productivity. In a letter to Zelter, who after Schiller's death had become Goethe's closest friend, he excuses his silence of nearly three months:

Ich will das nicht entschuldigen, denn zu ein paar Zeilen an einen Freund gäbe es immer Zeit; allein ich bin seit meiner Rückreise aus dem Carlsbad so wunderlich von der Gegenwart geklemmt worden, als wenn ich für jene vier Monate, die ich wie ein abgeschiedener Gymnosophist auf ungetrübter Bergeshöhe zugebracht, wieder büßen sollte. Zwar ist mir nichts unangenehmes wiederfahren; doch drängte sich so manches Liebes und Unliebes heran, daß meine Kräfte, weder physisch noch moralisch, recht ausreichen wollten. . . .
Werner, der Sohn des Thals, ist seit zwölf Tagen hier bey uns in Jena. Seine

Persönlichkeit interessirt uns und gefällt uns. Er liest von seinen gedruckten und ungedruckten Arbeiten vor und so kommen wir über die seltsamen Außenseiten dieser Erscheinungen in den Kern hinein, der wohlschmeckend und kräftig ist.

Soviel, mein liebster, für dießmal. Ich packe ein, um wieder nach Weimar zu gehen. Hier ist es mir ganz gut geworden, und was Sie wohl nicht rathen würden, ich bin ins Sonettenmachen hineingekommen. Davon schicke ich Ihnen gelegentlich ein Dutzend. . . . (WA IV, 19, 474–75)

It is apparent that Goethe is promising the dozen sonnets with an air of ease and assurance. A number had already been written. (Each of the three sonnets that shows a date of composition in the manuscript predates this letter.) Because of this buoyant assurance, Goethe's subsequent delay in fulfilling this promise is provocative. It seems to indicate a reevaluation by him of the sonnets and, perhaps, a failure to meet his own expectations in their composition. Six months passed, and repeated prodding by Zelter was necessary before any sonnets were sent. Then only six were offered, and these after several repeated letters which ignored Zelter's polite reminder that he awaited the poems. Zelter's final letter is an elaborately stylized plea, and it proved successful only because he made sizeable issue of Goethe's negligence, albeit with tact and wit. At the end of March Goethe had responded to Zelter that he had no poems suitable for composition. Zelter, still eager to see the sonnets, answered:

Sie werden erlauben, daß ich einen kleinen etwas großen Zank mit Ihnen anfange. Denn 1mo muß ich Ihre Sonette haben, weil sie mir versprochen sind und ich dagegen wieder versprochen habe, woraus ein Kontrakt entstanden ist, der um so heiliger gehalten werden muß, da nicht Brief und Siegel, wie zwischen Kaufleuten oder Potentaten, sondern Wort und Treue das Recht verwalten. 2do muß ich als Königlich Preußischer angesehner Bürger und Kaiserlich Französischer, Königlich Italienischer Heptarch der *ci-devant* Residenzstadt Berlin doch wohl wissen, was sich nicht singen läßt; denn wer es jetzt nicht lernen wollte—

Ergo und kraft dessen bitte ich demütigst um meine 12 Sonette, von denen ich mir keins abdingen lassen will und mich zugleich anheischig mache, das zu singen, welches Sir für das unsingbarste bezeichnen wollen.

Telemann (ein hamburgischer Komponist des vorigen Jahrhunderts) hat gesagt: "Ein ordentlicher Komponist muß den Torzettel singen können," und ich sollte die Schande auf meinen Kaiser kommen lassen, ein Sonett nicht singen zu können? Das sei ferne!—Also nur her mit den Sonetten! ich will sie biegen wie Salat.[22]

The letter demanded a response, and Goethe sent six sonnets and a prefacing remark that is often cited in defense of the sonnet form (WA IV, 20, 85–86). Zelter was enthusiastic, thanked Goethe in his

next letter, and never mentioned the sonnets again! Nor did Goethe
ever inquire after their fate!

This is unfortunate, because if Zelter had set them all to music, he
would have been the first to compose a lyric song cycle—a musical
genre soon to be brought to great popularity by Schubert.[23] Goethe
had not sent six isolated sonnets to Zelter; he had sent a small lyric
cycle. Zelter's failure to compose an appropriate setting for these six
sonnets cannot be completely explained by a resistance to the sonnet
form, for he did set three sonnets, including Goethe's "Natur und
Kunst," to music.[24] But as a child of the eighteenth century, he never
composed a cycle of songs. That the sonnets that Goethe had sent
invited a group setting may have contributed to his neglect of the
poems.

It is with these poems, the six-sonnet cycle that Goethe sent to
Zelter in 1808, that we will begin our discussion of Goethe's *Sonette*.
As a sequence the poems have been ignored. They are:[25]

1. "Mächtiges Überraschen"   (I)
2. "Freundliches Begegnen"   (II)
3. "Wachsende Neigung"   (V)
4. "Gewöhnung"   (III)
5. "Entsagen"   (VI)
6. "Jähe Trennung"   (VII)

Goethe's selection clearly suggests his hope that Zelter would compose a setting for the entire sequence. As the titles of the six poems
indicate, they together describe a progression in an affair of the heart—
somewhat like a five-act tragedy with prologue. It is, however, a
dramatic structure that the poems themselves only partially realize,
for each title, while aptly suited to the poem it heads, is at the same
time a playful misnomer. "Freundliches Begegnen" might better be
entitled "Trotziges Zögern" because of its dominant images of resistance and retreat. "Wachsende Neigung" culminates in the final tercet in an image of distance which ironically transforms the poet's
growing desire into a futile longing. "Gewöhnung" is a witty attempt
to counter the poet's growing dependency, the title more a record of
his failure than his success. "Entsagen" does not conclude, as one
might expect, with a successful renunciation of love but with an affirmation of its abiding presence. "Jähe Trennung," finally, while sepa-
rating the poet from his beloved, suggests in the final tercet that there
is no real separation at all and that the poet has recovered in his heart
all he possessed before. And throughout all of these poems images
and events of the first sonnet, "Mächtiges Überraschen," are recalled,
in both contrast and confirmation. The first sonnet functions in this

sequence, as it does again later in the seventeen-poem cycle, as both prologue and counter-statement to the other five.

On the narrative level, which is suggested in the titles more explicitly than in the poems themselves, the poems move from first encounter through acknowledged passion to sudden departure. The titles of numbers two to six indicate a symmetrical structure, with the middle poem ("Gewöhnung") marking the high point of the love relationship. This is not quite the case, however. Throughout the sonnets there is a playful interaction between the poet's asserted desire to be in the presence of his beloved and the record of hesitant resistance, distant homage, attempted separation, final renunciation, and departure that the poems themselves provide. The poet intensifies the paradoxical idea of distanced closeness as he casts his beloved as a poetic ideal, as a heavenly vision, as a regal lady and dispenser of favorable glances, and as both subject and audience of his songs. While moments of immediacy and fulfillment occur, their occurrence is asserted more than described, and they are not central to the poems. They pale as each sonnet continues its record of resistance to the growing love. As love triumphs, the separation of the lovers is final. And precisely at the moment when all physical bonds are severed, when the poet's keenest glance can no longer discern the outline of the shore from which he has departed, precisely at that moment he asserts the full possession of the love the sonnets record:

> Und endlich, als das Meer den Blick umgrenzte,
> Fiel mir zurück ins Herz mein heiß Verlangen:
> Ich suchte mein Verlornes gar verdrossen.

> Da war es gleich, als ob der Himmel glänzte;
> Mir schien, als wäre nichts mir, nichts entgangen,
> Als hätt' ich alles, was ich je genossen.
>
> (6 [VII], 9–14)

The use of the subjunctive effectively underscores the subjective quality of the poet's possession. The love he has sustained marks a change in him and in his perception. It is a love none the less real for the absence of the beloved; indeed, its meaning is not understood until this distance is felt. Rather than describing a five-act tragedy of lost love, the five sonnets plus "Mächtiges Überraschen," which will require a more detailed examination in its relationship to the group, record a passage from restless isolation to assured possession. Despite its suddenness and lack of sufficient motivation, the reversal of feeling described in the last tercet is meant as a positive conclusion to the poet's journey begun in the second sonnet.

Although the sonnets are formally uniform and organized by a certain progression in their titles, they are not tightly joined in a narrative development. A few formal links are, however, employed. There is a repetition in rhyme that joins the second and third poems:

> grauen/Auen/anzuschauen/Frauen
> Auen/bauen/schauen/vertrauen

and the fourth and fifth poems:

> gewöhnen/Schönen/versöhnen/Tönen
> verschönen/versöhnen/von jenen/entwöhnen

"Gewöhnung" and "Entsagen" are further linked as the second seems explicitly to answer the question posed by the first, although, like so much that transpires in these sonnets, the response is not quite as straightforward as it first appears. "Gewöhnung" begins: "Sollt' ich mich denn so ganz an sie gewöhnen?" and the response follows in the opening line of the next poem: "Entwöhnen sollt' ich mich vom Glanze der Blicke." In addition, the motif of the glance in this sonnet provides a bond between it and the third sonnet ("Wachsende Neigung"). The third sonnet closes: "Ich beuge mich vor deinem Blick, dem flücht'gen." The opening of the fifth poem explicitly recalls this poetic posture. Schematically, these various links combine to effect fair coherence for the group:

J ⌐ G   1. "Mächtiges Überraschen"
o │ l   2. "Freundliches Begegnen"
u │ a ⌐3. "Wachsende Neigung"   > rhyme
r │ n │ 4. "Gewöhnung"
n │ c └5. "Entsagen"   > rhyme
e │ e
y └   6. "Jähe Trennung"

But what of my assertion that all is not as straightforward as it may first appear? We have already noted that the titles of the sonnets are somewhat playful misnomers and suggest a sequence of love poems far more conventional than the sonnets themselves prove to be. Similarly, the correspondence between the first and second sonnets in the cycle, made obvious by the explicit repetition of structural patterns and selected images and words is more complex than one first realizes. In addition, the fourth and fifth sonnets are less directly aligned by their question-and-answer relationship than may be immediately apparent. What must be noted is that the grammatical parallel masks a shift in meaning. "Sollt' ich mich denn so ganz an sie gewöhnen?" (4 [III], 1) might be translated "Should I become so very much accustomed to her?" It is a question posed by the poet to himself out of an

instinct for self-protection: ought I? is it desirable? The apparent response, however, "Entwöhnen sollt' ich mich vom Glanz der Blicke"
(5 [VI], 1), is not best translated using the same words: "It is desirable
that I grow unaccustomed to the light of her glances." "Sollen" has
been repeated, but it no longer designates a question that the poet
poses to himself, an attempt to determine the most desirable course
of action. Destiny has intervened, the higher powers have moved the
decision outside the domain of the poet's musings: "Was man Ge-
schick nennt, läßt sich nicht versöhnen;/ Ich weiß es wohl und trat
bestürzt zurücke" (5 [VI], 3–4). Consequently, it is with a statement
of future necessity that the fifth sonnet begins: "I was to grow unaccustomed to the light of her glances." The continuity of the poems is
not as simple as it first appears. The meaning of the encounter and
the love that the poems record is far too complex for a simple narrative
structure. Poems that seem straightforward and unambiguous acquire
new interest in the, at times, problematic variation of the completed
cycle. Because this characteristic of the poems becomes even more
visible when all seventeen sonnets are considered as a cycle, our
discussion of it will be postponed until later. A comparison of the six
poems sent to Zelter with the final sequence of seventeen reveals that
these six were selected to minimize the most extensive differences in
the cycle and to effect the greatest coherence possible. For this reason,
our discussion of these six will focus on this intended unity.

The five-sonnet sequence (from "Freundliches Begegnen" [2 (II)]
to "Jähe Trennung" [6 (VII)]) is held together by the fiction of a
journey begun in the mountains and completed by the departure at
sea. An embrace closes the opening sonnet, and a final kiss begins
the last. The love relationship in between, as we have noted, does not
sustain these images of immediacy. Instead, in the third and fifth
sonnets it is the regal glance that provides the metaphor of relationship. In the fourth it is the poet's song—a song that is intended to
soothe a longing for the beloved's presence, and in a delightful turn
that closes the sonnet, fires the desire anew. The poet is a reluctant
lover whose desire is at odds with a constraint never really clarified.
The beloved is one who bestows upon him her favorable glances, but
she is a lady because he has cast her in this role: "Doch ach! nun muß
ich dich als Fürstin denken" (3 [V], 12)—a ploy that intensifies both
desire and the demands of restraint. The beloved is more poetic occasion than participant in the five-sonnet sequence. It is the poet
himself who is at the core, and his sensiblities structure the poems.
While it seems at times that the sonnet form more than any force
within him has dictated the shifts in his emotional experience, it is
nevertheless his experience that is central.

Unlike the *Römische Elegien*, the sonnets do not exhibit an interlocking network of imagery and metaphoric reference. One group of images is fundamental both to the structure and meaning of the poems, however. The woman the poet encounters so unexpectedly on his journey and who interrupts his defiant solitude is presented in images of light and heavenly revelation: "Auf einmal schien der neue Tag enthüllet:/ Ein Mädchen kam, ein Himmel anzuschauen," (2 [II], 5–6). Her glances in the fifth poem, glances which define her presence completely to the poet (for she is otherwise absent from this sonnet) sustain these images. And the experience of unanticipated revelation and heavenly light is repeated in the final tercet of the last sonnet: "Da war es gleich, als ob der Himmel glänzte" (6 [VII], 12). The attribute ascribed to the woman's appearance in the mountainside encounter has become part of the poet's perception of the world about him in the final sonnet. The love he sought to avoid is now transforming his vision of the world. Dissatisfied longing is replaced by inner composure. The final tercet is somewhat unprepared. But in both the sonnet before it, in which the poet's love is declared his sole provision for the approaching journey, and in the images of light and heavenly revelation, there is continuity. It is "Mächtiges Überraschen," however, more than any other poem, that makes the closing lines of "Jähe Trennung" a suitable conclusion to this cycle of six poems. Its relationship to the other five demands consideration.

"Mächtiges Überraschen" is generally recognized as one of Goethe's finest poems and has sustained critical interest more in spite of, rather than because of, its placement in the *Sonette*. The *Sonette*, when not altogether ignored by critics, are accorded, not entirely undeservedly, a status of second rank among Goethe's poems. Consequently, the relationship of "Mächtiges Überraschen" to the sonnets that follow has been of little interest in the past.

It has been repeatedly stressed by interpreters of this poem that it ought not be read as an allegory. While it is clearly linked to Goethe's personal experiences in the winter of 1807–08, it cannot be reduced to a set of biographical equations:

River = Goethe
Oreas = Minna Herzlieb, or Bettina, or Silvie von Ziegesar[26]
Lake = Their love

Both Hankamer[27] and Killy[28] stress the symbolic function of the images employed in this sonnet. Hankamer, more than Killy, is inclined to interpret the poems as confessional: "Die erste und autobiographisch unmittelbarste Darstellung seines Erlebens gab der Dichter in dem Eingangssonett 'Mächtiges Überraschen.'"[29] Nevertheless, he is careful to assert that the autobiographical element is preserved in the interplay of the forces that clash and seek resolution in the sonnet, in the process itself, and not in the component parts: "In diesem Sonett findet das Urphänomen des Übergangs und der Umgestaltung seine erste geistbewußte dichterische Deutung."[30]

Unlike the other five sonnets, "Mächtiges Überraschen" is conceived completely in terms of natural phenomena. There is no lyric "I" at the center to organize the poem and its movement. The driving undistracted motion of the river and the sudden and precipitous fall of the rocks are the images that dominate in the two quatrains. In the sestet, in a superb realization of the sonnet form, a resolution of these two opposing forces is achieved. In a chain of shifting responses— "sprüht und staunt zurück und weichet/ Und schwillt bergan"—the water settles into a new existence. The continuity in this transformation has been recorded, but the resulting phenomenon is radically opposed to the river of its origin. The river of the first quatrain is markedly oblivious to its surroundings in the downward course to the ocean: "Was auch sich spiegeln mag von Grund zu Gründen,/Er wandelt unaufhaltsam fort zu Tale." Yet it is precisely the interaction with these surroundings that defines its motion and the life of the lake that is formed in the final six lines of the poem:

> Sie schwankt und ruht, zum See zurückgedeichet;
> Gestirne, spiegelnd sich, beschaun das Blinken
> Des Wellenschlags am Fels, ein neues Leben.
>
> (1 [I], 12–14)

The old gives way to the new, "das Streben" is replaced by "ein neues Leben"—as the final rhyme so succinctly underscores.

The events, while conceived completely in terms of natural phenomena, invite an interpretation that speaks to human experience. Not only is anthropomorphic design conveyed in the intentional striving of the stream and the erotic interaction of stream and mountain nymph, but also in the naming of the goal of the stream's single-minded flow as both ocean and father, a fusion familiar since Goethe's earliest poetry.[31] Nevertheless, the poem resists a psychological interpretation. The events occur, but they are not explained. "Dämonisch" is the adverb that prefaces the intrusion of the rocks on the river's course. It is the experience of sudden and unexpected mutation within the natural order. The new life the sonnet proclaims is the result of an encounter, powerful and unexpected, erotic and fateful, that necessitated a new existence, a new relationship to the self and to the world about. Life continues, but it has a new form. The single-minded striving towards the ocean is replaced by a more pacific and receptive role as the stars engage in a reflection of themselves in the waters below.

The phrase "ein neues Leben" is used in apposition to this new interaction of heaven and earth, and at the same time, as in the poems we have previously noted in our discussion of the conclusion of the first of the *Römische Elegien*, it provides in abstract summation the meaning of the entire sonnet. Unlike the conclusion to the opening elegy of the first cycle, however, the phrase "ein neues Leben" does not offer an uneasy resolution to the tension established within the poem, and one that demands explication in the poems that follow. Rather, it provides conclusive affirmation of the transformation the sonnet has recorded.

At the same time "ein neues Leben" might well be regarded as the title of the five-sonnet sequence that follows, a sequence both in analogy and counterstatement to the introductory sonnet. One cannot read the second sonnet, "Freundliches Begegnen," without immediate recollection of the structural development and motifs of "Mächtiges Überraschen." One quatrain each is accorded the masculine and the feminine in the sonnet. He descends a mountain path, she appears suddenly—and his life is altered. A series of responses, linked as in the first tercet of "Mächtiges Überraschen," follows: "Doch wandt' ich mich hinweg und ließ sie gehen/ Und wickelte mich enger in die Falten." In the second tercet a resolution is accomplished, and an embrace signals the end of the isolation and unrest of the opening quatrain. Here the second sonnet differs from the first. The transformation is explicitly presented as one from negative self-absorption to receptive openness, a value judgment withheld in "Mächtiges Überraschen." It is furthermore a transformation that is not physical, but a spiritual encounter played out in a mountain landscape. The concluding rhymes of both the quatrains and the tercets underscore this basic tension. The quatrains end "Unruh'gen Sinns, zur nahen Flucht gewillet" and "Mein Sehnen war gestillet." The tercets conclude with two symbolic physical gestures: "Als wollt' ich trutzend in mir selbst erwarmen" and "Die warf ich weg, sie lag in meinen Armen." The conflict is internal. The mountainside encounter of the second, like the collision of stream and rock in the first, is not to be understood literally but rather is symbolic. To insist on a biographical analogy for either poem or to establish rigid parallels between them is to fail to appreciate how carefully Goethe has avoided such directness in these two poems. They are deceptive, and they are rife with poetic wit and playful restatement. Hankamer credits the opening sonnet with the establishment of a niveau that guarantees a seriousness of purpose and insight for the poems that follow.[32] It does this most certainly, but there are recurrent indications that no insight will be obtained in direct pursuit. To borrow from the imagery of the opening sonnet, we are no longer storming headlong down to the ocean but engaged in a reflection of the stars above. The *Sonette* are bringing a new poetic life and a new poetic experience.

The final sonnet "Jähe Trennung," together with "Freundliches Begegnen," demonstrates the most suggestive relationship to "Mächtiges Überraschen." "Freundliches Begegnen" records a transformation from defiant self-enclosure to receptive embrace, from restless longing to satisfaction. A second transformation concludes the cycle in the final tercet of the sixth poem. The imagery of the closing tercet of "Mächtiges Überraschen" is reintroduced to assert an abiding satisfaction. The stars above shine once more, and once more one might add, "ein neues Leben."

Since Zelter did not set these poems to music, this cycle of six poems has been forgotten. An attempt to guarantee the greatest possible unity for the sequence is evident, but the cycle is far from being a model of consistency. Only when compared with the even greater diversity of the seventeen-poem cycle that appeared in 1827 in the *Ausgabe letzter Hand*,[33] can the six-poem sequence be regarded as unified in purpose.

The *Sonette*, and with this title I am from now on referring to all seventeen poems as they appeared in the *Werke*, can be separated into five loosely defined groups for the purpose of discussion. In brief summary:

I-VII	The six Zelter sonnets plus Nr. IV begin the cycle.
VIII-X	They are followed by three epistolary sonnets penned by the beloved.
XI-XIII	The next three sonnets display little relationship to one another. All three have been written by the man.
XIV-XV	Two dialogue sonnets pose the problem of the sonnet form as an effective expression of love.
XVI-XVII	The cycle is concluded by two poems in celebration of the beloved and the day the love began.

The poem "Abschied" (VII), which concluded the sequence sent to Zelter (as "Jähe Trennung," 6), now only marks a turning point in the relationship of the poet and his beloved. The epistolary sonnets and the two dialogue poems provide distinctive variation within the sequence. The poems suggest a temporal continuity without specific stress on matters of narrative relationship or chronology. Goethe includes both coherent and incoherent groups in his cycle and the type of coherence is not always the same. There is no single focus for the collection. Nor is there a tangible and fixed setting within which to locate the poet and his verse, as in the *Römische Elegien*. Rather the *Sonette* are poems more internal, more witty and more elusive, and if they are centered in any one concept, it is "das neue Leben" the opening sonnet proclaims, a motif that is not, however, developed to any great effect in the span of seventeen poems. The overall planning of the cycle is loose, and the difficulties the sequence of poems presents are many.

The sonnet form itself contributes to the difficulty of the *Sonette*. As a form, the sonnet is unusually self-contained. In the economy of fourteen lines all is said, the final words rhyming their conclusion no sooner and no later than at the close of the second tercet. There is considerable poetic gain in the successful exploitation of the stanza structure. Digressions are few. Consequently, it is often a single idea that is conceived and developed in the poem with refinement and wit. In the *Sonette* this formal independence of the sonnet structure aggravates the already marginal continuity of the poems.

The sonnets are a study in contrasts. The most obvious is between the girl (young, spontaneous and straightforward) and the man (sophisticated and complex). He is much older, possibly famous (the suggestion is made by the bust in Sonnet IV) and he is a reluctant lover. Three of the sonnets in the first series speak of his hesitation and coldness (Sonnets II, III, IV). A sudden turn in the last tercet is common to all seven of the opening sonnets (I-VII) and underscores the complexity of the poet's response to the young girl he has met. (A much simpler sensibility is expressed in the three epistolary sonnets penned by the girl, VIII-X, and these poems are marked by a continuity of thought rather than sudden turns.)

The stylization of the young girl in the opening sonnets as a noble and distant lady is an indication of the poet's ambiguous response to her presence and her love. It begins at the moment of their encounter in the second sonnet:

> Ein Mädchen kam, ein Himmel anzuschauen,
> So musterhaft wie jene lieben Frauen
> Der Dichterwelt.

(II, 6–8)

Even before the poet has admitted his love, he has made the explicit comparison of his beloved to the women of poetic renown—Dante's Beatrice and Petrarch's Laura. His love from the very beginning is cast within the protective conceit of these literary relationships. He does not choose to perceive his beloved apart from it. Even as he tosses off his mantle at the close of Sonnet II, he is willingly assuming the cloak of a Dante or a Petrarch. The gesture of self-revelation is ambivalent.

Similarly, the admission of passion that concludes Sonnet III is hardly a moment of naive self-disclosure. It is stylized from the start in a medieval-Renaissance motif of a debate between Self and his Heart. The triumph of the Heart and the joke at the poet's expense (the escape from life into literary activity fails as the poet is turned back into life by the power of his own song) is so obviously a conceit that the confession of love pales. The distance lost (maintaining a distance from the beloved is the immediate goal of the poet's song) is immediately regained in the artifice of the poem's structure. The stylization of the girl as "Fürstin" (V) (and later as "Herrin" [XVI]) is an additional device borrowed from medieval minnesang and Renaissance poetry to sustain distance in the newly found relationship.

This distance is fundamental to the poet's expression of the new love the *Sonette* proclaim. Sonnet IV, "Das Mädchen spricht," underscores the poet's responsibility for the courtly metaphor that defines the relationship of the lovers while they are together (at least to the poet). The girl, when she is allowed to speak for herself, reveals what little basis this portrait has in reality. But this is precisely the point. The unexpected encounter that leads to a new love and a new life (as introduced in Sonnets I and II) is not a naive affair of the heart for the poet, and the sonnets are not conceived to enhance the love between the girl and the poet. Instead they arise (in implicit analogy to Petrarch's songs) out of the very failure of the love to achieve fulfillment. It is the unlived life that is productive of poetry in the *Sonette*, the renunciation of love that guarantees its creative potential. It is for this reason that the poet at every turn appears the hesitant lover, distancing himself repeatedly from the young girl who so eagerly seeks his love. It is for this reason also that the moment of renunciation in the final tercet of Sonnet VII is the moment in which the poet claims full possession of the love the *Sonette* proclaim.

There are two contrasting images of the beloved presented in the *Sonette*—she appears both as a young girl and as a lady of dignity and distance—and the two are not necessarily contradictory. Rather they assert, particularly in the first seven sonnets, the complexity of a love relationship that is as much literary experience as live encounter for the poet. Unfortunately, in the course of the seventeen-sonnet cycle discrepancies arise that cannot be explained by ascribing them to the complex sensibility of the poet. In some instances, as in Sonnet X, the surprising candid avowal of love is a fiction penned by the girl and not the man's voice: "Da läs' ich, was mich mündlich sonst entzückte:/

'Lieb Kind! Mein artig Herz! Mein einzig Wesen!'" (X, 8-9). Other poems are less easily reconciled to the relationship presented in the earlier sonnets. For example, the poet's pleading in "Warnung" (XIII) for a positive response to his words of affection only confuses the relationship. Not only does the sonnet "Das Mädchen spricht" (IV) give him little cause to call her silent and unresponsive, but the three epistolary sonnets are rich with her words of longing and love. These difficulties have led Staiger to suggest a comparison with the *West-östlicher Divan*. In the *Sonette* Goethe attempted, but failed, to create the poetic masks that sustain the later work: "In den *Sonetten* hat Goethe weder für sich noch für die Geliebte schon eine eindeutig bestimmte Rolle gefunden."[34] One must agree and note that this failure is the principal barrier to a satisfactory interpretation of the poems as a seventeen-member sequence.

We will consider each of the five groups suggested above in turn to clarify the organization of the seventeen poems and to note other interpretive problems they present.

The continuity of the cycle is strongest in the first seven sonnets. Even so, their connection is looser than in the poems sent to Zelter, because they have been rearranged and given new titles, and because an additional poem has been placed in the center of the sequence. We will not repeat all that was said before about these opening sonnets (in the discussion of the Zelter sequence), but rather will note the effect the inclusion of the new sonnet, "Das Mädchen spricht" (IV), has on the series.

The new poem that is introduced to the sequence of six that opens the cycle is actually one of the oldest, if not the first sonnet that Goethe wrote in 1807, and is based on a motif taken from one of Bettina's letters.[35] Once Goethe made the decision to include it in the final cycle, it necessarily had to be placed in the first seven poems, before the poet's departure to sea. The teasing scene of reproach and affection could not be played out effectively in the epistolary sonnets that follow. Furthermore, it is almost by necessity that it became the fourth poem. Sonnets I-II and VI-VII are thematically inseparable and their location within the sequence fixed. A transition between the new sonnet, entitled simply "Das Mädchen spricht," and either the second sonnet or the sixth would have been extremely awkward. The second sonnet proclaims the poet's surrender of his guise and the beloved's acceptance of his embrace. The sixth opens with his declaration of an unwillingness to depart from the beloved's presence. Neither is compatible with the cold withdrawal the girl ascribes to the poet in her poetic reproach in Sonnet IV. All that was left was to place the two remaining sonnets, "Kurz und Gut" and "Wachstum," on either side. Again thematic considerations and a desire for continuity clearly prevailed.

A reordering of the opening sequence of sonnets is not the only effect the inclusion of the poem "Das Mädchen spricht" has on the series. Even the slightest suggestion of symmetry has been removed— the titles no longer reinforce such a pattern. The sequence as a whole is lighter and more playful, much the effect of the impish threat the beloved poses. In the Zelter sequence she remained distant, visible only as she was able to effect great indecision and emotional turbulence in the poet. It was the image of the gracious lady and the poet's longing for her glances and favors that prevailed. In the extended collection, however, a second portrait is drawn. The girl who speaks in IV is anything but distanced and ennobled. She is, indeed, young, affectionate, witty, and more than willing to share in the love the poet can bring to her. The disparity is intentional, as we have noted, and it is the girl of "Das Mädchen spricht" (IV) who later returns in Sonnets VIII-X to express her love for the man from whom she is separated.

The three epistolary sonnets (VIII-X) provide a welcome variation in the cycle. Written by the beloved, they witness to a love that has meant fulfillment and happiness. They are direct and communicate, as far as the sonnet form allows, a simplicity of thought and devotion. No dialogue with the man is established, but the tone is conversational, using rhetorical questions and imagined replies to suggest his response. A comparison with "Buch Suleika" is inevitable; there are similarities in both tone and message:

> Sag' ihm, aber sag's bescheiden:
> Seine Liebe sei mein Leben,
> Freudiges Gefühl von beiden
> Wird mir seine Nähe geben.
> (WA I, 6, 187)

But unlike Suleika's, the girl's letters have a plaintive note, for the man remains silent. Her recollection of the past asserts a fullness and immediacy of love that the letters hope to sustain. In the first sonnet it is the exchange of glances, the kiss that is recalled; in the second, a speechless gazing upon him that brought self-fulfillment; in the third, words of affection and tenderness. But this recollection brings her no comfort; there is no sudden reversal as in the seventh sonnet, no assertion that all that has gone before is not lost, but once more the lover's possession. The man has renounced his love and through renunciation has recovered his loss. The girl, by contrast cannot and will not renounce (the thought never crosses her mind) and must, therefore, continue to long and pine.[36] Why did he leave? Why shouldn't he come back? The girl was happy in his love and cannot understand that he should not be happy too. Her sonnets are not great poetry, but agreeable and straightforward and successfully augment the portrait of her introduced in Sonnet IV.

The three epistolary sonnets are not isolated within the cycle but are linked in various ways to the poems that precede and follow them. By specific reference in the first of the epistolary sonnets to the moment of the poet's departure, as well as in the continuing metaphor of the "Blick," the three poems are linked to Sonnets V, VI and VII. "Wachstum" (V) concludes: "Ich beuge mich vor deinem Blick, dem flücht'gen" (V, 14), and the sixth sonnet continues immediately: "Entwöhnen sollt' ich mich vom Glanz der Blicke" (VI, 1). The retreating shoreline and the poet's longing gaze at its vanishing images structures the seventh sonnet. Finally, the motif is sustained in the first of the epistolary sonnets to augment the transition: "Ein Blick von deinen Augen in die meinen" (VIII, 1). The repetition of selected motifs is also used to relate the epistolary sonnets to other poems in the cycle. For example, in the eighth sonnet the beloved makes reference to "das Lispeln dieses Liebewehens" (VIII, 12), and in the tenth sonnet this is repeated, but now in reference to the poet's speech, "dein Lispeln" (X, 12). In a similar manner, the beloved confesses in the tenth sonnet a fond memory: "Wie du so freundlich meine Sehnsucht stilltest" (X, 10), and recalls explicitly the poet's words in the second: "Mein Sehnen war gestillet" (II, 8). She adds in the same poem: "Und mich auf ewig vor mir selbst verschöntest" (X, 14). As the poet's departure had drawn near in the sixth sonnet he had stated: "Mein Leben sollten sie nicht mehr verschönen" (VI, 2). The repetition is somewhat misleading, however, for it suggests a love that is wholly reciprocal. But the mutual satisfaction that this repetition of selected phrases suggests is never central to the sonnets of the cycle. Although it is indirectly asserted in a number of poems, and it serves to strengthen the bonds between the various sonnets in the cycle, it is not the focus of the collection. It cannot be, for a mutually satisfying love is not the love the sonnets proclaim. It is indicative of the interpretive difficulties the sonnets pose that these repetitions, used to augment the structure of the sequence, should be thematically misleading.

The epistolary sonnets are placed to enhance the thematic continuity of the cycle and form a cycle within the cycle. The three sonnets that follow (XI-XIII) are far less continuous. They are the most loosely defined of the five groups in the cycle. They have been placed together between the epistolary sonnets and the dialogue sonnets, but there all similarity ceases. The poems are structurally disparate, thematically unrelated, and share neither imagery nor diction. Yet the three do not prove wholly disruptive because the previous poems provide a secure context for the playful expression of love they bring. Indeed, they are a welcome variation to the two extended sequences that have gone before, somewhat like the shorter of the *R·omische Elegien* that Goethe used to provide relief after his longer and more ponderous elegies. None is compatible with any of the other groupings in the cycle, and that is as good cause as any for their placement together.

In each of the three poems the poet speaks, and in two of them he addresses the beloved directly. The titles are brief. "Christgeschenk" (XII) reveals a thematic link to the epistolary sonnets and to the imagery that concludes both the first and seventh poems. In contrast, both "Nemesis" (XI) and "Warnung" (XIII) introduce entirely unexpected subject matter. The question why Goethe disregarded the thematic kinship of "Christgeschenk" and the epistolary sonnets (as well as the relationship of "Nemesis" to the dialogue poems) in his ordering of the three sonnets is difficult to answer. Perhaps he preferred the juxtaposition of dissimilar works to create more interesting space between the poems and to augment the tension within the cycle. Perhaps he chose the arrangement he did because of the difficulty of finding a suitable place for "Warnung." "Warnung" would follow the epistolary sonnets very badly. In this sonnet the courtier of the opening seven sonnets has returned. The poet's address to the beloved as if she were a reluctant lady is a troubling contradiction of the affectionate letters she has penned. The discrepancy cannot be explained away. It can only be minimized by careful placement of the poems.

Unlike the first seven sonnets of the cycle and Goethe's skillful attempt to adapt a traditional form to his purposes by using its conceits and conventions in his stylized proclamation of a new love, poems XI and XIII are heavy-handed. "Nemesis" (XI) is wildly extravagant. "Warnung" (XIII) is contrived. These two poems attempt a witty tone of self-irony and provide a sharp contrast to the open affection of the beloved's letters. In contrast, in "Christgeschenk" (XII) the poet makes an attempt to adapt his style to the simplicity of the beloved's letters. He begins by letting her have her way and addresses her as she wishes to be addressed. But then step by step he draws back. The dominant image is that of Christmas sweets which, however, grow more abstract in each successive repetition. The sweets in the first strophe are cookies; those in the second are flattering sonnets which the lover might, but disdains, to write; and those in the third are the loving remembrance which the man feels and wants the beloved to feel. In "Christgeschenk" the poet continues the verbal images of bridged space that run through the epistolary sonnets ("in diese Stille herlieben," "in die Ferne reichen" [VIII], "hinübertragen," "hinüberwenden" [IX], "hinüberwehen" [XII]) and offers a gift of love to span the physical distance. What he offers is cold comfort, however. She wants him to come back, or at least write her love letters. He wants her to be content with "ein freundliches Erinnern"— which is considerably less than passion. The "very small gift" which he sends her is, literally, the box of sweets; figuratively, the kind remembrance born of renunciation:

> Und fühlst du dann ein freundliches Erinnern,
> Als blinkten froh dir wohlbekannte Sterne,
> Wirst du die kleinste Gabe nicht verschmähen.
>
> (XII, 12–14)

The stars once more bear poetic witness to the power of renunciation. The parallel to the image used in the closing tercet of "Abschied" (VII) is unmistakable. The beloved is invited to renounce her passion as the poet has renounced his.

"Nemesis" concludes with the words: "Doch trennet mich von jeglichem Besinnen/ Sonettenwut und Raserei der Liebe." As plague and punishment are visited upon the scornful, sonnet writing and love's madness are indivisibly paired at the poem's end. While the self-irony is exaggerated, the direct association of love with the writing of sonnets is not meant simply as a passing joke. In the two dialogue sonnets that follow (XIV-XV) this fusion is given thematic status.

Dialogues in poetic form are not new to Goethe's poetry; nor were they new to sonnet composition in 1807. Zacharias Werner, among others, had written several notable sonnets in which two, three, and even four voices were engaged in poetic exchange. The two dialogues again bring structural variety to the sequence of sonnets, putting to rest any facile claim that a sonnet is a sonnet. They are obviously paired. In each the sonnet is greeted skeptically. A distrust of artifice is expressed, and a confession of love is sought. The two dialogues are staged in defense of the probity of the love sonnet.

In these two sonnets a number of inventive metaphors are employed. The critics in the fourteenth poem ("Die Zweifelnden") offer a comparison between the writing of a love sonnet and the labored and vain toils of Sisyphus. The poet in the fifteenth poem portrays himself as an explosive engineer. The exaggeration is part of the polemic, but the metaphors are not random selections. In both query and response, motifs and images that have been present throughout the cycle are reintroduced in new combination.

Fire, warmth, passion, and love have been associated since the opening sonnets, and the images have been consistently conventional ("im ersten Feuer," "heißes Liebetoben," "mein heiß Verlangen"). Stone, inertia, coldness, and concealment have also been joined and have been used to describe the poet's resistance to new love. It is this elemental opposition of fire and stone that is sustained in the dialogue sonnets.

The objections raised against the sonnet form in these exchanges are not new. The heart, we are told in the first, even when not constrained by the requirements of a strict form, finds it difficult to reveal itself. The constraint of rhyme and rhythm makes revelation impossible. The sonnet is no vehicle for a confession of love. In the next sonnet, it is not the resistance of the heart that disturbs, but the polish of the form. Can a confession of love be deemed candid if it has been so carefully filed and honed to poetic perfection? Furthermore, isn't this probing of passion a poet's way to protect himself from the power of his own emotion?

The responses to these charges are at once inappropriate and revealing. A direct answer is not given; instead, a metaphor is employed. It is the detractors who cast the first stone. The burden of prescribed poetic form, as hopeless an encumbrance as the rock of Sisyphus, is their description of the sonnet form. In a response that echoes far beyond this simple image of vain labor the metaphor of the stone is retained:

> Das Allerstarrste freudig aufzuschmelzen
> Muß Liebesfeuer allgewaltig glühen.
>
> (XIV, 13–14)

"That's no way to write love poetry," the detractors have said. "But it is the best way to write sonnets," the closing lines proclaim in a deft reworking of the conflict. Stone and fire, the sonnet form and the passion that renders it fluent, the resistant coldness on the mountain path and the love that overcame it, are joined in this proclamation of elemental fusion.

In the second dialogue stone and fire are again engaged in the concluding metaphor, and once more they prove an elusive response to the opening query. Even as the poet asserts the integrity of his passion he provides tacit affirmation of the beloved's suspicion: "Yes, the writing of poetry can serve to cool the passion, but it's dangerous work, and if I'm not careful I'll be blown up by my own craft." The analogy the poet draws to an explosive engineer is a hyperbole, and both he and the girl know this. This does not belie the danger that he describes, but, in truth, he has successfully controlled the explosive charges within the resistant rock and used them to his own purposes. He is skilled in his profession. The *Sonette* have been written; the poet has not been destroyed by either rock or fire, but found a new poetic life in their controlled interaction.

In 1827 Goethe wrote to Iken of his poetic composition: "Da sich gar manches unserer Erfahrungen nicht rund aussprechen und direkt mittheilen läßt, so habe ich seit langem das Mittel gewählt, durch einander gegenüber gestellte und sich gleichsam in einander abspiegelnde Gebilde den geheimeren Sinn dem Aufmerkenden zu offenbaren" (WA IV, 43, 83). One thinks immediately of the juxtaposition of "Das Sonett" and "Natur und Kunst" (and of "Prometheus" and "Ganymed"), and in the *Sonette* this same principle has been used. Both the opening sonnets "Mächtiges Überraschen" and "Freundliches Begegnen" and these two poetic dialogues illustrate this complementary process of reflection. Furthermore, in the interaction of fire and rock, as in the initial interaction of rock and water that began the cycle, Goethe has created two symbols of elemental and creative power. Together they frame the sequence of sonnets, providing two separate images of encounter and creative transformation that are conjoined within the cycle itself.

The dialogue sonnets closed the sequence of sonnets in the *Werke* of 1815. I am inclined to agree with Hankamer that they were originally intended to mark the conclusion of the *Sonette* and lost this position in 1827 only because of Goethe's reluctance to disrupt a sequence already formalized by publication.[37] The two poems originally withheld for personal reasons were appended to the conclusion rather than integrated into the cycle. "Epoche" and "Scharade," the two sonnets that were appended in 1827, are poems written for the company of friends in Jena. They are at once more private and more public—more private because they make direct reference to the events that produced the *Sonette*, references that are not to be found in the other fifteen sonnets; but also more public, for they were written to be read aloud and enjoyed. Here I acknowledge the persuasion of Schlütter's argument.[38]

The circumstances that led to the composition of the last sonnet are known. Werner wrote a "Scharade," or lyric riddle, for recitation at the Frommann house on 16 December. The poem celebrates the name "Herzlieb" as a word of love and happiness. Unlike Goethe's "Scharade," which he showed to Riemer the following day, the poem is quite explicit and reveals the beloved's name in the very first line: "Herz ist was Liebes, was so lieb wir haben."[39] Goethe is more elusive and does not repeat the beloved's name. It is introduced to the cycle in the first tercet of Sonnet X.

It is not unusual that two poets should celebrate the same woman in this manner. The charade, ever since Petrarch an established sonnet form,[40] was read far more for its skillful play on words than as a confession of love. It was an approved guise, a public display of affection without offense. Goethe's "Scharade" is a suitable enough conclusion to the sequence of sonnets. The revelation of the poet's secret, the identity of his beloved, has been reserved for the final poem. The sonnet itself is not distinguished, however. It is a pleasantly conventional homage that lacks as do so many sonnets in the cycle both the forcefulness and insight of "Mächtiges Überraschen," the first poem of the cycle. It is as easy to imagine that Goethe read his "Scharade" in the Frommann circle (even in the presence of Minna) as it is difficult to imagine that he introduced the opening sonnet of the cycle to these social gatherings.

The curious rhymes and diction of "Epoche" (XVI) reveal that it, too, was conceived for social purposes. In sequence it becomes a droll acknowledgment of the Petrarchan pose struck at various moments in the *Sonette*. The syntax is strained, particularly in the final tercet. The diction is uncertain (now high-flown, now prosaic): "Ebenso, ich darf's wohl sagen," "Doch stets erscheine, fort und fort, die frohe,/ Süss, unter Palmenjubel, wonneschaurig." The story of Petrarch's love for Laura *is* sad, but the poet chooses a tone of exaggerated sympathy: "leider unbelohnt und gar zu traurig." The rhyme words at the close of the stanzas are far-fetched. The poet is clearly engaged in play, but his purpose is not clear. The association of the sonnets he has written with the poetry of Petrarch is no ruse. (It corresponds to the invocation of Dante's *Vita nuova* at the end of Sonnet I.) There is clear delight in the skillful contrast drawn between Petrarch's first encounter with his beloved Laura on Good Friday and Goethe's first meeting with the beloved of his sonnets in Advent of 1807. Using the traditional Gospel text for the first Sunday in Advent, Matthew's account of the Palm Sunday entry into Jerusalem (Matthew 21:1–9), he moves from the dead of winter to a springtime of love and celebration. The unusual association of winter and new love is not unfamiliar to the cycle. It was on a wintry mountainside that the poems began and the new life found in a new love was first proclaimed.

"Epoche" and "Scharade" end the cycle of seventeen with a festive air. They are poems of celebration and reveal none of the internal uncertainty, longing, and resistance that began the cycle. Sonnet I tells of violent interference. XVI and XVII, like the final tercet of "Mächtiges Überraschen," show that the violence has not proved to be destructive. The poet's sovereignty over his passion and his craft has created new life in a new poetry of love. The day of its beginning will always be a day of fond recollection, and the beloved an image of happiness.

Zelter wrote to Goethe after he had received the six-sonnet cycle: "Für die schönen Sonette danke ich fürs erste herzlich. Viele, viele Male habe ich sie schon gelesen, und da ich die Situation und den Zusammenhang noch nicht erraten konnte, habe ich sie abgeschrieben, welches eins von meinen Hausmitteln ist."[44] His curiosity to know "die Situation und den Zusammenhang," just how all this meshes with Goethe himself, is natural, but it is a curiosity not satisfied within the course of the cycle. It is this curiosity that Goethe uses to conclude the sonnets. After "Epoche" and "Scharade" it's all been told, one feels, and the *Sonette* are over, the riddle solved. The fact that it is not all solved, that the *Sonette* have remained an enigma to scholars and critics who have seen in the poems the most intimate confession and the most contrived artifice, a tangled but intriguing blend of "Ernst und Scherz," signals anew that the poems never really do come to a resolution in any single poem.

The *Sonette* have long troubled Goethe scholars. The poems have so long been the object of biographical speculation that they have been neglected as works of art.[42] It has proven easier to cite selectively from them than to confront the entire sequence of sonnets as a group. Often the *Sonette* are simply omitted in surveys of Goethe's poetry.[43] They are a source of uneasiness, and the reasons for this discomfort are many. Gundolf, for example, claims that the *Sonette* fail to achieve genuine self-expression. They are lyric craft and not lyric confession: "Die Sonette sind entstanden aus der handwerklichen Freude am sprachlichen Bilden, ja Bosseln unter der Anregung des romantischen Modespiels mit den südlichen Formen."[44] In short, they are not *naiv*. For Gundolf, as for so many critics of Goethe's poetry, poetic integrity is synonymous with spontaneous self-expression. The *Sonette* are too self-aware: "Der künstlerische Spieltrieb und das überlegende, fast ironische, selbstbespiegelnde Wissen um die Liebe und um das Dichten als Handwerk wie als Seelenausdruck"[45] is their fatal flaw. Gundolf dismisses the poems as "bloß technische Meisterstücke ohne dichterisch seelischen Wert, artistische Musterbeispiele."[46]

Critics willing to deal with the text without fixed notions of poetic integrity are also disturbed by the *Sonette*. Staiger confesses at the outset that the sonnets are "nicht so leicht zu deuten."[47] He nonetheless attempts to find meaning in the contradictions and confusion of the poems. Schlütter, on the other hand, abandons the attempt to seek coherent meaning. He believes that the cycle "enthält nebeneinander inhaltlich und qualitativ die heterogensten Gedichte,"[48] and, in the face of "eine so offenbare Uneinheitlichkeit,"[49] he mounts an argument concerning the genesis and composition of the *Sonette* to account for the disparity of the collection.

One of the few critics of the *Sonette* who remains completely persuaded of their excellence and coherence is Hankamer. Hankamer's probing interpretation of the *Sonette* is not directly concerned with the cyclical structure of the poems. Rather he seeks to discover the meaning of Goethe's unexpected selection of the sonnet as an expressive vehicle for his attachment to Minna Herzlieb in the winter of 1807–08. Hankamer's argument is concerned, primarily, with the proper evaluation of this erotic experience as a markstone in Goethe's maturity—the point at which, independent of plan or desire, the course of his old age was altered, and a new personal and poetic existence took shape. The sonnets, especially the opening sonnet "Mächtiges Überraschen," together with *Pandora* and *Die Wahlverwandtschaften*, are the central documents of this turbulent period of reconstitution. Hankamer's discussion of the *Sonette* focuses on the first sonnet of the cycle. In an attempt to articulate the significance of the sonnet form he does not completely neglect the other sixteen.

Hankamer opposes two forces in his interpretation, "die Leidenschaft" and "der selbstsichere gefaßte Geist." The sonnets are the product of neither of these alone, but a synthesis, a synthesis made possible because the unanticipated full possession of both qualities gave Goethe, at this point in his life, new insight into the "Spiel der Mächte," the powers at work within his life and within the changing world. The sonnets are, therefore, not the record of this passion alone, but of the personal and poetic epoch to which it gave rise. "Die gewußte und gewollte Spannung von geistigem Spiel und seelischer Leidenschaft ist die innere Form des Zyklus geworden, das ironisch wissende Spiel mit der tragischen Gefahr, wie das Spiel der Mächte sie barg."[50] It is an elusive interplay of passion and wit that characterizes the poems.

Hankamer's concept of "Epoche" and his description of the threatening intrusion of passionate feeling that is productively contained in the sonnet form are credible and find support in one of Goethe's later statements in the *Tag- und Jahreshefte*:

Es war das erste Mal seit Schillers Tode, daß ich ruhig gesellige Freuden in Jena genoß, die Freundlichkeit der Gegenwärtigen erregte die Sehnsucht nach dem Abgeschiedenen und der auf's neue empfundene Verlust forderte Ersatz. Gewohnheit, Neigung, Freundschaft steigerten sich zu Liebe und

Leidenschaft, die, wie alles Absolute, was in die bedingte Welt tritt, vielen verderblich zu werden drohte. In solchen Epochen jedoch erscheint die Dichtkunst erhöhend und mildernd, die Forderung des Herzens erhöhend, gewaltsame Befriedigung mildernd. (WA I, 36, 391–92)

The difficulty is that the *Sonette* are not adequately described by the synthesis of passion and wit alone. It is the advantage of Hankamer's critical approach that he is not compelled to deal with the cycle sonnet by sonnet. It is not possible to locate within all the poems the monumental struggle he describes, and many of the difficulties the sonnets pose are not admitted in his account.

Schlütter has done a great service by calling our attention once more to the social purpose that originally motivated Goethe's sonnet writing. The poems were conceived in the beginning to be read aloud and enjoyed by an intimate gathering of friends. It is safe to assert that not all of the sonnets were written for presentation, but a number were.[51] Only secondarily did they find a place in a lyric collection. Unlike the *Römische Elegien*, where there is evidence that specific elegies were selected for the final collection and others excluded, the *Sonette* apparently include all the sonnets Goethe had written in 1807–08. Goethe gave his "Sammlung" the most meaningful order possible when he published the poems in 1815 and again in 1827. A closer examination of the poems has revealed that the sonnets vary so greatly in tone and poetic excellence that no attempt to reduce them to a single descriptive norm can be successful. Rather, one must affirm the purposeful organization and continuity of the poems and admit that some of the interpretive difficulties they present are insuperable.

I have resisted the temptation to define any single structural scheme that organizes the sonnets and have attempted instead to indicate varying reasons for the way in which the collection of poems is ordered. I have indicated as well the difficulties that a single and comprehensive interpretation of the cycle must necessarily encounter. There are three critics, however, who are less troubled by the barriers to unity in the *Sonette* and who have sketched schematic interpretations of the cycle. The arguments of Elisabeth Reitmeyer, Helen Mustard and Joachim Müller deserve brief consideration. Elisabeth Reitmeyer and Helen Mustard share an interest in structural symmetry. They both regard the epistolary sonnets as the axis in the geometric alignment of the *Sonette* and declare this symmetrical arrangement to be the decisive characteristic of the cycle. For Reitmeyer the symmetry elevates the cycle to paradigmatic status within her category of classic (as opposed to romantic) lyric cycles: "Die Sonette haben sich zum Ganzen gefügt, und zwar nicht nur zu einem los gebundenen Kranz, sondern zum klassisch symmetrischen, wohl-proportionierten Bau."[52] This structure, according to Reitmeyer, is symbolically appropriate to the content of the sonnets, to the central themes of moderation and renunciation. The arrangement is argued to be deliberate, and thematic correspondences between the poems thereby paired (I + XVII, II + XVI, III + XV, and so on) are sought. For the sonnets that reveal no clear thematic relationship when paired in this manner, she offers the dubious declaration that this variation is further proof of poetic excellence: it is a sign that the collection grew naturally ("wie natürlich gewachsen, wie wenig konstruiert").[53] In the very act of constructing a geometric model, she celebrates the organic metaphor!

Mustard is more cautious as she argues for a recognition of structural symmetry in the *Sonette*. Again the epistolary sonnets form the core of of the structure, but linear links and contrasting pairs are also introduced to modify the rigid symmetry. She offers the following schematic design:[54]

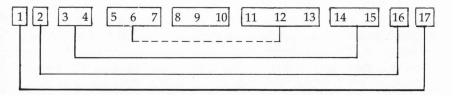

Furthermore, Mustard remarks that this symmetry is probably not the result of any consciously conceived scheme on Goethe's part. The progression of the sonnets is not meant to relate a connected story, but to highlight various stages in the love relationship being depicted. Finally, a value judgment is made on the *Sonette*'s composition: "Goethe's sonnet cycle is, indeed, one of the few true cycles in the sense that the construction is circular; the end returns to the beginning and thus the circle is completed."[55]

Reitmeyer's reductive structural scheme is self-defeating, as she demonstrates in her attempt to mask its deficiencies by a nod to the organic metaphor. Mustard's more cautious and more qualified assessment of the poems is preferable. But in both instances, too facile a balance within the cycle is posited. While it is not possible to deny the central placement of the epistolary sonnets in the cycle, the pivotal role assigned to them is unclarified. The candid affection and devotion the poems disclose is refreshing. They are effectively bound together in a trilogy of tender passion. But the suggestion that this frank and gentle love is the effective core of the cycle cannot be supported, nor can the

implication that all other sonnets have been arranged in careful symmetrical support. Rather, it is helpful to recall that these poems could
hardly have been placed elsewhere in the cycle, and that in their
judicious location provide a continuity and a deepening of the love
experience the *Sonette* record.

Neither Reitmeyer nor Mustard deals adequately with the continuity of the opening seven sonnets, nor with the marked diversity
of the other ten. The successive shifts from the opening poems to the
epistolary sonnets, to the wit of "Nemesis" and "Warnung," and
finally to the dialogue poems and the cycle's end cannot be justified
as marking turns in a developing love relationship. Rather, the thematic material is being consciously extended as the poems progress,
the possibility for play as well as passion is being probed, and their
fusion in the sonnet form becomes the central focus. In this way the
Sonette recall the deliberate turn at the end of the *Römische Elegien* to
an acknowledgement of the distich as the proper lyric vehicle for the
love those poems celebrated. Mustard's description of the *Sonette* as a
"true" cycle must be greeted critically. The sonnets are no more circle
than triangle, and the "true" cycle is a critical fabrication.

Joachim Müller does not offer so schematic an explanation of the
cycle's organization, but he is nonetheless insistent that the sonnets
display marked continuity. His argument is unfocused. He claims
that two principles are basic to the sonnets' organization. The first is a
principle of "lyrische Verfremdung," which he introduces as one of
several (unspecified) "motiv symbolische Bezüge" that unite the poems.[56] Sonnets IX, XIV, and XV are said to illustrate the technique.
The second is the love narrative, "eine lyrisch gefaßte Liebesge-
schichte mit tiefen Konflikten und mannigfaltigen Phasen, die von
enthusiastischer Unmittelbarkeit bis zu ironisierender Distanzierung
und zu versöhnlichem Verzicht reichen."[57] The "mannigfaltige Phasen" of the love story are not adequately explained, however. Müller's terminology is frequently obscure, and his discussion fails to
elucidate the organization of the poems. In his concluding remarks
Müller asserts that a contrapuntal principle is fundamental to the
cycle's organization and with rhetorical flourish (but without specific
elaboration) he lists eighteen contrasting pairs to support his claim.
Some of the pairs are legitimate if somewhat trite: "Kunst und Leben,"
"Jugend und Alter"; others are not contrapuntal as he suggests, but
sequential: "Hoffnung und Erfüllung," "Begegnen und Epoche"; still
others are simply ill-chosen: "Jüngstes Gericht und ewiger Maitag,"
"drohende Nemesis und poetisches Charadenspiel."[58] An attempt to
sum up this list with the catchwords "Systole und Diastole" only un-

derscores his failure to clarify the continuity of the sonnets that the title of his monograph proclaims.

That the *Sonette* are ordered to enhance the continuity of the seventeen poems and to minimize disruptive contradictions has been the argument of this study. That some contradictions remain must be acknowledged. Goethe wrote the sonnets and joined them in sequence without a fixed notion of cyclical structure. An interpretation of the poems that begins with such a notion can only prove inadequate to the difficulties they pose. For this reason the interpretations of Reitmeyer, Mustard, and Müller fail to convince. For this reason also, this discussion of the *Sonete* has sought to concede those problems the sonnets pose that are insuperable, suggest possible reasons for the diversity of the sequence, and assert the purposeful organization of the cycle that is nevertheless apparent and that joins the individual poems in the expression of the new love and the new life the sonnets celebrate.

In 1817 Friedrich Rassmann published an anthology entitled *Sonette der Deutschen* in response to what he called the "Sonetten-Legion" of recent years. Single sonnets and sonnet sequences are represented (none are called cycles) and attest to the variety in subject matter and in group organization that characterized the German sonnet by 1817. Bürger's and August Wilhelm Schlegel's poems are included in the collection, as are most of Goethe's *Sonette* (XV is inexplicably omitted; XVI and XVII had not yet been published). There are love poems, laments, obituaries ("Todtenopfer"), and descriptions of works of art, all in poetic sequence.

As their presence in Rassmann's collection indicates, Goethe's *Sonette* were recognized as part of the widespread enthusiasm for the sonnet that swept German letters in the early decades of the nineteenth century. It is clear that he did not initiate the craze; neither did he radically alter its course.[59] Goethe's sonnets did not have a marked influence on the sonnet sequences written by his contemporaries. The *Sonette* were not published until 1815. The number of sonnets being written declined greatly between 1820 and 1830,[60] and after 1825 it was Platen (*Sonette aus Venedig*) who set the future course of the German sonnet.[61]

Goethe wrote no more sonnet cycles, and he wrote very few poems of note in the immediate years that followed. Instead he worked intensively on the *Farbenlehre*, prepared manuscripts for the 1815 edition of the *Werke* (at which time he added the mottos that introduce a number of the lyric rubrics, including the *Römische Elegien* and the *Sonette*), and drafted *Dichtung und Wahrheit*. It was not until 1814 when Goethe discovered the poems of Hafis and began his extensive study of the Orient and its verse that lyric poetry again became a central preoccupation. To what extent the *Sonette* prepared Goethe for the far more ambitious and more successful composition of the *West-östlicher Divan* can only be conjectured. It is the *West-östlicher Divan*, that "wunderliches Ganze" (WA IV, 25, 333), that was written in the years that followed, that marked the return of the lyric cycle to his writing.

IV

The Trilogies

*The "Müllerin" Ballads, the "Paria" Trilogy,
"Trilogie der Leidenschaft"*

The three major lyric compositions by Goethe to which the word "Zyklus" is most generally applied today (the *Römische Elegien*, the *Sonette*, and the *West-östlicher Divan*) never enjoyed this common designation during his lifetime. Rather, as we have demonstrated in our discussion of the *Römische Elegien* and the *Sonette*, a variety of descriptive terms, related to the diverse literary origins of these lyric collections, were employed.

In this chapter we shall turn to a selection of poems that differ markedly from these well-known compositions. These are poems often overlooked in a discussion of lyric cycles, for as vague as the definition of the cycle remains, it is commonly understood to mean a series of at least four poems. We intend to explore the relationship of Goethe's trilogies to the emerging structural concept of the lyric cycle, however, because they, as much as the major compositions, offer insight into the variety of literary traditions and designs that informed the organization of poems into lyric groups at the turn of the nineteenth century.

Goethe's trilogies are not part of a response to a flourishing poetic genre, as were his *Sonette*. Soret writes: "J'observe qu'il y a peu d'exemples à moi connus de trilogies hors les siennes. Goethe répond qu'en effet cette form est très rare chez les modernes."[1] They also do not represent a conscious revival of ancient poetry in modern idiom, as did the *Römische Elegien*. While it is true that the word "Trilogie" has a specific classical referent, it is a term derived from drama rather than lyric poetry. "Trilogie"—literally, three utterances or words, from the Greek "tri" and "logos"—describes the three Greek tragedies chosen for sequential performance in ancient Athens. It is in this limited sense that the word "Trilogie" was first used in German. It entered the German language as a technical dramatic term about 1800.[2] Grimm documents the extension of the term in the course of the nineteenth

77

century beyond classical Greek drama to the works of German drama-
tists, to other literary genres, and finally to the visual arts.

Goethe played an active role in the extension of the word "Trilogie"
beyond its original classical meaning. He did not hesitate to regard
selected dramatic works of his contemporaries as trilogies (WA I, 41²,
66–68). He also did not find it inappropriate to call a series of three
pictures on a grave stone a trilogy (WA IV, 22, 360). In poetry as well,
trilogies were to be found and Goethe identified three of his lyric
sequences as trilogies in the winter of 1831. They are the "Müllerin"
ballads of 1797–98, the "Paria" trilogy, and the "Trilogie der Leidenschaft."

These three trilogies (the four "Müllerin" ballads are treated as a
trilogy, a problem which we will pursue later) could hardly suggest a
less immediate relationship to one another. They were written in
distinct periods of Goethe's life, in varying poetic genres, and are
distinguished more by diversity of structure than by any common
conceptual origin. None of the three was originally conceived as a
trilogy. Each was, however, published as a sequence and later designated a trilogy by Goethe. The four "Müllerin" ballads ("Der Edelknabe und die Müllerin," "Der Junggesell und der Mühlbach," "Der
Müllerin Verrath," and "Der Müllerin Reue") were written in 1797–98
and published the following year in Schiller's *Musenalmanach*. They
appeared in sequence in the journal, but were separated from one another by the insertion of a single unrelated poem (not written by
Goethe). Goethe took them into volume 7 of his *Neue Schriften* in
1800, and published all four in direct sequence under the rubric "Balladen." The "Paria" poems were completed in 1823. Goethe had read
the material that provided a basis for the poems well over three decades earlier and had tried without success to adapt the legend. The
actual writing of the trilogy extended over at least a year, from December of 1821 into 1823. The poems were first published in *Kunst
und Altertum* in 1824. The poems of the "Trilogie der Leidenschaft"
were originally written as independent pieces: the first, "Aussöhnung," in August of 1823; the "Elegie" in early September of the
same year; and the final poem "An Werther," in March of 1824. They
were first published together in the *Ausgabe letzter Hand*.

How did these three diverse sequences come to be joined under the
single designation "lyric trilogy" in the winter of 1831? It was Soret[3]
who first asserted their kinship, an observation that Goethe enthusi-
astically endorsed. Soret approached Goethe in the winter of 1831
with a selection of his poetry. Like so many younger poets of this era,
he sought critical approval for his lyric compositions from the acknowledged master of German verse. The poems he brought were

not scattered samples of his craft, however, but a short series of related sketches depicting a shepherd boy and the anguish of unrequited love. They were originally published in separate issues of the Weimar court literary pamphlets *Chaos* and *Création*.[4] Now Soret hoped to join the poems formally into a trilogy. Goethe's own works, the three trilogies that are the subject of this chapter, were introduced into the discussion of Soret's poems as exemplary models. They became the basis for an extended exchange on poetic composition.

This exchange is recorded by Soret in his memoirs, in Eckermann's *Gespräche*,[5] and documented by correspondence. A significant portion is, however, only partially retrievable—the conversations that took place during the long winter afternoons and evenings: "Daß Sie, mein Theuerster, in die Geheimnisse der Trilogie einzudringen wünschen, freut mich ganz besonders, und nur desto mehr, als ich Sie auf dem rechten Wege finde. Doch ist dieses Capitel wegen großer Zartheit und Mannigfaltigkeit, nur mündlich zu behandeln" (WA IV, 49, 160).

Because it was Soret's inquiry about how his own poems ought to be organized into a single work that was the catalyst that provoked Goethe to reflect on the structure of the trilogy, Goethe's comments are at times specific suggestions to Soret about the reorganization of his texts, at times general remarks on the most effective way to link poems in sequence. In their conversations and correspondence, admonition, recollection and analysis mingle. It will be the task of this study to examine the three trilogies that Goethe wrote and to relate the poems and the observations made by Goethe and Soret on their organization to the broader issue of the lyric cycle and the question of how single poems ought to be joined together into larger poetic units.

The "Müllerin" Ballads

The first of the three lyric trilogies, the "Müllerin" ballads, is the least well-known of the works that Goethe discussed with Soret and, poetically, the weakest. We will discuss the poems and the problems they pose in some detail. The ballads figure prominently in Soret's discussion with Goethe because they are closely related to the trilogy that Soret was writing. As a lyric sequence the "Müllerin" ballads are not completely successful, but it is the flaws as well as the successful innovations in the sequence that mark its participation in the emerging definition of the lyric cycle.

Each of the four "Müllerin" ballads ("Der Edelknabe und die Müllerin," "Der Junggesell und der Mühlbach," "Der Müllerin Verrath," and "Der Müllerin Reue") presents a young miller maid and a lad eager to win her affection. The setting is rural. Although the various scenes of flirtation and wooing are linked in the person of the heroine, the continuity of the poems is problematic. The four poems are uneven in quality, which in itself would not preclude a successful comprehensive intrepretation, were it not that they are also formally quite disparate and do not compose a continuous narrative.

The first poem, "Der Edelknabe und die Müllerin," introduces the setting of the ballad sequence. The poem presents a young and desirable miller maid in her rural environment, the attempt to seduce her by means of flirtation and bold affront, and the rejection of the would-be seducer. The poem is a conversation in rhythmically irregular lines which are selectively rhymed. The conversation is initiated by the young squire, and, at first, the miller maid eagerly rhymes her responses to the questions he poses. As he grows bolder and suggests that they retreat to an arbor at mid-day, his words and hers rhyme no longer. Rather, the conversation ends with a firm refusal, expressed in lines of emphatically rhymed exclusion:

Edelknabe
Nicht wahr, im grünen vertraulichen Haus—

Müllerin
Das gäbe Geschichten.

Edelknabe
Ruhst du in meinen Armen aus?

Müllerin
Mit nichten.

The interaction has ended. The miller maid's rejection of the squire turns on the saying "Gleich und gleich, so allein ist's recht," noting the social distance expressed in the title and visually marked by the image of the squire's dark coat spotted with white flour. She asserts her preference for one of her kind, a journeyman miller, and adds quickly: "An dem ist nichts zu verderben."

In the second poem, "Der Junggesell und der Mühlbach," both the "Edelknabe" and the "Müllerin" have vanished and have been replaced by a solitary lad lamenting his unrequited love. The bold attempt at swift seduction has been replaced by a direct and heartfelt lament. The poem is a dialogue between a dejected youth and a brook. The brook, at first reproached by the youth as indifferent to his sorrow, is recognized by him as a companion. In the brook the lamenting love of the youth finds its expression, for everything the brook does is but a response to the presence of the miller maid. The attraction of the miller maid has occasioned inner turmoil in both. "Ich war ein Bächlein," the stream tells him, implying, "but I am no longer." The brook has been forced to become a millrace. Similarly, the youth's emotions have been channeled by the allure of the young maid. The millrace is a symbol for the involuntary direction of the youth's thoughts and emotions. The water of the millrace turns into steam when the maid opens the shutters and shows her face and bosom, a sign of heated passion at her arrival. The speedy flow of the stream reflects the energy of her erotic attraction, and the meandering path through the meadows below the mill is the lingering desire to catch a final glance of her. Unfortunately, the poem is flawed by its last stanza. In it the unhappy youth who confides in the running water charges the stream to murmur a confession of love to the girl. The brook is thought of as a continuous flow of water which constantly passes by the mill and can tell the girl about the young fellow's hopes and wishes. In the previous stanza, however, the brook had lamented that it could not reverse its course and return to the mill. Despite this discrepancy, the poem effectively depicts the sorrows of unrequited love and proclaims the desirability of the young miller maid.

The appearance of a narrator at the beginning of the third poem, "Der Müllerin Verrath," would seem to offer an opportunity to clarify the relationship of the two previous poems. They are not completely disparate, but their continuity is not self-evident. The narrator even implies a familiarity with the scene. The seasons have progressed, the brook is now frozen, and "der Freund" is observed on a curious early morning errand in the winter woods.

The narrator does little, however, to reveal any purposeful development of the poems. After his opening remarks he steps aside and encourages our sympathy for the plight of the lad who tells of his treacherous reception in the bedroom of the miller maid. His expulsion from her bed is accompanied by exasperation and self-righteous protest. He bitterly attacks the virtue of the young maid. It is not chastity that is at issue, however, as one might expect in so idyllic a setting, but rather her abuse of the social convention of well-timed escapes and her failure to play the nocturnal game of illicit pleasures with discretion. The narrator intervenes and concludes the poem with an unexpected lack of sympathy for the suffering hero (in marked contrast to the tone established at the end of the previous poem). At the same time, he shows no real interest in the miller maid either (in marked contrast to the approval she wins through her wit and alertness in the first poem). The mill has been cast as the setting for treacherous love. The narrator's voice is authoritative, and the rustic idyll is now a scene of heartless exploitation.

The title of the fourth poem, "Der Müllerin Reue,"clearly parallels that of the third, "Der Müllerin Verrath." The poem is a conversation between a young man and the miller maid, who is at first disguised as a gypsy. The exchange, cast in the form of a dialogue, recalls the second poem in the series in its tone of heartfelt devotion and reconciliation. Allusion is made to the events of the third poem, but there is no attempt to accomodate the narrator's caustic remarks that concluded the poem. The mill has been replaced by the young man's house and a spring, and the spring functions as the symbol of enduring love and fidelity that closes the sequence.

In sequence the four ballads present a number of problems. The poems are a tale of wooing and winning centered on the figure of the "Müllerin." Their continuity is disrupted by a failure to clarify the identity and role of her various suitors. While it is clear that the "Edelknabe" of the first poem cannot be identified with the "Jüngling" of the others, one is invited by the progression of the ballads to think of the youths in the next three poems as being one and the same person. Both the titles of the poems and a certain familiarity that the narrator expresses with the youth of the third poem ("Woher der Freund so früh und schnelle") argue for this identification.

Most critics, however, have concluded that each of the four poems presents a different youth in pursuit of the artful miller's lass. There are two reasons for this. First, it is difficult to reconcile the portraits of the young men in the second, third, and fourth poems. The sincerity of the youthful suitor in the second poem does not prepare us for the amorous adventurer of the third. Second, there are narrative discrepancies. The fourth poem contradicts the third. Both the chastity of the miller's lass and the events of the ill-fated night of intended pleasure are given two distinct renderings. In "Der Müllerin Reue" the young girl states that no man has touched her: "Nimm hin das vielgeliebte Weib/ Den jungen unberührten Leib." In "Der Müllerin Verrath" the young man has no doubts that he is not the first to make a nighttime call in the miller maid's bedroom. The two can be tenuously reconciled—one can insist that the young man is speaking in anger and without factual knowledge—but such speculation is awkward at best and disturbing when it is demanded to insure the narrative continuity of the sequence.

It is not only the absence of a continuous narrative that makes interpretation of the four poems as a sequence difficult, but also the contrasting style of the poems. Three of the poems ("Der Edelknabe und die Müllerin," "Der Junggesell und der Mühlbach," "Der Müllerin Reue") are dialogues suggesting a tone of naive immediacy. The stylized speech of "Der Müllerin Reue," the operetta-like duet that concludes the sequence, and an interruption by the poet halfway through the conversation to narrate a shift in scene evoke, however, less the simple directness of the folk song and more a costumed conclusion to a pastoral comedy. The third poem, unlike the others, introduces a detached narrator who feels compelled to pass a moral judgment on the events related. The narrator's remarks frame the youthful suitor's tale of consternation and distress as he recounts his unfair treatment at the hands of the seemingly guileless miller's lass. Because of the frame the narrator imposes on the bucolic setting and his censure of the nighttime pleasures being pursued within it, it is only with difficulty that "Der Müllerin Verrath" is reconciled with the other three poems in the sequence. The narrator's unexpected approval of the young man's punishment and his condemnation of illicit pastoral pleasures seriously alter the tone established in the previous poems.

"Der Müllerin Verrath," the third poem in the series, is also in its genesis an anomaly among the four "Müllerin" ballads. The ballads began, according to a letter that Goethe wrote to Schiller en route to Switzerland in August of 1797, as "Gespräche in Liedern":

Nach allem diesem . . . muß ich Ihnen sagen: daß ich unterwegs auf ein poetisches Genre gefallen bin, in welchem wir künftig mehr machen müssen, und das vielleicht dem folgenden Almanach gut thun wird. Es sind *Gespräche in Liedern*. Wir haben in einer gewissen ältern deutschen Zeit recht artige Sachen von dieser Art und es läßt sich in dieser Form manches sagen, man muß nur erst hineinkommen und dieser Art ihr eigenthümliches abgewinnen. (WA IV, 12, 280)

Goethe perceived the dialogue poem as a distinct genre and one closely tied to the popular folk poetry of Germany. His letters and journals attest to a renewed interest in the village arts and rural life of the German farmers and craftsmen he encountered en route to Switzerland. It is not surprising, then, that his attraction to folk poetry was renewed and that he began to experiment with its forms. The "Müllerin" ballads began as such an experiment.[6] Two weeks after Goethe announced his discovery of the new poetic genre he sent Schiller the first of the "Müllerin" ballads, "Der Edelknabe und die Müllerin."[7] The second followed a month later, and the fourth was completed and mailed to Schiller in November of 1797.[8] The third poem in the sequence, however, which Goethe entitled "Der Müllerin Verrath," was not completed until the summer of the following year.[9]

In other ways "Der Müllerin Verrath" differs from the first, second, and fourth ballads in the sequence. Not only was it completed more than six months after the first three, and then as the only poem in the sequence not written as a dialogue, but the poem also did not really begin, as did the others, with Goethe's trip to Switzerland. The original idea for "Der Müllerin Verrath" predates Goethe's second journey to Switzerland and his writing of the other "Müllerin" poems by almost ten years. "Der Müllerin Verrath" is an adaptation of the French romance "En manteau, en manteau sans chemise," which Goethe first read in 1789 in the novel *La folle en pèlerinage*. He attempted, and failed, to translate the poem at that time.[10] In a letter to Knebel in July, 1798, after he had completed the adaptation and entitled it "Der Müllerin Verrath," Goethe recalled his first attempts to translate the poem:

Du erinnerst dich wohl, daß vor 10 Jahren ein kleiner Roman, *la folle en pelerinage*, an der Tagesordnung war, in demselben stand eine kleine Romanze, die wegen ihrer Artigkeit allgemein gefiel, ich legte mir schon damals die schwere Pflicht auf sie zu übersetzen; allein es wollte nicht gehen. Nun habe ich sie umgebildet, wie du in der Beylage siehst, ich wünsche daß du an dem Scherz einiges Vergnügen finden mögest. (WA IV, 13, 231)

"Der Müllerin Verrath" is thus the only poem of the four for which there is a specific poetic model. When Goethe sent the first of the ballads to Schiller, he indicated that three more would follow: "es folgen auf diese Introduction noch drey Lieder in deutscher, französischer und spanischer Art" (WA IV, 12, 302). When the poems were published the following year in Schiller's *Musenalmanach*, subtitles were afixed to each: "Altenglisch," "Altdeutsch," "Altfranzösisch," "Altspanisch." Except for "Der Müllerin Verrath," however, the four national subtitles do not indicate a specific poetic model. Rather, they attest to the conscious stylization of the poems. They recall the subtitles Herder used in his *Volkslieder* to indicate the national origin of each poem. The four subtitles suggest that the "Mullerin" ballads were conceived as four variations on common folk motifs, the vagaries of love presented in the rustic costumes of different lyric traditions. Attempts to clarify what is specifically Old English in the first poem, Old German in the second, and Old Spanish in the fourth have proven arbitrary. Goethe removed the subtitles when he took the poems into the *Werke* and published them under the rubric "Balladen."

Goethe's design of the "Mullerin" sequence reflected his renewed interest in the folk song—both in his description of the poems as "Gespräche in Liedern" and in his attempt to identify each with a different national tradition. There is another factor that influenced his writing of the four ballads. Goethe attended a performance of Paisiello's opera *La Mulinara o L'amor contrastato* in Frankfurt on 8 August 1797 (WA IV, 12, 221). He was already familiar with the popular work and its comic plot centered on the winning of the charming miller maid. In the opera, three suitors, two making a double entrance in comic disguise, vie for her hand. Intrigue, betrayal, and an idyllic intermezzo culminate in the triumph of the notary Pistofolo in the rustic disguise of a miller. At what point Goethe's concept for the dialogue poems he intended to write began to center exclusively on the figure of the "Müllerin" and the various attempts at wooing and winning her favor is uncertain. Doubtless his attendance at the opera in Frankfurt contributed to his selection and organization of the materials for the ballads. It may also account, in part, for the operetta-like finale that closes the four-ballad sequence.[11]

In addition to the rediscovery of the dialogue poem in a folk setting, the different national modes of folk poetry, and a comic opera, there was a fourth structural concept for the "Müllerin" ballads in Goethe's mind—a concept which, to use his own words, is best described as "ein kleiner Roman." In a letter to Schiller that accompanied the draft of "Der Edelknabe und die Müllerin" he wrote: "Zum Schlusse lasse ich Ihnen noch einen kleinen Scherz abschreiben; machen Sie aber noch keinen Gebrauch davon, es folgen auf diese Introduction noch drey Lieder in deutscher, französischer und spanischer Art, die zusammen einen kleinen Roman ausmachen" (WA IV, 12, 302). Most critics, however, have argued that Goethe's characterization of the poems as a short novel is inappropriate. Viehoff concludes that if one must view these poems as "ein kleiner Roman," they must be judged unsuccessful.[12] Baumgart dismisses Goethe's comments to Schiller as a chance observation and denies the existence of any internal unity for the poems.[13] Only Kommerell defends both the coherence and quality of the four poems, but when pressed to define their coherence, he reaches rather lamely for the categories of Goethe's "Balladen" essay and asserts it to be "geheimnisvoll."[14]

What is surprising is that Goethe used the term "ein kleiner Roman" to describe a lyric sequence that does not present a continuous narrative. The term is not without precedent, however, and it becomes a less curious choice once its previous occurrences are recalled. In 1777 L. F. G. von Göckingk published a collection of poems entitled Lieder zweier Liebenden. Göckingk did not call his collection of poems exchanged between the rococo lovers Amarant and Nantchen a novel, but his allusion to Werther in the "Vorbericht" to his cycle connects the Lieder zweier Liebenden with the epistolary novel. The poems themselves are less than bold in their conception and execution, but earned praise from Göckingk's contemporaries for their "sapphische Zärtlichkeit" und "süsseste Naivität."[15] Although their popularity was assured by their adherence to rococo convention and their confessional tone,[16] they did not generate any immediate interest in the possibility of grouping poems into cycles.

In the April 1784 issue of Wieland's *Teutscher Merkur* there appeared a collection of five poems entitled "Ein Roman in fünf Liedern von W——r."[17] They are prefaced by the remarks of a fictive editor, B., who explains to the readers the origin of such an unusual poetic production:

Die Idee, einen ganzen Roman ohne Erzählung, blos durch eine Reyhe Lieder zweyer Liebenden zu liefern, und den Scenen desselben dadurch mehr Darstellung, Ausdruck und Energie zu geben, ist neu, und, soviel ich weis, bis jetzt nur noch von Göckingk bearbeitet worden. Folgende 5 Lieder, die ich unter den Papieren eines meiner Freunde fand, sind höchstwahrscheinlich treue Ausflüsse seines Herzen bey wahren Scenen des Lebens, und nichts weniger als planmäßige Producte seiner Muse am Schreibepulte. Ich las sie zusammen, stellte sie so, und da gaben sie ungesucht die ziemlich vollständige und sich immer ähnlich Geschichte eines liebenden Herzens.[18]

The reference to Göckingk's *Lieder zweier Liebenden* is instructive both because it points to E. W. W. von Wobeser's model and because it connects the incipience of the lyric cycle with the epistolary novel.

Wobeser's idea to pen a complete novel in verse was as new to his readers as his preface indicates, but it was not unprecedented. He went beyond Göckingk only in characterizing his collected poems as a novel. It is a designation that proved in the next decades well-suited to the growing number of larger lyric compositions and frequently served to describe these works until "Cyklus" finally emerged as the standard literary term. In these compositions, as in Wobeser's work, the individual poems are often referred to as "Lieder." Ludwig Kosegarten, for example, described a series of poems he submitted to the *Horen* in these terms. In a letter to Schiller he called them "eine Art von poetischem Roman in drey Liedern, eine harmlose, demüthige Spielerey."[19] It is in a similar manner that Goethe used the terms "Roman" and "Lieder" to describe his four ballads: "es folgen auf diese Introduction noch drey Lieder in deutscher, französischer und spanischer Art, die zusammen einen kleinen Roman ausmachen" (WA IV, 12, 302). The term "Roman" does not intend to prescribe the organization of the poems. It does indicate an attempt to mark their sequence as purposeful and assert the coherence of the group.

While he was writing the "Müllerin" ballads Goethe characterized the four-poem sequence as "Gespräche in Liedern," as folk poems in four different national styles, and as "ein kleiner Roman." We have noted a fourth concept that was a factor in his design of the four-ballad sequence, the comic opera. At no time during these months, however, does he refer to the poems as a trilogy. The description of the "Müllerin" ballads as a trilogy was not made until 1831, when Goethe discussed the sequence with Soret. Soret recorded Goethe's remarks on 27 November: "En particulier, dit-il, mes poésies du Jeune homme et de la Meunière sont une véritable trilogie. Elles sont placées dans ce but les unes à côté des autres. C'est une suite complète présentée sous trois faces diverses: l'amour naissant, la perfidie, le repentir."[20] In a letter to Goethe on the following day Soret spoke again of the triadic scheme Goethe had suggested to him. Soret had re-read three of Goethe's trilogies (the "Müllerin" ballads, the "Paria" trilogy, and "Trilogie der Leidenschaft") and commented to Goethe:

Das brachte mich auf einige Gedanken über das eigentliche Wesen dieser Dichtart: innere Einheit, die in drei verschiedenen, gegensätzlichen Bildern zum Ausdruck kommt, wahre dichterische Dreifaltigkeit. Das ergibt sich . . . aus der "Müllerin," wo die Liebe des Junggesellen drei ganz verschiedene Vorgänge entstehen läßt: die keimende Liebe, den Verrat und die Reue.[21]

Soret's description of the "Müllerin" sequence is an exact repetition of Goethe's remarks.[22]

In his description of the "Müllerin" ballads as a trilogy, Goethe is clearly trying, at this late date, to fit the existing poems into a triadic scheme. The attempt is not quite satisfactory: the incipient love is the young man's, the treachery and repentence are the woman's. Furthermore, to fit the "Müllerin" ballads into the proposed scheme and to present them as a trilogy, Goethe had to leave aside the first poem, "Der Edelknabe und die Müllerin." His description of the sequence as "l'amour naissant, la perfidie, le repentir" involves only "Der Jung-gesell und der Mühlbach," "Der Müllerin Verrath," and "Der Mülle-rin Reue."

Soret declared that he was unwilling to lose the first poem, "Der Edelknabe und die Müllerin," from the sequence of ballads. Instead, he suggested that it be affixed as an introduction to the trio and added parenthetically that Goethe had not considered this possibility before:

Nous avons repris le sujet des trilogies. Il a été question des trois trilogies de Goethe et surtout de la *Meunière*. Goethe faisait commencer par le jeune homme et le ruisseau; j'ai propose de joindre cette poésie à celle qui précède et à laquelle Goethe ne pensait pas, le *Gentilhomme et la Meunière*, parce que l'ensemble est à la fois plus complet et plus vrai et aussi pour éviter de mettre en première ligne une action avec un objet inanimé, chose à laquelle Goethe répugne en général.[23]

The point is not simply to recount a conversation of some 140 years ago, but to stress how little Goethe was interested in the "Müllerin" ballads for their own sake. He was instead intent on seeking an a posteriori justification of the poems as a trilogy. Goethe enjoyed systematizing and schematizing in his old age. In his conversations with Soret, it was the problem of how lyric trilogies ought to be written that was at issue. The ballads themselves were of secondary interest. It hardly need be noted that Goethe's claim to have never thought of linking "Der Edelknabe und die Müllerin" to the other three is simply absurd, as both his letter to Schiller cited previously and the publication in the *Musenalmanach* confirm.

What became of Soret's trilogy? Soret had been intent on accomodating all four of his poems in one "trilogy." It was for this reason, in part, that he was so keenly interested in Goethe's four "Müllerin" ballads. In addition, Soret admitted to an unconscious imitation of the second of Goethe's poems, "Der Junggesell und der Mühlbach," in his own dialogue, "Le jeune homme et l'étoile," and he recalled his translation of Goethe's entire sequence a few years previously. Soret intended to create a trilogy from his four poems by subordinating his second poem to the principal three poems of the trilogy. He explained to Goethe: "Ich glaubte, die erste Nacht ["L'invocation du Berger. 1ere nuit," the first poem of the trilogy] nur etwas erweitert zu haben durch den Dialog zwischen dem Jüngling und dem Stern ["Le jeune homme et l'étoile"], er sollte zugleich als Umschreibung und Vorbereitung dienen."[24] In Goethe's "Müllerin" ballads Soret perceived a similar arrangement:

Wie enttäuscht war ich, als ich in der "Müllerin" dasselbe fand, die Unterhaltung zwischen dem Junggesellen und dem Bach steht ebenfalls zwischen dem ersten und zweiten Teil! Diese Ihre Gedichte habe ich vor Jahren übersetzt, sie werden mir, ohne daß ich es wußte, als Vorbild gedient haben. Es ist doch fast unmöglich, etwas Neues zu erfinden! Aber ich berufe mich jetzt auf dieses Vorbild und lasse den Dialog da stehen, wenigstens bis auf weitere Order.[25]

Goethe complimented Soret's poems and urged him to continue in his writing. In his final conversation with Goethe on the trilogies, Soret announced that he hoped to translate all three of Goethe's trilogies into French.[26] By making Goethe's trilogies better known in France, he hoped to be able to promote his own poems as well. Goethe agreed to the plan. Doubtless, it was Goethe's death three months later that caused Soret to abandon the project. His poems were never published as a trilogy.

The "Müllerin" ballads were never called a "Cyklus" by Goethe and his contemporaries. Goethe's designation of the poems as "ein kleiner Roman," however, is significant. For a time, both "Cyklus" and "Roman" coexisted as descriptive terms for lyric sequences. "Cyklus," for example, was adapted by the popular epigone Tiedge to describe his pastoral sequences—poems unabashedly grounded in the anteceded costumed idylls of an earlier epoch. He wrote in the "Vorwort" to his composition "Das Echo oder Alexis und Ida. Ein Ciclus von Liedern:" "Sein [Vergil und seine Schäferwelt] Beispiel veranlaßte folgenden Zyklus kleiner idyllischer Lieder. . . . Wenn gleich ein leichtes Band von Wechselbeziehungen durch den Zyklus hinläuft: so kann doch jedes einzelne Lied, als ein kleines Ganze, für sich bestehen und ausgehoben werden." [27] The use of the word "Roman," on the other hand, to describe lyric collections continued well into the nineteenth century. In his praise of Petrarch's *Canzoniere*, August Wilhelm Schlegel even implies that the idea of a lyric novel is completely new: "Die Sammlung von Petrarcas Gedichten ist schon Roman. Es gibt ja dergleichen in Briefen, warum nicht in Kanzonen und Sonette?" [28] He defends the poems as a true and complete novel, "Petrarcas Sammlung [ist] ein wahrer und vollständiger lyrischer Roman," [29] and calls this concept truly romantic: "Von dem Geist seiner Liebe, und endlich der Sammlung seiner Gedichte aus einem Ganzen, einer wahrhaft romantischen Komposition, eines rhapsodisch lyrischen Romans habe ich in voriger Stunde gesprochen." [30]

It is indicative of the general flux in nomenclature that in the 1840s and 1850s a debate took place among critics on the appropriate use of the terms "Cyklus" and "Roman" in reference to the *Römische Elegien*. Viehoff explicitly denied that the *Elegien* could be considered a "Roman" and asserted that the poems were an "Elegiencyclus." Everything "dramatisch fortstrebend" (as he characterized the structure of the "Roman") would be inappropriate to the genre "Elegie" and to the word "Cyklus." [31] Lehmann countered that he did not see the point of the implied difference between "Cyklus" and "Roman" and used the "Müllerin" ballads as an example of how the term "Roman" is used to assert that the poems in question do not stand alone, but rather are joined in a loose narrative progression. [32] Thus, even more than half a century after the "Müllerin" ballads were written, they continued to play a small part in the gradual emergence of the lyric cycle as an acknowledged poetic structural device.

The "Paria" Trilogy

The second of the three trilogies that Soret and Goethe considered in their discussion of poetic form is the "Paria" trilogy, but, unlike the "Müllerin" ballads, which occupy so central a position in Soret's record of his conversations with Goethe, the "Paria" trilogy is afforded only a cursory nod. Soret's first discussion with Goethe on the "Müllerin" ballads had taken place on 27 November. That afternoon, as Soret noted in his memoirs, he reread both the "Müllerin" poems and the "Trilogie der Leidenschaft": "Rentré chez moi, j'ai repris les deux trilogies, La Meunière et Les Passions, ce qui m'a suggéré quelques réflexions que je compte soumettre demain à Goethe, dans une lettre."[33] In his letter to Goethe written the following day, Soret suggested a third trilogy that might be of interest in their conversations on the organization of poems into lyric sequences: "Ich las gestern nachmittag wieder Ihre Trilogien, um ganz in das Wesen dieser Form einzudringen; zuerst die 'Trilogie der Leidenschaft', dann 'Die Müllerin' und schließlich den 'Paria', der auch als Trilogie gelten kann."[34]

It is not curious that the "Paria" trilogy was slighted in Soret's recorded conversations with Goethe, for the poems, both in form and content, bear little relationship to Soret's own poems and the trilogy he hoped to organize. Neither Goethe nor Soret mentioned the "Paria" poems again in their correspondence. The only other reference to the poems occurs in Eckermann's (not completely reliable) record of 1 December. He attributes to Goethe the following remark: "Auch mein 'Paria' ist eine vollkommene Trilogie, und zwar habe ich diesen Cyclus sogleich mit Intention als Trilogie gedacht und behandelt."[35]

The "Paria" poems were begun in December of 1821 and completed in 1823. They were written as a trilogy. The idea for the poems is much older, however, and can be traced back to Goethe's first reading of the legend of a Hindu noble woman whose head was tragically joined with the body of a common criminal in Sonnerat's Reise nach Ostindien. Although Goethe must have read Sonnerat's account shortly after it appeared in 1783,[36] it was almost four decades before he was to rework the legend and write the "Paria" trilogy. He had tried several times without success to adapt the legend. In 1817 he wrote to Zelter that "Das Gebet des Paria dagegen hat noch nicht pariren wollen" (WA, IV, 27, 302).[37] It was not until 1823 that he found the proper poetic form for the material.

Once Goethe had completed the "Paria" trilogy, he expressed his satisfaction with the composition. We are not forced to rely simply on Eckermann's report that Goethe called the poems "eine vollkommene Trilogie."[38] In all of Goethe's discussions of the "Paria" there is an emphatic assertion that the poems display formal excellence. In his essay "Bedeutende Fördernis durch ein einziges geistreiches Wort" (1823) he employs an organic metaphor to clarify the extended period of time between his first acquaintance with the "Paria" materials and the writing of the poems: "mir schien der schönste Besitz solche werthe Bilder oft in der Einbildungskraft erneut zu sehen, da sie sich denn zwar immer umgestalteten, doch ohne sich zu verändern einer reineren Form, einer entschiedneren Darstellung entgegen reiften" (WA II, 11, 60). The extended gestation period allowed the maturation of the poetic image. Abandoning the organic metaphor for one of honed craftsmanship he also described the poems as "eine aus Stahldrähten geschmiedete Damaszenerklinge."[39] Both comments convey the sense of precision and refinement of poetic image. While neither is specifically related to the structure of the poems as a lyric trilogy, each clearly expresses Goethe's conviction that the poems are excellent and that their meaning is most fully realized in the poetic form he has given them. A careful examination of the poems will reveal that their three-part structure is essential to this meaning.

The three poems of the "Paria" trilogy are formally and functionally distinct. The central "Legende" is framed by prayers that open and close the three-poem sequence: "Des Paria Gebet" is a prayer of supplication, and "Dank des Paria," one of thanksgiving. All three poems are written in trochaic tetrameter, but the opening poem of three eight-line stanzas and the closing prayer of three four-line stanzas contrast sharply with the unrhymed narrative of the "Legende" and its considerable length.

The pariah's prayer that opens the trilogy is both a confession of faith and a plea for confirmation. Despite his lowly stature, which he does not challenge, the pariah claims significance in the created world. Although the lowest of men, more comparable to animal than human life ("Oder bist auch du's, der Affen/ Werden ließ und unseresgleichen?"), he asserts a claim on the remote divinity of Brahma, the great creator. "Alles ist von deinem Samen" is the opening declaration, and with cautious argument the suppliant seeks some tangible affirmation of this credo. An assurance of kinship, an assurance that despite the distance between the highest of gods and the lowest of men, a bond exists—this is his request.

The second of the three poems, "Legende," is the answer to this prayer. The mediator the pariah has sought is revealed. In the retelling of the legend of a brahman's hapless wife whose head is affixed to the body of a lowly pariah woman and who eternally suffers the knowledge and the agony of this dual existence, the truth of the Great Brahma's universal paternity is made visible. The newly created goddess (half-goddess, half-demon) is an abiding image to assure the pariah of access to the remote Brahma. She incorporates the highest and the lowest in the created world and has become a mediator between these two extremes. She charges her husband and son, witnesses to the revelation of Brahma's goodness, to travel through all the world and through all times announcing that Brahma hears the

prayers of even the lowliest of men. Brahma's accessibility and participation throughout the world and in the life of the pariah are celebrated in the closing poem, "Dank des Paria."

To understand what Goethe has accomplished in this trilogy, and
to understand why the poems are deemed so successful by their
author, the opening and closing prayers cannot be regarded merely
as a preface and afterword to the central "Legende." It is only through
the framing request and response of the troubled pariah that the full
significance of the "Legende" and consequently, of the trilogy, is
made visible. The pariah closes his prayer:

> Oder Eines laß entstehen,
> Das auch mich mit dir verbinde!
> Denn du hast den Bajaderen
> Eine Göttin selbst erhoben;
> Auch wir andern, dich zu loben,
> Wollen solch ein Wunder hören.

The miraculous tale of the bayadere's redemption through her self-
sacrificing love that is already known (for it has been told, and by
Goethe, of course) brings no assurance to the pariah of Brahma's
attendance to his needs. Rather he seeks a confirmation that speaks
to him and his class (the outcasts)—he seeks a tale and a miracle that
will produce an image of the fusion of the greatest with the least.

The "Legende" as it is told in the second poem is the answer to his
prayer. The creation of a goddess from the fateful fusion of a brahman
wife and a pariah woman is not an event occasioned by the pariah's
plea. It is not an event at all in the sense that it can be placed in the
1–2–3 sequence of the trilogy's progression. What does occur and can
be placed in this progression is the telling of this legend, the revealing
of this promise of continuing mediation. There the pariah finds the
assurance he has asked for, and the "Legende" is the vehicle of its
disclosure. Brahma's promise of continuing accessibility to the eager
supplicant is made visible in the poem. It is this revelation that the
pariah celebrates in his closing prayer of thanksgiving.

In the "Paria" trilogy it is the telling of the tale that mediates between the divine and the earthbound. Poetry is proclaimed a means
of revelation, a concrete realization of an otherwise ineffable truth.
The concept is not new. In our discussion of the *Römische Elegien* we
asserted this understanding of the poetic image, or "Bild," as fundamental to Goethe's use of poetic language. In the "Paria" trilogy this
process of mediation is the thematic core of the poems.

The simple diction and syntax of the framing poems suggest a
naïvety that effectively enhances the narrative power of the "Le-

gende" and its rhetorical devices. The first two stanzas of "Dank des Paria" contain a summary of the message proclaimed in the "Legende." The pariah addresses his Creator in grateful thanks. In the third stanza he turns to his fellow pariahs and announces his intention to devote himself in the future to the contemplation of this great god. The pariah dares to put himself on the same level as the highest caste, the priests, who spend their lives in study, in contemplation, and in teaching. His words emphatically affirm the efficacy of the poetic image in "Legende." The pariah does not need to understand how the fusion of the highest and the lowest is realized. The inner life of the brahman wife remains closed to him: "Was ich denke, was ich fühle/ Ein Geheimnis bleibe das." It is sufficient to know *that* it is a reality.

Goethe judged his "Paria" poems to be excellent and spoke of them with justifiable satisfaction. Nevertheless, the three poems remain of limited significance in the discussion between Goethe and Soret on the trilogy. This is not surprising. Soret's real interest, as we have noted, was the "Müllerin" ballads; they, both in form and content, bore the closest relationship to his own poems and to the trilogy he hoped to write. For Goethe, however, only one trilogy was of central importance and that was the "Trilogie der Leidenschaft."

"Trilogie der Leidenschaft"

Neither of the two trilogies we have considered prepares for the third series of poems, the "Trilogie der Leidenschaft." This trilogy is an unrivaled testament to despair and desolation. It is rooted in a personal crisis that seriously threatened the acquired composure and self-mastery of the aging poet. The lyric response is unique in its presentation of destructive passion and life-renewing grace.[40]

The poems in the "Trilogie der Leidenschaft" are the last of Goethe's poetic trilogies and the most personal. Unlike so many of his lyric poems, which Goethe never considered again once they were completed, the "Elegie," the second poem in the trilogy, was read and reread by Goethe, according to Zelter's account, recorded on costly paper, and set aside as a private and treasured document (WA IV, 38, 11).[41] Only the "Trilogie der Leidenschaft," not the "Müllerin" ballads or the "Paria" trilogy, sustained any personal interest for Goethe by 1831.

The "Trilogie der Leidenschaft" was not begun as a trilogy. The poems were written as independent pieces; the first, "Aussöhnung," in August of 1823; the "Elegie" in early September of the same year; and the final poem, "An Werther," in March of 1824. Not until October did Goethe take note of the possible relationship between "An Werther" and the "Elegie" (WA IV, 38, 278). The first reference to all three poems as a single trilogy was made in January of 1825 (WA III, 10, 8).

Consequently, there was no plan for the trilogy: "Meine sogenannte 'Trilogie der Leidenschaft' dagegen ist ursprünglich nicht als Trilogie concipirt, vielmehr erst nach und nach und gewissermaßen zufällig zur Trilogie geworden." [42] The three poems were not purposefully conceived as complementary. Goethe later insisted that the final linking of the poems occurred quite apart from any conscious plan. He ascribed their final continuity to an autonomous process at work within the poems themselves. Speaking of the final poem in the trilogy, "Aussöhnung," he stated: "Die Strophen, die ich dieser Freundin widmete, . . . fügen sich dieser ["Elegie"] *wie von selbst* als versöhnender Ausgang." [43] Of "An Werther" he said: "Da ich aber immer noch einen Rest jener Leidenschaft im Herzen hatte, so *gestaltete sich* das Gedicht *wie von selbst* als Introduction zu jener Elegie." [44] In conclusion he stated: "So kam es denn, daß alle drei jetzt beisammenstehenden Gedichte von demselbigen liebesschmerzlichen Gefühle durchdrungen worden und jene Trilogie der Leidenschaft *sich bildete, ich wußte nicht wie.*" [45]

Invoking once again the mysteries of the creative process as he had done so often before, Goethe nevertheless acknowledged a fundamental continuity—that of his own painfully passionate attachment to Ulrike von Levetzow, a complex of poetically productive emotions· so strong and so consuming that they were only exhausted in the final and wearily bitter self-assessment of the first poem in the series, the last to be written, "An Werther." This emotional reservoir is described by Goethe as both the source of the poems and the guarantee of their continuity. Three poems were written because one did not exhaust the reservoir of passion, Goethe suggests. The three proved continuous because they shared this common origin. The poet is as much observer as participant in the creation of the trilogy, at least as Goethe chose to describe its composition seven years later.

These feelings that Goethe asserts permeate the poems and sustain the continuity of the sequence become, in the poet's struggle to articulate them and to bring them into a productive relationship with his creative past, the thematic focus for the lyric trilogy. The arena for the struggle portrayed by the poems is the internal life of the poet himself. His emotional turmoil is both source and theme of the trilogy.

The three poems were written in inverse order of their final publication. In the writing of the poems one can trace a process of slowly regained distance and self-understanding. The persona moves from complete isolation and passivity in "Aussöhnung," where he is the grateful recipient of a grace proffered and affirmed, but not really understood, through the painful retelling of the encounter that led to this immobilization—now easier to tell because of the knowledge of the release that has been granted, more horrifying to tell because the telling itself does not, as in the past, bring with it the longed-for resolution—and, finally, yet another step further distanced from the immobilizing present in "Aussöhnung" to a sharpened sense of himself as a poet and as a man with a past and a future in "An Werther." Goethe proclaims the troubled and yet productive relationship of passionate engagement and expression a repeating event in his own history in the opening poem of the trilogy. This new distance brings self-recognition coupled with despair, for the familiarity of the spectre does not guarantee its banishment. Quite to the contrary, the demon once driven out has returned to haunt with a power seven times greater than the first.

In the structure of the completed trilogy, however, the movement is quite different. It is the self-presentation of the poet that opens the trilogy. The opening poem, "An Werther," not only introduces the poet of the *Trilogie der Leidenschaft* as the aging and renowned Weimar patriarch, but also places the entire sequence under the shadow of his literary past. Werther's return becomes the occasion for the poet's frank remarks on his spent career and at the same time is a grim foreboding of the events that follow. The trilogy begins abruptly. It is the boldness of the apparition that shocks, its audacity to emerge into a world of flowers and light when it so long ago was consigned to the night of forgetfulness. The "vielbeweint" is ironic, for as much as Werther's death was mourned by Goethe's readers, his departure was a relief for his author. His unhappiness and longing, his inability to deal with himself and his social environment, his submission to an all-consuming passion that finally destroyed all contact with the external world—all these were washed away in the literary creation. According to the fiction that Goethe later cast for himself as *Werther's* author, the poet proceeded onward to new and productive life. Now the shadow returns, not nearly so neatly buried as Goethe had hoped, and it is with a tone of frank intimacy that the poet acknowledges the presence. Not for the first time, but "noch einmal" the aging Goethe is confronted with a spectre of himself. In "An Werther" a new bitterness is linked to this lifelong struggle.[46]

The second poem "Elegie" becomes in this sequence an explanation of the opening lament and, at the same time, its intensification. The bitterness revealed in "An Werther" is now given a present cause.

The poet's attempt to contain and control his plight in poetic activity, a recourse so often used in the past and one Werther's presence specifically recalls (as does the figure of Tasso, introduced at the conclusion of "An Werther" and again as the motto to the "Elegie"), now fails.

The present moment of relief is found in the third poem, "Aussöhnung." The separation that immobilized, that was death, has become a new movement forward, a return to life. The poet is reconciled with himself, with his life and his art. It is this moment of reconciliation that concludes the trilogy.

There is a formal continuity to the three poems, despite their contrasting length and stanza forms. Each of the three uses an iambic pentameter line. The strophic organization of the poems becomes more pronounced in each successive poem. The final despair and reawakening to life in "Aussöhnung" is expressed in sharply defined stanzas, each marking a specific stage in the recovery of hope and renewal.

Goethe ascribed the continuity of the three poems to his painfully passionate attachment to Ulrike von Levetzow and to the emotional turmoil that followed his separation from her in 1823. Among the verbal motifs and allusions that are introduced in the first poem of the series, "An Werther," and that are used to express the poet's growing despair are several that recur in the other two poems of the trilogy. This repetition is fundamental to the continuity of the series.

"Paradies," "Scheiden," "verworren," "umgarnt" are four examples of terms introduced in "An Werther" that are developed in "Elegie" and swiftly recapitulated in "Aussöhnung." In the process they are not unchanged. The "Scheiden" that is central to the opening lines of the first poem, Werther's departure from this world and the poet's continuing presence in it, becomes in the course of the poem the focus of the poet's lament and despair: "Scheiden ist der Tod." It is not Werther's departure that he laments, however, but the inexorable "Scheiden" that accompanies the constriction, entanglement and confusion of life itself, a life no longer a paradise as it first appeared (l. 13), but a labyrinth of pain and despair. Isolated, helplessly confused, a pawn of passion, the poet desperately attempts distance and understanding in his "song." The opening poem of the trilogy concludes with yet another allusion to the sorrows of Werther; the desperate cry of Tasso echoes in the closing lines as well. The way is prepared for the "Elegie" that follows.

The complex of lament and confusion, poetic power and intense suffering that marked the lives of Werther and Tasso, these creations of a much younger Goethe, are visible again in the "Elegie," and in this second piece in the trilogy the motifs of the opening poem, "An Werther," acquire new significance. The paradise that is the beloved's presence and the celebrated entanglement in her love ("Ein herrliches Geflecht verschlungner Minnen," l. 20) are abruptly severed and replaced by oppressive isolation. Far more effective than the catalog at the close of the fifth stanza, "Und Mißmut, Reue, Vorwurf, Sorgenschwere/ Belasten's nun in schwüler Atmosphäre," are the subsequent attempts to reclaim the bliss of the paradise lost in a paradise recalled—in nature, in the imagination, in the poetic word. "Elegie" concludes as did "An Werther" in isolated helplessness, but the saving grace of self-expression, that lingered as a hope at the end of the first poem, has now proven a vain longing:

> Fehlt's am Begriff: wie sollt' er sie vermissen?
> Er wiederholt ihr Bild zu tausendmalen.
> Das zaudert bald, bald wird es weggerissen,
> Undeutlich jetzt und jetzt im reinsten Strahlen;
> Wie könnte dies geringstem Troste frommen,
> Die Ebb' und Flut, das Gehen wie das Kommen?

The expulsion from paradise culminates in the poet's separation not only from the beloved, but from the world about him, his art (a part of his productive relationship to this world), and finally himself.

The motifs are given a final recapitulation in the opening stanza of "Aussöhnung." "Die Leidenschaft bringt Leiden!"—so the poem begins; the sufferings of Werther and of Tasso, the labyrinth of confusion, the pain that permeates the "Elegie" are recalled in an etymological play on the word "Leidenschaft" that has been elaborated in the preceding poem with painful poignancy. Explicit motifs are repeated ("Trüb ist der Geist, verworren das Beginnen"). The resolution that follows is a belated answer to the plea that closed the first poem: "Geb ihm ein Gott zu sagen, was er duldet." The grace is not a return to paradise (a recovery of the beloved's presence) but a recovery of the poet's feeling for his life and his art, a feeling for the divine value of art (here represented by music) and a feeling for the value of life itself. Tears and musical tone combine to convince the heart of its desire to live.

Helen Mustard, in the conclusion to her chapter on Goethe's lyric cycles, states: "Though not significant or at all complicated in its form, the trilogy ["Trilogie der Leidenschaft"] possesses a unity of theme and illustrates once more Goethe's fondness for arranging related poems together."[47] Mustard has no interest in the formal organization of the three poems in the "Trilogie der Leidenschaft." She dismisses the topic as insignificant and asserts that a thematic unity guarantees the continuity of the three works. She is mistaken. The organization of the poems is more complex than she suggests. The trilogy cannot be described as a mere arrangement of thematically related poems.

Between 1823 and 1827, the years in which Goethe wrote and organized his "Trilogie der Leidenschaft," he also began a closer study of Greek drama and Aristotle's theory of tragedy. The early decades of the nineteenth century had not only produced the first dramatic trilogies in the German language, as we have noted previously, but also extensive and notable studies of the Greek tragedy by classical scholars such as Süvern, Hermann, and Welcker. Goethe was aware of these investigations and reread Aristotle with new interest. He concluded that the Aristotelian concept of catharsis had been misinterpreted in the past. Regarded as an affective device, catharsis had been wrongly understood as a description of the emotional response of the individual in the audience (the result of the experience of fear and pity aroused in the viewer). Goethe argued that catharsis is more properly understood as a structural principle. It is a part of the literary text itself, and he asserted that all poetic works, not just the drama, conclude in this act of reconciliation: "Er [Aristotle] versteht unter Katharsis diese aussöhnende Abrundung, welche eigentlich von allem Drama, ja sogar von allen poetischen Werken gefordert wird" (WA I, 41², 248). Furthermore, Goethe observed that the Greeks specifically used the structure of the trilogy to accomplish this final reconciliation: "Ferner bemerken wir, daß die Griechen ihre Trilogie zu solchem Zwecke benutzt" (WA I, 41², 249).

Goethe's "Trilogie der Leidenschaft" is not simply three related poems that have been conveniently grouped together, but a trilogy that moves purposefully toward an "aussöhnende Abrundung" in the final poem, "Aussöhnung." Elizabeth Wilkinson, who first noted the close relationship between Goethe's essays on Greek tragedy and the "Trilogie der Leidenschaft," has suggested that the trilogy was conceived as a poetic illustration for Goethe's theory of catharsis. She asserts that the poems are an "Urbild tragischer Gefühlsstruktur."[48] While her attempt to specify Goethe's poetic intent remains necessarily speculative, as she admits, her observations on the structure of the "Trilogie der Leidenschaft" underscore the purposeful progression of the poems.

Wilkinson has noted, as well, the absence of any single thematic motif to unify the poems. Rather, the trilogy moves from Werther and the poet's past (including allusions to his drama *Tasso*) to his present crisis in "Elegie" and to the release granted in the music of "Aussöhnung." In the move from the historic present as it is used in the opening poem to the lyric present of the final poem, Wilkinson perceives a "Steigerung." She traces a similar pattern in the progression of literary references in the trilogy, a progression of external forms, from the novel to the drama to poetry and finally to music.[49] Wilkinson is eager to identify such a progression, or "Steigerung," in order to relate the poems more convincingly to an essay Goethe wrote in 1823 entitled "Die tragischen Tetralogien der Griechen." The dramatic trilogy (and tetralogy), Goethe wrote in this essay, does not demand an increasingly intense treatment of one and the same subject matter, as scholars had previously asserted. Rather, it demands that different subjects be treated in an increasingly effective way. "Es kann nicht geläugnet werden, daß man sich die Tetralogien der Alten sonst nur gedacht als eine dreifache Steigerung desselben Gegenstandes," he begins and then continues: "eine Tri- oder gar Tetralogie habe keineswegs einen zusammenhängenden Inhalt gefordert, also nicht eine Steigerung des Stoffs, wie oben angenommen, sondern eine Steigerung der äußern Formen, gegründet auf einer vielfältigen und zu dem bezweckten Eindruck hinreichenden Gehalt" (WA I, 41², 64–66).

The trilogy, and by extension, we can include at this point the lyric trilogy, is not organized, according to Goethe, by a simple principle of thematic continuity. Goethe did not perceive the Greek trilogies as dependent on such a principle for their unity, nor did he impose such a limitation on his lyric trilogies. Goethe's remarks indicate a far more subtle understanding of the trilogy's structure.

The unity of the three poems of the "Trilogie der Leidenschaft" is guaranteed, according to Goethe, because the three are an expression of a single emotional upheaval. We have noted as well that a formal continuity and a repetition and development of selected verbal motifs enhance the progression of the poems. But the organization of the three poems of the "Trilogie der Leidenschaft" is not fully described by the identification of these selected examples of formal and verbal continuity. There is another structural concept of equal significance which demands consideration, and it is a structural device Goethe used intentionally and skillfully. It is the principle of discontinuity.

It should be noted that the three poems of the "Trilogie der Leidenschaft" do not proceed in an unbroken continuity. While the first two poems conclude with an expression of utter despair, the opening lines of the poems that follow ("Elegie" and "Aussöhnung") do not directly acknowledge this desolation. The opening lines of "Elegie" present an ongoing struggle—the poet is anything but resigned. Expectation prevails. In the linking of the two poems "An Werther" and "Elegie" there is no explicit statement of sequence. Similarly, the helplessness that closes "Elegie" and the expectation found in the opening lines of

"Aussöhnung" are discontinuous. The question posed at the beginning of "Aussöhnung"—"Wer beschwichtigt/ Beklomnes Herz, das allzuviel verloren?"—expresses a hopefulness not conceivable in the aura of alienation and isolation at the end of "Elegie."

It is not simply that the opening lines of the second and third poems in the trilogy do not provide a direct continuation of the lines that concluded the poem preceding. In the "Trilogie der Leidenschaft" a number of central motifs are discontinuous. The figure of Werther and of the beloved, for example, as well as the music motif, each central to one of the three poems, are not repeated in the other two. The thematic continuity of the trilogy is not guaranteed by simple repetition. The reader cannot avoid seeing the break between the poems.

This is intentional, for Goethe's basic conviction is that the poems in a trilogy cannot be joined by explicit connecting links. A break between poems is necessary:

Là-dessus, Goethe pense qu'il est absolument nécessaire de faire les coupures sans liaisons trop senties, d'abord parce qu'une partie de l'effet produit dépend justement du travail d'imagination que le lecteur est appelé à faire pour rejoindre les trois membres épars, ensuite parce que si la liaison était plus prononcée, ce ne serait plus une trilogie, mais un seul poème un peu long en une partie au lieu d'être en trois parties distinctes.[50]

It is the structural intention of the trilogy to actively engage the reader's imagination in the creative process. He is not to be confronted with a long poem in three stages, but rather with a lyric composition that consists of three poems together with the spaces in between— spaces in which the reader is enjoined to pursue the disjunctive as well as the continuous relationship of the poems.

The technique of discontinuity was introduced very early into Soret and Goethe's discussions of the lyric trilogy. In their conversation of November 27, the first conversation on the trilogy that Soret records, Goethe described his "Müllerin" ballads as the presentation of a growing love in three distinct stages. Soret, considering his own poems, asked Goethe whether his sequence was not flawed by the absence of a sufficient time lapse between individual poems. Goethe withheld any explicit judgment on Soret's poems, but stated unequivocally that the poems of a trilogy must not be joined too explicitly. According to Eckermann, in the conversation of 1 December, Goethe stated that it was necessary "daß zwischen jeder der drei Productionen eine fühlbare Lücke bleibe."[51]

Discontinuity is the one principle of composition that is fundamental to each of the three trilogies we have considered in this chapter. At times, as in the "Müllerin" ballads, the discontinuity of the individual poems can be so great that the coherence of the series is lost. Used successfully, as in the "Paria" trilogy and the "Trilogie der Leidenschaft," it is a technique that not only awakens the reader's imagination but also invites him to join in the creative process itself and to complete the poem's meaning.

The technique of discontinuity is clearly not restricted to cycles of three poems. It can be demonstrated in Goethe's longer lyric sequences as well. Goethe never discussed the lyric cycle as a poetic structural device. It is doubtful that he perceived it as a distinct poetic form. But he did reflect on the distinctive organization of the lyric trilogy. Goethe's discussion of his three trilogies in 1831, and his effort to assist Soret as a poet and a promoter of the art, provides the reader of all his poetic sequences, and not just of his trilogies, with insight into the craft of his poetry. At the same time, Goethe's three trilogies, innovative in their structure, document the diversity of concept and composition that even the smallest of lyric cycles, a lyric trilogy, can exhibit.

The Smaller Cycles of 1821

The Howard Poems, Wilhelm Tischbeins Idyllen, Zu meinen Handzeichnungen

The three smaller cycles we will consider in this chapter are all products of the immediate post-*Divan* years. Each was completed in 1821. The poems are not well-known. Each cycle was first published in one of Goethe's Weimar journals (The Howard poems in *Zur Naturwissenschaft überhaupt; Wilhelm Tischbeins Idyllen* and *Zu meinen Handzeichnungen* in *Kunst und Altertum*) and later placed in the *Ausgabe letzter Hand*, the Howard poems under the rubric "Gott und Welt," the other two under "Kunst."

No immediate connection is apparent between the Howard poems, which are clearly linked to Goethe's scientific investigations, and the other two cycles, written as poetic commentary to two series of drawings: the first a group of sketches by Tischbein, the second a series of etchings based on sketches by Goethe himself. Despite obvious differences among them, however, two points should be made about the common features of the three cycles. First, unlike the *Römische Elegien*, the *Sonette*, or the *West-östlicher Divan*, in these three cycles Goethe makes no deliberate thematic reference to his literary models.[1] Consequently, one of the standard fictions that he uses to organize his larger cycles is absent. No longer is the figure of a poet central to the cycle and no longer is one of the basic themes the discovery of a new language and a new love within the poetic world created from the idioms of an older tradition. Rather, each of the three cycles is organized on the most obvious level by an external scheme—the sequence of clouds described by Luke Howard, a sequence of sketches drawn by Tischbein, and a series of etchings based on Goethe's drawings. In each case the coherence of the sequence arises from a coherence and continuity the poet has perceived within the phenomena themselves and consequently expressed in the poems.

This brings us to our second point. It is important both to the design and to an interpretation of the three cycles that Goethe began each in an expressed attempt to make the meaning of the original series—be it clouds or drawings—more accessible to his audience. He quite explicitly links the writing of them with an impulse towards clarification and commentary.[2] In this they are not unique. In the immediate post-*Divan* years, Goethe was continually occupied with the process of clarification, both of his life and of his work. The *Italienische Reise* was completed in 1817, *Campagne in Frankreich* was written from 1820 to 1822. Goethe regarded the preparation of the *Ausgabe letzter Hand*, which he began in earnest in 1822, as an opportunity to demonstrate a reasonable unity within his life's work.[3] For his poetry Goethe's growing interest in his collected work and in his own past meant that his characteristic silence about his writing was, at least in part, abandoned.[4] Prose commentaries were added to selected poems in the hope that they could be made more accessible. Scattered poems were gathered and re-ordered, and new rubrics conceived. Numerous "Inschriften, Denk- und Sendeblätter" were arranged in a single rubric and explanations attached. Old projects were revived, and a collection of drawings, like the collected inscriptions, became the occasion for reflective comment.[5] This is the setting for the three smaller cycles we will examine in some detail, a period of poetic activity unique within Goethe's career and one marked by concerns that are immediately visible in the conception and design of the three works.

The Howard Poems

We will begin with the poems written in honor of Luke Howard and his meteorological discoveries, not only because they are the first of the three smaller cycles which Goethe wrote, but also because they have a rather complex genesis and illustrate in an almost paradigmatic fashion the multiple concerns that occupied Goethe as a poet in these transitional years between the conclusion of the *Divan* and the writing of the late poetry. The three poems, "Atmosphäre," "Howards Ehrengedächtnis," and "Wohl zu merken," have been considered a trilogy by some recent critics.[6] In our discussion of the poems we have chosen to avoid this description, in part because Goethe never referred to the poems as a trilogy and failed to include them in his discussion with Soret, but also because the identification of the three poems as a trilogy is simply inadequate. It describes only one of several stages in the composition of this rather unique sequence of poems. The poems neither began nor ended as a trilogy.

The writing of the three Howard poems spans the years from 1817 to 1821; it proceeded in several distinct stages. Goethe first wrote

lines 23–52 of the second of the three poems, "Howards Ehrengedächtnis," and gave the work this same title when he published it in
Zur Naturwissenschaft überhaupt in 1820. The poem is in four parts;
each part is named for a basic cloud formation as described by Luke
Howard: "Stratus," "Kumulus," "Cirrus," and "Nimbus." The
twenty-two lines that precede the cloud stanzas were written in March
of 1821. The prefacing poem "Atmosphäre" and the last poem "Wohl
zu merken" were completed by October of the same year.[7] When the
poems were first published in *Zur Naturwissenschaft überhaupt* in 1822,
"Atmosphäre" and "Wohl zu merken" were untitled; "Howards Ehrengedächtnis" was accompanied by an English translation. In the
Ausgabe letzter Hand "Atmosphäre," "Howards Ehrengedächtnis," and
"Wohl zu merken" were all placed under the rubric "Gott und Welt,"
but not in direct sequence. "Wohl zu merken" was separated from
the others by "Entoptische Farben. An Julien," a poem written much
earlier and unrelated to Goethe's meteorological observations.

   There are four stages in the composition of the Howard poems: the
writing of the first four stanzas of the "Howards Ehrengedächtnis,"
the subsequent expansion of the poem by twenty-two lines, the addition of two short poems, one before and one after the central "Ehrengedächtnis," and the final placement of the three poems under the
rubric "Gott und Welt." Each stage reveals in turn a new and different
aspect of Goethe's concerns during these years. In various ways the
poems are related to a wide selection of Goethe's later poetry, including "Urworte. Orphisch" and "Um Mitternacht," the poems in the
collection "Gott und Welt" and the other two cycles of 1821. The
significance of these relationships will become apparent as we consider the contribution of each stage to the final structural design of
the small cycle.

   The year 1817, the most probable year for Goethe's composition of
the cloud stanzas, together with the first months of 1818, mark a brief
respite for him from the writing of the *Divan*. The majority of the
cycle's poems had been written, but the collection was not to achieve
its final form until 1820. During the pause Goethe wrote a number of
shorter poems, most of them of little interest. He also wrote two
poems which clearly signal the beginning of new lyric possibilities.
The first of these is "Urworte. Orphisch," written in October of 1817,
the second "Um Mitternacht," written in February of 1818.

   The four cloud stanzas of "Howards Ehrengedächtnis" (technically
they are five, as the first of the four, "Stratus," is written in two
stanzas) have much in common with these two poems. The relationship has not been noticed. Rather, "Howards Ehrengedächtnis" has

been repeatedly linked to Goethe's earlier didactic nature poetry, particularly to "Die Metamorphose der Pflanzen" and "Metamorphose der Tiere," and rightly so. Meteorology was the last of Goethe's scientific interests to find a direct expression in his poetry and he himself underscored the significance of the poems within his scientific and philosophical thought by placing them in "Gott und Welt" in 1827.[8] The relationship of the four cloud stanzas to "Urworte. Orphisch" and "Um Mitternacht" is less apparent. It is one of structural design rather than thematic intent.

The cloud stanzas of "Howards Ehrengedächtnis" present four contrasting stages of cloud formation. The stages are based on Howard's system of cloud classification, first made available to Goethe in 1815 in an essay in L. W. Gilbert's *Annalen der Physik* entitled "Über die Modificationen der Wolken von Lucas Howard, Esq."[9] Goethe selected four of Howard's seven cloud categories and rearranged them to suit his purposes. Like Howard, Goethe was concerned to describe the unique identity of each cloud formation. More than Howard, Goethe was also concerned that each individual formation be understood as part of a total and continuing process of cloud transformation. The poem, therefore, is distinguished by a very clear tension established by the poet between the independent, individually titled stanzas, in which the unique identity of each cloud pattern is stressed, and the central, almost unspoken assertion that becomes apparent in the course of the poem that in their uniqueness, each of the cloud formations is part of a larger process, that the progression of the clouds is not arbitrary but meaningful, and that, finally, it is the recognition of how the four individual stages together describe a single ordered continuity that is the poem's purpose. No single cloud formation, no single stanza is sufficient to define the entire process; at the same time, no single stanza is dispensable. In sequence their meaning becomes clear.

The same tension between independently defined stanzas and a unity that arises from the sequential process they describe is basic to the design of both "Urworte. Orphisch" and "Um Mitternacht." Goethe wrote in his commentary to "Urworte. Orphisch": "Diese wenigen Strophen enthalten viel Bedeutendes in einer Folge, die, wenn man sie erst kennt, dem Geiste die wichtigsten Betrachtungen erleichtert" (WA I, 41[1], 215). The five stanzas of "Urworte. Orphisch," each with individual titles taken from the Orphic mysteries, together describe the passage of an individual through the ages of man from birth to an implied death. Each individual stanza depicts a single constitutive aspect of human experience. It is only in the sequence of five stanzas, however, in the alternating images of constriction and freedom, and in the ultimate movement upwards towards greater spirituality and material release that the meaning of the poem can be found.

Similarly, in "Um Mitternacht," a poem concerned with three ages of man, and specifically with the insight born of a maturity achieved in the final age, the single stanza is at the same time an independent unit and a part of a carefully conceived sequence. Although no subtitles are employed as in "Urworte. Orphisch" and "Howards Ehrengedächtnis" to underscore the autonomy of the single stanza, each clearly depicts a separate stage in the progression from childhood to early manhood and finally to old age and insight. The sequence of three stanzas is characterized by contrasting images of light and varying depictions of the midnight hour. The meaning of the persona's maturity and the insight he has acquired in the third and final stage of his life is not to be found in the third stanza alone, however, but in the succession of stanzas and in the complex interplay of the images within them. The patterns described are more elusive than those used by Goethe to organize "Howards Ehrengedächtnis," but the basic design is quite the same.

Goethe wrote the cloud stanzas of "Howards Ehrengedächtnis" in the months between the writing of "Urworte. Orphisch" and "Um Mitternacht." In an essay he wrote in the fall of 1817, "Wolkengestalt nach Howard," he relates how he had long been fascinated by the variety of cloud formations, but unable to perceive any ordering principle in their varying shapes: "In meinen Tagebüchern bemerkte ich daher manchmal eine Folge von atmosphärischen Erscheinungen, dann auch wieder einzelne bedeutende Fälle; das Erfahrne jedoch zusammenzustellen fehlten mir Umsicht und wissenschaftliche Verknüpfungszweige" (WA II, 12, 6). The discoveries of Luke Howard and his system of cloud classification enabled Goethe to perceive the unity that had previously eluded him and he responded with a poem to honor the British scientist. In his poem Goethe addresses the very problem that had troubled him for so long: how to perceive order and unity in the variety of cloud formations. He provides no abstract response to the problem, however, but rather offers four individual descriptions of four types of clouds. It is in sequence that the four reveal the unifying patterns he perceived. In the progression of the stanzas in "Urworte. Orphisch," according to Goethe, "das Absolute, die moralische Weltordnung" is revealed (WA IV, 29, 358). Similarly, one might describe the progression of the cloud stanzas as the revelation of the "natürliche Weltordnung." The principles that govern the transformation of the clouds are revealed to be none other than "die zwei großen Triebräder aller Natur," the principles of "Polarität" and "Steigerung" (WA II, 11, 11). Werner Keller's excellent discussion of the cloud stanzas, and particularly of the function of polarity, metamorphosis, and heightened intensification ("Steigerung") in them, examines in detail Goethe's development of these principles in the sequence.[10] First, Goethe employs the familiar polarities of earth and sky, heaviness and lightness to mark the central opposition, and he concludes the first stanza, "Stratus," with explicit reference to the contending forces:

> . . . . so umdüstert's weit
> Die Mittelhöhe, beidem gleich geneigt,
> Ob's fallend wässert oder luftig steigt.

In subsequent stanzas the polarities are constantly reinforced. Second, he describes a diastolic and systolic pattern in the alternation between the broadly layered stratus cloud, the compact density of the cumulus, the dissolution of the cirrus, and the concentrated energy of the nimbus. Finally, Goethe clearly associates the entire process with a movement towards the most free, most spirit-filled state, a "Steigerung" he links metaphorically in these stanzas as well as in other works with both ascendance and lightness. The cirrus stanza of "Howards Ehrengedächtnis" marks the high point in the sequence:

> Doch immer höher steigt der edle Drang!
> Erlösung ist ein himmlisch leichter Zwang.[11]

Like the sequences in both "Urworte. Orphisch" and "Um Mitternacht," the cloud stanzas progress towards a moment of greatest freedom and spiritual (non-material) existence. The peculiar ethical diction Goethe employs in the Howard poems to describe this progression provides an interesting complement to the meteorological language he uses in the last stanza, "Hoffnung," of "Urworte. Orphisch":

> Ein Wesen regt sich leicht und ungezügelt:
> Aus Wolkendecke, Nebel, Regenschauer
> Erhebt sie uns . . .

For Goethe, the two dimensions are not radically distinct. He writes of metamorphosis that the process "dergestalt sich veredelnd vorschreitet, daß alles Stoffartige, Geringere, Gemeinere nach und nach zurückbleibt und in größerer Freiheit das Höhere, Geistige, Bessere zu Erscheinung kommen läßt" (WA II, 6, 190).

Clouds, however, while drawn (at least figuratively) to the airy regions above, are fundamentally material as well, and the cycle of four transformations concludes with a decisive return to earth. (A similar return marks the conclusion of both the other smaller cycles we will consider in this chapter.) Goethe asserts in the final stanza, "Nimbus," that the return to earth is necessary, but it does not mean that the higher regions have been abandoned altogether. Descriptive speech records events in their natural sequence, it follows the rain downward into the physical world, but the meaning of the total process is not lost. It is in the images of the poem, or more precisely, in the poem itself as an image, a *Bild*, that it is preserved:

> Doch mit dem Bilde hebet euren Blick:
> Die Rede geht herab, denn sie beschreibt,
> Der Geist will aufwärts, wo er ewig bleibt.

Poetry has accomplished what descriptive language cannot—a representation of the total process of cloud transformation that reveals the secrets of its varying modifications. Goethe wrote, "Wem die Natur ihr offenbares Geheimnis zu enthüllen anfängt, der empfindet eine unwiderstehliche Sehnsucht nach ihrer würdigsten Auslegerin, der Kunst,"[12] and "Poesie deutet auf die Geheimnisse der Natur und sucht sie durchs Bild zu lösen."[13] Like all of nature's secrets, the clouds are an "offenbares Geheimnis." Goethe has found a way to solve the riddle once posed by the shifting clouds, and he has solved it in images that point to the clouds themselves as the revelation of nature's secrets.

As we have demonstrated, Goethe's original design for a poem to honor Howard consisted of four independent stanzas together defining a greater unity. Nothing more would have been written, but for a letter he received in February, 1821, from John Christian Hüttner, a London contact, who admitted his difficulty in understanding the meaning of the poem: "In dem bewußten Gedichte hat keiner von uns hier Spürkraft genug, die Beziehung auf Howard ausfindig zu machen. Wollen Ew. Excellenz geruhen, ein paar Winke darüber zu ertheilen, so daß die Verse auch einem größeren Publicum verständlich werden" (WA IV, 34, 366). In response Goethe wrote twenty-two additional lines introducing the cloud stanzas and provided a brief prose commentary in a letter to Hüttner (WA IV, 50, 47–48). Correspondence as well as Goethe's later remarks in the *Tag- und Jahreshefte* leave no doubt that he expanded the poem specifically to meet the request made by Hüttner: "Ich schrieb ein Ehrengedächtniß in vier Strophen, welche die Hauptworte seiner Terminologie enthielten; auf Ansuchen Londoner Freunde sodann noch einen Eingang von drei

Strophen, zu besserer Vollständigkeit und Verdeutlichung des Sinnes" (WA I, 36, 186–87).

While it is not unusual for a poet to want his works to be read and appreciated, it is quite unlike Goethe to give a great deal of thought to the reception of his work or to modify a poem because readers found it difficult. Yet, a concern for a proper understanding of his work is revealed over and over again in the years from 1819 to 1822. While "Howards Ehrengedächtnis" seems to be the only poem he actually expanded at a reader's request, he wrote explanatory statements for several other poems at this time. In the introductory comments to the *Noten und Abhandlungen zu besserem Verständnis des West-östlichen Divans* he himself notes his earlier reluctance to comment on his work:

Ich habe die Schriften meiner ersten Jahre ohne Vorwort in die Welt gesandt, ohne auch nur im mindesten anzudeuten, wie es damit gemeint sei: dieß geschah im Glauben an die Nation, daß sie früher oder später das Vorgelegte benutzen werde. Und so gelang mehreren meiner Arbeiten augenblickliche Wirkung, andere, nicht eben so faßlich und eindringend, bedurften, um anerkannt zu werden, mehrerer Jahre. Indessen gingen auch diese vorüber und ein zweites, drittes nachwachsendes Geschlecht entschädigt mich doppelt und dreifach für die Unbilden die ich von meinen früheren Zeitgenossen zu erdulden hatte.

Nun wünscht' ich aber, daß nichts den ersten guten Eindruck des gegenwärtigen Büchleins hindern möge. Ich entschliesse mich daher zu erläutern, zu erklären, nachzuweisen, und zwar bloß in der Absicht daß ein unmittelbares Verständiniß Lesern daraus erwachse, die mit dem Osten wenig oder nicht bekannt sind. (WA I, 7, 3–4)

While Goethe explains that it is because the *Divan* placed unusual demands on readers unfamiliar with the Eastern world that his accompanying remarks are necessary, this is not the complete explanation. The *Noten* are the first in a series of commentaries he wrote between 1816 and 1822, together revealing a new impulse towards elaboration and clarification of his work. Goethe's retreat from public life as he grew older has been amply documented in the critical literature. Goethe signaled it as early as 1816 in remarks to Zelter about the writing of the *Italienische Reise*: "Ich führe meine eigene Art zu leben, die du kennst, immer fort, seh wenig Menschen und lebe eigentlich nur in der Vergangenheit, indem ich alte Papiere aller Art zu ordnen und redigiren trachte" (WA IV, 27, 208). Similar remarks echo in later letters: "Meinen Winter bring ich beynahe in absoluter Einsamkeit zu, dictire fleißig, so daß meine ganze Existenz wie auf dem Papiere steht, zu Ostern sollst du allerley zu lesen haben. Hören und reden mag ich nicht mehr, sondern vertraue, wie des Königs Midas Barbier, meine Geheimnisse den verrätherischen Blättern" (WA IV, 35, 261). The retreat is accompanied, however, by various attempts to assure that a satisfactory record of his life and work would remain available to the public. The preparation of the *Ausgabe letzter Hand* has already been mentioned. Goethe's clarifying statements on both "Urworte. Orphisch" and "Harzreise im Winter," as well as the prose remarks sent to Hüttner on "Howards Ehrengedächtnis," are further examples. The short essay "Ballade. Betrachtung und Auslegung" was written at this time as well. In several cases Goethe directly attributes his commentary to a request from readers for clarification of the work: "Aufgeregt durch theilnehmende Anfrage schrieb ich einen Commentar zu dem abstrusen Gedichte: 'Harzreise im Winter'" (WA I, 36, 179). In reference to "Urworte. Orphisch" he wrote: "Auch haben Freunde gewünscht, daß zum Verständniß derselben einiges geschähe, damit dasjenige, was sich hier fast nur ahnen läßt, auch einem klaren Sinne gemäß und einer reinen Erkenntnis übergeben sei" (WA I, 41 1, 215).

The expansion of "Howards Ehrengedächtnis" is but one more example of a general interest in elaboration and explanation. What is it that the additional lines specifically accomplish? More than anything else, they clarify the problem to which the four cloud stanzas provide the solution. They explain that the seemingly endless variety of clouds admitted of no pattern or purpose and they assert that it was Howard's system of cloud classification that made it possible for Goethe to perceive the underlying order. In short, they do not alter the basic thrust of the original poem, but simply state the problem more clearly.

The additional twenty-two lines, which precede the cloud stanzas, are divided into three parts. In each a different interpretation of clouds and their varying shapes is presented. In the first stanza the clouds seem to vary in an arbitrary manner. Their modification is explained by identification with the divinity Camarupa (a figure Goethe borrowed from his reading of the Indian epic "Megha-Duta"), meaning the "wearer of shapes at will" (WA IV, 50, 47). Goethe remarks that the clouds are both "leicht und schwer," and at times gathered in, at times dispersed, but the basic patterns are not understood as ordering principles (as they will be in the cloud stanzas). Rather, they are attributed to the divinity's passing.

In the second stanza the imagination of the observer intervenes to impose order on the shifting cloud formations. The images defined by the imagination are delightful (exotic and mythological beasts predominate)[14] but they fail to clarify—metaphorically, the army of figures beaks apart on the rocks.

In the third stanza Goethe proclaims the final solution. The human desire for clarifying order need not depend on imaginative constructs in order to be satisfied. The phenomena themselves yield the answer when properly understood. In the ever-changing shapes an unchanging order can be perceived, and what eluded conceptualization can be comprehended:

> Was sich nicht halten, nicht erreichen läßt
> Er [Howard] faßt es an, er hält zuerst es fest;
> Bestimmt das Unbestimmte, schränkt es ein,
> Benennt es treffend!—Sei die Ehre dein!—

Just how Howard has done this so successfully is not stated. The succinct pattern that follows, "Wie Streife steigt, sich ballt, zerflattert, fällt" is much like the formulas that were used to conclude the opening poem of both the *Römische Elegien* and the *Sonette* and at the same time to begin the cycle that followed—an abstract statement of the essential idea of the poem, but one that must be given its full meaning in the poems that follow. In a sense the poem "Howards Ehrengedächtnis" is like a small cycle itself.

When Goethe, in the months after completing "Howards Ehrengedächtnis," prepared two poems to place before and after the central text, he chose to use the opening poem to give direct voice to the confusion that first prompted his appreciation of Howard's ordering system. A single voice states:

> "Die Welt, sie ist go groß und breit,
> Der Himmel auch so hehr und weit,
> Ich muß das alles mit Augen fassen,
> Will sich aber nicht recht denken lassen." [15]

The problem is posed more abstractly than in "Howards Ehrengedächtnis"; the clouds do not alone elude the mind's grasp, but everything, the world and the sky above it. The response is familiar in its epigrammatic succinctness:

> Dich im Unendlichen zu finden,
> Mußt unterscheiden und dann verbinden.

In the next couplet Howard's work is explicitly linked with the first part of the recommended solution, "unterscheiden." He taught us how to differentiate. Where does the relinking, the "verbinden," occur? The question is not even posed at this point. In our discussion of the cloud stanzas, however, we have already noted the answer. It occurs in the poet's words, in the poem itself.

The first line of the third poem, eventually entitled "Wohl zu merken," continues the presentation begun in "Atmosphäre," and in a meter and stanza form identical to it. The issue of rebinding is now explicitly raised, and Goethe suggests in the opening line ("Und wenn wir unterschieden haben") that the necessary second step, the rejoining of what has been divided into parts, has not yet occurred. He is, of course, being somewhat misleading. Even as he has presented the clouds in Howard's categories and noted how to differentiate among them, he, as the poet, has assured their continuity. The scientist divides, describes, and clarifies, but the world cannot be understood by the scientist alone. In partnership with the artist, the poet, a proper appreciation of nature is possible. This is the message made explicit in "Wohl zu merken." The artist does not disregard the definitive character of each of the four types of clouds he observes; indeed, he carefully notes their differences as the first step towards comprehending their unity. But he grasps as well a reality that eludes scientific description, for it is a reality of a permanence and a unity that is constantly changing and yet ever present. While it is visible if one learns to perceive correctly, it is visible only in the fleeting transitory shapes of an everchanging nature:

> Da läßt er den Charakter gelten,
> Doch ihm erteilen luftige Welten
> Das Übergängliche, das Milde,
> Daß er es fasse, fühle, bilde.

A reality that eludes scientific description, but that is nonetheless real—this is the province of poetry: "Die Kunst ist eine Vermittlerin des Unaussprechlichen." [16] The task Goethe assigns the poet in "Wohl zu merken" is one he has already accomplished in the cycle. The poem urges the reader not only to perceive the significance of Howard's teaching, which Goethe gladly celebrates, but of the poet's accomplishment as well.

"Atmosphäre," "Howards Ehrengedächtnis," and "Wohl zu merken" were published together in 1822 in *Zur Naturwissenschaft überhaupt*. This was not to be their final placement. When Goethe sent the poems to Riemer on 24 October 1821, they were returned with the suggestion that Goethe consider compiling his philosophical nature poetry into a single collection. Riemer reminded him that he had a fair start on the collection already, specifically naming the poems "Die Metamorphose der Pflanzen," "Howards Ehrengedächtnis," "Weltseele," and "Urworte. Orphisch" in a letter of 29 October (WA IV, 35, 354). Two days later, on 31 October, Goethe began gathering poems for "Gott und Welt." He wrote to Riemer the following day:

Ihr guter Gedanke, mein Werthester, hat wie billig eine gute Wirkung ge-than: schon sind ältere und neuere Gedichte, wie sie sich auf *natura naturans* beziehen, abgeschrieben und zusammengesteckt. Es findet sich schon mehr als man denkt und wie man auf Vollständigkeit sinnen kann, so erweist sich auch der große Vortheil, daß man sich nicht wiederhole. (WA IV, 35, 165)

The three Howard poems were placed in the *Ausgabe letzter Hand* in this collection. Curiously, "Wohl zu merken" was separated from "Howards Ehrengedächtnis" by the short unrelated poem "Entop-tische Farben. An Julien." It has been suggested that the two poems were switched accidentally in printing (numerous editions have qui-etly reversed the original order without comment). [17] Goethe appar-ently raised no objection to the published sequence. In "Gott und Welt," a collection of both older and more recent poems of varying quality, the poems are selectively ordered ("nach Bezug und Folge" according to Goethe) (WA I, 36, 187). He placed the three Howard poems within a series of metamorphoses that progress from plants ("Die Metamorphose der Pflanzen") to animals ("Metamorphose der Tiere") to man ("Urworte. Orphisch") and finally to clouds. The Ho-ward poems have reached a wider audience only within this larger collection. This fact, coupled with the displacement of "Wohl zu mer-ken," has hindered appreciation of the poems as a short sequence in their own right. Trunz's publication of the poems as a trilogy in the *Hamburger Ausgabe* (HA I, 349–52) has guaranteed continued interest in them apart from "Gott und Welt." The poems reveal, in their rather complex genesis, the major poetic concerns that distinguish Goethe's lyrical writing and publication in the years after the *Divan*. Not only did Goethe develop a structural design for individual poems that can be considered a kind of mini-cycle, but his marked concern for clarifi-cation, elaboration, and a final summing up of his life and work led to the completion of a number of new lyric groupings in the post-*Divan* years. *Wilhelm Tischbeins Idyllen* and *Zu meinen Handzeichnungen* pro-vide two further examples of his poetic activity.

Wilhem Tischbeins Idyllen

In 1821, the year Goethe completed the sequence of three Howard poems, he wrote two other smaller cycles: *Wilhelm Tischbeins Idyllen* and *Zu meinen Handzeichnungen*. While the *Idyllen* are the better known of the two, neither has attracted much critical attention. [18] Both cycles were written to accompany a series of drawings (in the case of the second cycle, etchings based on Goethe's drawings) and both were begun, according to a later explanation provided by Goethe, because the pictures alone were not adequate and needed some kind of clarification.[19] Apparently, Goethe was less concerned that the poems needed the drawings, however. He published both cycles in *Kunst und Altertum* and later placed them in the *Ausgabe letzter Hand* under the rubric "Kunst."

The plan for an *Idyllen* cycle began with Tischbein in Rome in the first months of Goethe's visit in 1786. As Goethe notes in the *Italienische Reise*, the work was conceived as a joint project between artist and poet. Together they hoped to express something which neither of them working alone in his own medium would be able to do:

Da uns die Erfahrung genugsam belehrt, daß man zu Gedichten jeder Art Zeichnungen und Kupfer wünscht, ja der Mahler selbst seine ausführlichsten Bilder der Stelle irgend eines Dichters widmet, so ist Tischbeins Gedanke höchst beifallswürdig, daß Dichter und Künstler zusammen arbeiten sollten, um gleich vom Ursprunge herauf eine Einheit zu bilden. . . . Tischbein hat auch hiezu sehr angenehme idyllische Gedanken, und es ist wirklich sonderbar, daß die Gegenstände, die er auf diese Weise bearbeitet wünscht, von der Art sind, daß weder dichtende noch bildende Kunst, jede für sich, zur Darstellung hinreichend wären. (WA I, 30, 220)

The project never advanced beyond the planning stage and the friendship between the two artists waned. Goethe returned to Weimar, and Tischbein, after ten more years in Italy, returned to northern Germany. There, in 1808, he was appointed court painter in the Duchy of Oldenburg by the reigning Duke Peter Friedrich, an enthusiastic patron of the arts.[20]

In 1819, however, Tischbein revived his plan for an *Idyllen* cycle and in the next year completed forty-three smaller oil paintings and a larger canvas entitled "Ideale Landschaft." The paintings hang today in Oldenburg as he grouped them. On 1 May 1821 Tischbein wrote to Goethe and told him of the belated realization of the earlier scheme. Contact between the two former friends was cautiously resumed. Tischbein sent Goethe a selection of seventeen ink and water-colored sketches: nine identical with nine of the smaller oil paintings, six related closely to them, and two details from the large painting, "Ideale Landschaft."[21] Goethe never saw the original oil paintings and had no idea how they were to be grouped. Tischbein enclosed no plan indicating how the sketches were to be ordered.

Goethe arranged the drawings to his purposes and wrote the first fifteen of the short poems known as *Wilhelm Tischbeins Idyllen* in July of 1821. Shortly thereafter he completed a prose description of the sketches and published the poems, inserted in the prose commentary, in *Kunst und Altertum* in 1822 (WA I, 49¹, 306–30). In 1827 he placed the poems, without any prose commentary, in the *Ausgabe letzter Hand*. Six additional poems had been added, poems written in October of 1821 in response to a second set of sketches Tischbein had sent. Together these twenty-one poems are known as *Wilhelm Tischbeins Idyllen*.

All twenty-one poems are a response to Tischbein's sketches and appropriately grouped together in the *Ausgabe letzter Hand*. In its original design, however, the cycle consisted of only fifteen poems, the fifteen Goethe wrote between 16 and 22 July 1821. A discussion of the *Idyllen* will necessarily focus on these fifteen. The final six are an afterthought, poetically less engaging, and should be regarded as a kind of coda rather than as works basic to the cycle's design.²² Tischbein sent seventeen sketches. Goethe wrote fifteen poems and an introduction, "Titelbild." (A sketch for the title page was made by Clemens Wenzeslaus Coudray, court architect, at Goethe's request [WA IV, 35, 21].) Goethe omitted Tischbein's drawing, "Ein Stilleben, Pfirsich, Aprikosen, Apfelblüte," from his sequence.²³ The remaining sixteen sketches were ordered (in his journal Goethe refers to the "schematische Aufstellung" of the series [WA III, 8, 79]) and fifteen poems were written. One of the sketches, "Drei Nebelnymphen," which Goethe compares in his prose commentary with the flashy finale to a series of fireworks (WA I, 49¹, 328), has no accompanying poem. Goethe had placed the sketch fifteenth in the series of sixteen, among a group of drawings of air and water nymphs. In his poems he uses the series of nymphs to trace the gradual transformation of the material (water) to the immaterial (air), a "Steigerung" familiar to his late poetry and fundamental to the design of "Howards Ehrengedächtnis," as we have already noted. The problems with the sketch "Drei Nebelnymphen," Goethe explained later, was that its three ascending figures suggested so clearly to him the sequence of three clouds, stratus-cumulus-cirrus, that any poem he wrote about them would seem a repetition of the three cloud stanzas in "Howards Ehrengedächtnis." "Es ist als wenn der Künstler die Howardische Terminologie anthropomorphisch auszudrücken den Vorsatz gehabt. . . . [Wir] bringen deßhalb kein Gedicht hier bei, weil solches nur als Wiederholung von Howards Ehrengedächtniß erscheinen dürfte" (WA I, 49¹, 328–29). Just a few months earlier Goethe had written the twenty-two-line introduction to the Howard poem. One senses in his remarks a basic satisfaction with the completed work.

The poems of the *Idyllen* cycle are short, visually oriented pieces written with little variation in either rhythm or rhyme scheme. While a single image or motif is central to each, the poems are not filled with descriptive detail, but rather are themselves suggestive sketches. The progression of nymphs, fauns, satyrs, and the like, may cause the poems to seem somewhat out of place among Goethe's other poetry of this period. The world of the *Divan* seems distant indeed, as does the weighty speculation of the philosophical nature poetry. The Tischbein poems are light in contrast, a deliberate imaginative indulgence, free from personal passion; yet they are also clearly poems of Goethe's old age. The isolated symbolic figures such as Chiron (poem 8) and the language of the poems identify them as part of Goethe's late poetry, as does the actual design of the cycle.

The sequence of the Tischbein poems, like the sequence of the four cloud stanzas in "Howards Ehrengedächtnis," is informed by the basic principles of "Polarität" and "Steigerung." Not only does the complete cycle chart a course from earth to the heavens, but each of the smaller groups of poems within it is characterized by the same general pattern. The first of the three (poems 1–4) is a series of natural landscapes, and it culminates in the image of the single majestic oak. The second (poems 5–8) is an arcadian landscape filled with shepherds, music, fauns, and satyrs. It culminates in the image of the worthy centaur Chiron. In the third and longest sequence (poems 10–14) a series of water and air nymphs describe a symbolic ascent from earthly regions to the heavenly sphere. Poems 4, 8, and 14, the final poems in each of these sequences, present three separate images of heightened existence. In themselves the three core images mark a progression. While the oak remains the visual statement of solitary greatness and retains its superlative characterization ("Einsamkeit ist höchstes Gut") in the progression from oak, rooted in the earth, to the centaur, half animal but half spiritual, and finally to the interweaving play of the air spirits in poem 14, Goethe leaves no doubt about the direction man's imaginative longing as well as the cycle must take. In the middle lines of poem 9, a poem which functions as a turning point in the cycle, he clearly states:

> Alles habt ihr nun empfangen,
> Irdisch war's und in der Näh'
> Sehnsucht aber und Verlangen
> Hebt vom Boden in die Höh'.

The cycle begins, however, firmly grounded with a series of four natural landscapes. Although Goethe ordered Tischbein's sketches to suggest a progression towards various moments of heightened existence within the idyll, the poems themselves do not underscore this sequence except by very subtle means. In each poem a single image or motif is central. The encompassing design emerges only gradually in the course of the cycle.

In the first poem a ruin overgrown by vegetation provides the central image.[24] The crumbling ancient structure is depicted in four lines, the regenerative power of the earth in another four. The poem in its two parts suggests a two-part process. But when the poem is understood as a picture, as one of Tischbein's idylls (indeed, the word derives from the Greek *eidyllion* meaning "little picture"),[25] there can be no temporal sequence. Both decline and renewal are bound together as a single process. Nature is identified as the active agent in this process, and the poem concludes with an abstract proclamation of her achievement: "Der Natur ist's wohlgeraten." Goethe will echo this phrase to conclude the cycle in poem 15.

The second poem continues the pattern of decline and renewal as well as the celebration of nature's activity. It begins with a grateful nod towards the artist: "Der Geist,/ Der uns in das Freie weis't." A vast landscape is sketched, and the sun, evoked as both rising and setting in the noun compound "Sonnen-Auf- und Untergänge" acclaims the ceaseless activity of "Gott und die Natur,"[26] even as it unites the expansive landscape. All of nature is, in truth, part of the celebration. In the opening poems the past and the present, morning and evening, have been conjoined in the images of nature's ceaseless activity. Goethe does not press the linking. The motif is temporarily set aside, only to be recalled quite explicitly in poem 14, the final poem in the third sequence of the cycle.

The third poem presents two contrasting images, a forest and a small cluster of trees. The trees in the forest are undifferentiated; the trees clustered together are individual in character. Bosshardt suggests that the poem is concerned with the evaluation of the first landscape as a natural setting and of the second as a landscape created by man and concludes: "Die Entscheidung zwischen Natur und Kunstlandschaft wird wiederum nicht eindeutig gefällt. Goethe schätzt sowohl das eine wie das andere."[27] This is not the issue, and Goethe's evaluation of the two landscapes is less equivocal than Bosshardt suggests. He clearly favors the second, but not because it is a "Kunstlandschaft." The forest seems to provide a positive enough setting as it is introduced in the opening lines of the poem:

> Wenn in Wäldern Baum an Bäumen
> Bruder sich mit Bruder nähret,
> Sei das Wandern, sei das Träumen
> Unverwehrt und ungestöret.

When the contrast is completed in the final four lines of the poem, however, a reevaluation is necessary:

> Doch wo einzelne Gesellen
> Zierlich mit einander streben,
> Sich zum schönen Ganzen stellen,
> Das ist Freude, das ist Leben.

For the observer, according to Goethe, real joy and real life are not to be found in landscapes that in themselves command no interest, where the wanderer lapses into his own private dreams. The clustered trees are of far greater interest. But the poem is not concerned simply with the wanderer in the forest. Like the poem that follows, it is anthropomorphic in its design. The small cluster of trees, striving with each other towards a higher unity, is not simply a landscape, but an image of human aspiration. A community of individuals, individually active and yet defining a greater whole—this, rather than the undifferentiated masses, ought to be man's ideal.

The fourth poem completes the sequence begun in poem 3, and the cluster of trees is replaced by the single majestic oak. Like the image of Chiron in poem 8, the oak stands as a symbolic statement of a realized excellence. Its solitary position in the middle of a small lake, uniting heaven and earth in its self-reflective gazing, is proclaimed the greatest good: "Einsamkeit ist höchstes Gut." What began in poem 1 with seeds and tendrils close to the earth is crowned now by a majestic figure: "Majestätisch Fürstensiegel/ solchem grünen Waldesflor," the grandest representative of the natural world.

In the opening four poems Goethe has intorduced a number of motifs that will be recalled later in the cycle: nature as a ceaseless creator, the artist as the one who points the way into the idyll, the value of solitary greatness. He has moved the first four poems towards a high point in the image of the solitary oak that will be answered in the later sequences by other images of heightened existence. Finally, he has prepared a way to end the cycle, for the scene in poem 1 will find its complement in poem 15. All this has been done, however, with very few words and little obvious linking of the individual poems. Four separate images of idyllic delight open the cycles: the overgrown ruin, the sunrise-sunset, the cluster of trees, and the solitary oak. The significance of the sequence and the final unity of the cycle are only apparent when the second sequence of poems (poems 5–8) repeats in a general sense the progression of the opening poems.

The second series of poems marks a departure from the natural landscapes of poems 1–4. It is set in the timeless arcadian world of shepherds, satyrs, and enchanting music. As in the opening four poems, various motifs are used to link the four sketches, but no single one dominates the sequence. The poems are not complex; each suggests with a playful lightness a broader canvas and stories left untold. Young women in poem 5 await the enticement of music. The presence of two instrumentalists, one with a flute and the other with Pan's pipes (Goethe identifies him as a faun in the prose commentary), promise not only hours of enchantment but a sprightly rivalry as well. In poem 6 the characteristic elements of the idyll are gathered: gentle lambs, frolicking goats, bountiful natural foods, a father with a flute in his hand, and the mother with a child, all united in the joys of their simple existence. It is a life freed from all that distorts original goodness and simplicity, according to Goethe: "Menschlich natürliche, ewig wiederkehrende, erfreuliche Lebenszustände, einfach wahrhaft vorgetragen . . . , freilich abgesondert von allem Lästigen, Unreinen, Widerwärtigen, worein wir sie auf Erden gehüllt sehn" (WA I, 49[1], 315). The image is one of paradise unchanged, "Und Natur ist's nach wie vor." In poems 7 and 8 Goethe employs maxims in his presentation of the pastoral scene, forms of wisdom which likewise attest to unchanging values. Like father, like son begins poem 7: "Wie die Alten sungen, so zwitschern die Jungen"; poem 8 echoes the saying "Würde bringt Bürde" in its closing rhyme. The two poems are linked by the task of education. The perpetuation of the idyll is at issue and it is presented as a spiritual task. In poem 7 the task is portrayed in the teaching of music by father to son—even fauns, with animal ears, are educated to the appreciation of beauty. In poem 8 the centaur, the spiritual animal, the noble pedagogue (cf, *Faust* 7337) marks the culmination of the sequence. At home in the idyll and yet keenly aware of greater tasks, he is called "edel-ernst" by Goethe, recalling the diction of "Howards Ehrengedächtnis" ("der edle Drang"). The education of man points beyond the physical setting—it is a spiritual direction that must be given. An awareness of the significance of the project is the burden that occupies the worthy teacher. Like the solitary oak in poem 4, the centaur transcends the landscape into which he has been placed.

With Chiron, Goethe prepares to close the arcadian idyll. A scene of parting, with its tragic potential, is the focus of the ninth poem. In Tischbein's sketch two lovers take leave of one another. In Goethe's poem it is we who take leave of the idyll we have enjoyed. The physical loss is real; it is, however, not without compensation. Goethe has twice suggested in the opening eight poems that the idyll is not permanently lost to man. In poem 2 the artist points the direction out into nature where the continuing creative renewal assures multiple images of life in its fullness. In poem 6 we are told that the earth

itself takes on shades of paradise ("silbern, golden") when man declares his allegiance to the unchanging goodness nature reveals. With
this Goethe prepares the way for poem 9, the scene of parting. The
sketches of idyllic pleasure must pass, but there is a sense in which
the idyll is sustained:

> Lasset Lied und Bild verhallen
> Doch im Innern ist's getan.

The images of the idyll continue to inform the longing of man's imagination, to assist his participation in the heightened existence to which
it points. The sequence of ascending spirits in poems 10–14, and their
culminating image of countless hours interwoven with delight mark
the goal. *Natura textor*, nature the weaver, continues her creation.[28]
Man, through the eyes of art, perceives the scheme.

The significance of the "Steigerung" represented by the sequence
of water and air nymphs in poems 10–14 and of the culminating image
of interwoven hours (14) is not rendered less serious when Goethe
begins the series with a fanciful tale of discord. In poem 10 the undu-
lating flow of the stream is represented by two water nymphs. The
stream must part as one portion of its channel is routed through the
mill, and this becomes the occasion for Goethe's tale of strife. He
suggests that a shepherd is the object of the nymphs' desire and his
presence gives rise to a feud that divides the two. The end of the tale
is left untold. While the stream flows downward to its rendezvous,
Goethe's poems begin their ascent.

The rising mists mark the first step in the gradual removal from the
earth-bound settings that have characterized the idyll thus far. Goethe
calls attention to the new direction that both the cycle and the water
have taken. A symbol for all that is drawn downwards to the earth,
the water, quite unexpectedly, rises upwards in poem 11. "Künstler-
wille macht es leicht," Goethe states, proclaming simultaneously the
ease with which the artist effects a transformation of the landscape
and the airy lightness that will become the central characteristic of the
new setting in poems 11–14. The rising mist is not actually named in
poem 11. Goethe does not depend on nouns, but rather employs
verbs to evoke the new landscapes. He pays little attention to the full-
bodied beauties Tischbein has sketched (in one of the six poems later
appended to the cycle he comments on Tischbein's penchant for "ap-
petitliche Leiber") and transforms their physical presence into symbolic movement. In the rising motion of the nymphs he charts the
passing hours until in the final poem of the series, poem 14, the
nymphs are themselves the interwoven hours of ceaseless delight.

An image of dawn follows the rising mist of poem 11; the morning hour of poem 12 gives way in poem 13 to the long day. The daytime hours are proclaimed troublesome sisters by the poet, who favors the anticipation of the morning to the toil of the day. He dwells in the end, however, not on the burdens of life, but on its pleasing moments, and there is, in truth, no end to the delights of the idyll. Both warp and woof of the interwoven hours in poem 14 are "lieblich." Here is the answer to the parting of poem 9, for in the continuing coming and going suggested by the weaving metaphor in 14, there is no final separation. Nature continues her creation (the image of poem 1 is recalled) and guarantees that moments of idyllic delight are yet possible.

But poem 14 does not mark the end, and the final poem, poem 15, seems both a strange sequel to 14 and an equally strange conclusion to the cycle. The landscape it evokes stands in stark contrast to the verbal lightness of the preceding poem and is far removed from the pastoral pleasures of the earlier portion of the cycle. It is elemental, characterized by a density that belies motion. In four lines only one verb is used, and then not to describe the landscape, but rather its impact on its viewer. The landscape is said to address the soul in aweful ("schauderhafte") tones. Water, stone, air, and light, each self-contained and remote, define the scene.

But there are links to the rest of the cycle, and specifically to the opening poem. Goethe encourages the connection in his commentary. Poem 15 presents a scene, "welche Bezug auf das erste Bild zu haben scheint"; he continues, however, "mit welchem sie jedoch einen auffallenden Gegensatz bildet" (WA I, 49[1], 329). Like the opening scene, poem 15 is a landscape. Unlike the opening scene, the setting in poem 15 is devoid of both plant life and signs of human activity. There is little to charm or delight the viewer, yet, Goethe repeats the affirmation that closed the first poem: "So erweist sich wohl Natur." In what is "lieblich" as well as in what is "schauderhaft" the natural world provides the artist with images of heightened existence. Goethe has returned his reader to the earthly regions at the close of the cycle, much as he did at the end of the cloud sequence of "Howards Ehrengedächtnis." In doing so he is not denying the direction the idyll has taken. Rather, he describes the concluding sketch as a kind of epilogue to the cycle. The curtain has fallen—"der Künstler [läßt] auf einmal den Vorhang fallen" (WA I, 49[1], 330)—but the show isn't quite over. He concludes poem 15 as he began poem 2, with a nod towards the artist who has made all this possible. He affirms that it is, and always has been, the artist who is able to perceive the wonders of nature and assist others to retrieve images now remote which both delight and astound:

So erweist sich wohl Natur,
Künstlerblick vernimmt es nur.

With a similar affirmation of the artist Goethe closes the cycle a second time in poem 21:

Wie herrlich ist die Welt! wie schön!
Heil ihm, der je sie so gesehn.

A second conclusion became necessary because Goethe had received an additional series of sketches from Tischbein. The poems that he wrote to accompany these drawings (poems 16–21) are little more than an afterthought, however, and have almost nothing to do with the design of the cycle. In them Goethe even expresses his dissatisfaction with some of the new sketches he has received. He proclaims them confusing (16), extravagant (17), and unintelligible (20) in part.[29] His criticism is, however, generally accompanied by words of affection for the artist and does not diminish the enthusiasm the earlier poems reveal for Tischbein's achievement. What the final six poems do reveal is how carefully Goethe planned his original sequence of fifteen. The cycle of fifteen is not distinguished by consistently outstanding verse.[30] But even though a number of the poems are not Goethe's best, all the poems contribute to the overall design and bring to the original Tischbein sketches a considered poetic statement.

In his concluding comments on the cycle Goethe describes the poems as an attempt to reawaken images in the imagination that have grown very remote or indeed disappeared from the world altogether (WA I, 49[1], 330). In the cycle that he began just a few months later, *Zu meinen Handzeichnungen*, he is concerned once more with the images from the past that have been reawakened. This time they are a bit less remote, for it is his own past that Goethe recalls in the new cycle.

Zu meinen Handzeichnungen

Two months after completing the first fifteen poems of *Wilhelm Tischbeins Idyllen* (but before writing the six that conclude the cycle), Goethe wrote another series of poems to accompany a collection of pictures, this time a series of etchings based on his own drawings.[31] The project began with the decision to allow two young Weimar artists, Karl Lieber and Karl Wilhelm Holdermann, to prepare a series of Goethe's sketches for publication. It is not clear whether Goethe intended from the beginning to write poems to accompany the six etchings, or whether the idea arose later as he was working on the

Tischbein cycle. Goethe's journal suggests that the selection of the drawings for the sequence was already completed in June of 1821: "Drey frische Zeichnungen an Lieber und Holdermann" (15 June 1821); "Abends Hofrath Meyer die radirten Landschaften bringend" (30 June 1821). [32] The poems were written from 23 to 25 September 1821, like the Tischbein poems, in a very few days. The six etchings and the six poems were published together the same year by Carl August Schwerdgeburth, a Weimar artist. The poems and a prose introduction were published a short time later in *Kunst und Altertum* in the same issue as the *Tischbein Idyllen*. [33] When they were placed in the *Ausgabe letzter Hand* the earlier title "Radirte Blätter, nach Handzeichnungen (Skizzen) von Goethe" was changed to *Zu meinen Handzeichnungen*.

In his introduction to the six poems Goethe readily admits his shortcomings as an artist and acknowledges the assistance he received in the preparation of the sketches. Lieber and Holdermann not only did the etching, but touched-up the original sketches, adding starker contrasts and greater detail. Even so, according to Goethe, the sketches are not great works of art. But sketches, like other kinds of jottings, can be valuable despite aesthetic failings, he continues, for they prove to be indispensable aids in a person's attempt to recall his own past: "also ist es auch mit flüchtigen Skizzen nach der Natur, wodurch uns Bilder, Zustände, an denen wir vorüber gegangen, festgehalten werden und die Reproduction derselben in der Einbildungskraft glücklich erleichtert wird" (WA I, 49[1], 332). The six sketches that are the basis for the poems *Zu meinen Handzeichnungen* have precisely this function. If they fail to communicate to the viewer what Goethe once perceived in the landscapes he sketched and hoped to express in his drawing, they nevertheless succeed in retrieving the experience for the aging poet. In the six poems of *Zu meinen Handzeichnungen* Goethe is not attempting to describe a set of drawings. Rather, in each poem he is attempting once more to evoke the significance of a setting he once knew, a setting that a sketch has helped him to recover out of his own past. The poems are retrospective pieces, an invitation to perceive the world as Goethe once saw it and at the same time to join the elderly poet in a reflective assessment of his younger self. Each landscape has become for Goethe a symbolic setting and it is his presentation of himself within each landscape that commands our interest.

For this reason the six poems of *Zu meinen Handzeichnungen*, to a much greater extent than the *Tischbein Idyllen*, can be read apart from the drawings on which they are based. When Goethe chose to publish the poems without the sketches, he did not, as in the Tischbein series, add a prose description to the sequence to assist the reader's visualization of the original drawing. His reason is clear. It is not the sketches themselves that are the focus of the cycle. The six poems, with far greater skill and more subtlety than the drawings, are able to evoke the settings Goethe once knew. The sketches remain of interest—it is they that made the poems possible in the first place—but they add very little to our understanding of the cycle.[34]

Goethe admits as much in his introduction to the poems. What he once attempted to express in his drawings, and failed to do, is now accomplished in verse:

Im Gefühl übrigens, daß diese Skizzen, selbst wie sie gegenwärtig vorgelegt werden, ihre Unzulänglichkeit nicht ganz überwinden können, habe ich ihnen kleine Gedichte hinzugefügt, damit der innere Sinn erregt und der Beschauer löblich getäuscht werde, als wenn er das mit Augen sähe, was er fühlt und denkt, eine Annäherung nämlich an den Zustand, in welchem der Zeichner sich befand, als er die wenigen Striche dem Papier anvertraute. (WA I, 49[1], 333)

While it remains fundamental to the cycle's design that each poem be understood as a comment on a single sketch (so that the reader necessarily pauses to try to frame the suggested scene in his imagination), the poems prove a far better aid to the recovery of the original setting than any one of Goethe's drawings.

When Goethe decided to publish the series apart from the etchings, he added individual titles to each poem.[35] The six titles Goethe chose are clearly conceived to suggest a coherence for the sequence. As an amateur, according to Goethe, he was attracted to a subject, in this case, a landscape, because it was distinctive in character. He sketched "was einen auffallenden, sich besonders aussprechenden Charakter hat" (WA I, 49[1], 333). The title that Goethe gave each of the poems calls attention to that unique characteristic of the landscape that at one time spoke directly to him and that now in retrospect defines its essence to him as a symbolic setting. In a sense the titles replace the original drawing. The six titles are:

1. "Einsamste Wildnis"
2. "Hausgarten"
3. "Freie Welt"
4. "Geheimster Wohnsitz"
5. "Bequemes Wandern"
6. "Gehinderter Verkehr"

The basic scheme they suggest is one of alternating images of openness and enclosure. Titles 1, 3, and 5 introduce the images of openness, titles 2, 4, and 6 those of enclosure. The pattern is familiar, the diastolic and systolic principle now defining the rhythm of Goethe's recollected memories. The fundamental opposition expressed in images of expansion and contraction, openness and enclosure, informs not only Goethe's perception of the physical world, as his scientific writings amply demonstrate, but his self-understanding as well.[36]

The opening poem, "Einsamste Wildnis," functions as the title page to the cycle, and like Goethe's "Titelbild" in the Tischbein cycle, it does not belong, strictly speaking, to the sequence that follows. It introduces the project, acknowledges Goethe's limitations as an artist and the role of the young artists, Lieber and Holdermann (unnamed in the poem), in the preparation of the cycle. The use of the past tense (in the opening "Ich sah die Welt. . . . " it is rhythmically underscored) marks both the young would-be artist's revel in the natural world and his dismay at repeated failure to capture its delights on paper as part of a bygone era. It is a youthful world the poet evokes— alive, fragrant and vigorous. But he is not deceived. He claims a permanence neither for it nor for the pictures that it brought forth. Indeed, his closing lines are rather pessimistic: "Und wie dem Walde geht's den Blättern allen, / Sie knospen, grünen, welken ab und fallen."

The five poems that follow evoke five scenes from Goethe's past. Each assumes a symbolic significance as Goethe pauses to comment both on the setting and his presence within it. The poems are linked, as we have noted, by alternating images of openness and enclosure. In the first of the five the opposition of home (or more precisely, the garden, as the title states) and the wider world is made explicit in the closing lines:

> Wir wenden uns, wie auch die Welt entzücke,
> Der Enge zu, die uns allein beglücke.

Also linking the five scenes is the image of the path. Various paths cut through the landscapes of the poems, each a part of the particular experience the poet now recalls. In the varying images of how the path was traversed, what goals accompanied the walk, and what was encountered along the way, each landscape becomes more than a natural scene once sketched by an amateur artist. Each is revealed as a symbolic setting expressive of a unique aspect of Goethe's experience along life's path. The metaphor is never explicitly stated in the poems, although in a later letter recommending the poems Goethe does refer to "die mancherlei wunderlichen Lebenspfade" he has recalled in the cycle (WA IV, 37, 105). It lingers in the background, however, assuring for the poems a significance that the mere description of five landscape sketches could never claim.

Each of the five settings is unique, and for each Goethe skillfully evokes its distinctive qualities. "Hausgarten" opens the series. The scene is characterized by images of protective enclosure, an enclosure that nourishes a life of friendship and joy. Nothing disturbs the stillness. Wandering, the wider world, strange lands—all serve but to enhance the appreciation for the familiar, the private and the narrowed perimeters. Goethe opens the series with the home, using it symbolically to mark both the beginning of the various paths that lead out into the world and as the complementary setting to all the distant landscapes that follow in the cycle.

The next poem, "Freie Welt," places us in the outside world. It is not a limitless horizon that Goethe evokes to express the freedom of this world, but a path that is traversed without pressing speed, without any set goal, in the luxury of shifting gaits, and with the assurance of youth and good health. In Goethe's younger days he often undertook such a vague and rather aimless wandering.[37] In the poem it becomes a symbol for a freedom unique to one untroubled by age, illness, or rigidly defined goals. The path is the symbolic setting for a youth without fixed plans, but with half-defined hopes, a setting in which encounters lead to love and love to a transformation of both the self and the surrounding scenery. The path had a purpose after all, if not a geographical goal. In this image of the path and how it was walked, Goethe provides a positive portrait of himself in early manhood. The path is still there, he tells us, but the poet proceeded on to a new landscape.

Poem 4, "Geheimster Wohnsitz," is the most enigmatic setting in the series. The structure is most secret, we are told, and Goethe carefully shrouds its origins in mystery in the opening lines of the poem. At the same time he teases the reader: "Wer Buchten kennt, Erdzungen, wird es finden." The character of the secret residence is presented in religious images: a temple, built on a firm foundation and dedicated to the loftiest purposes, visited by pilgrims, protected from the outside world by walls, and more importantly by the ideals of light and right, and returning its apprentices to the world after a year with new stature. Goethe carefully avoids any further specification of the "temple's" identity and yet adds, somewhat mysteriously, "Wir hofften selbst uns im Asyl zu gründen." He suggests that the hope was never fulfilled, but readily asserts the attraction of the retreat. While the language of the poem recalls Goethe's description of his "pilgrimage" to Rome and his quest for a new life as an artist, the poem is concerned far less with specific biographical circumstances than with the longing for retreat that it evokes. Goethe's reference to bays and peninsulas assumes that this most secret residence will be sought and can be found. Yet, there is irony in this, for the secret dwelling has remained well-hidden. Indeed, attempts to identify the landscape in Goethe's sketch have proven inconclusive.[38] If it can be found, according to Goethe, by those who know the meaning of places of separation and retreat ("Wer Buchten kennt, Erdzungen, wird es finden"), then, perhaps, it remains most secret precisely because each person must find the place for himself. The outer structure is but a symbol for an inner place. He concludes the poem with a statement of regret that no true artist accompanied him to sketch the scene. Is this meant as a clue to the setting's identity? The poem leaves a number of questions unanswered. It remains a most enigmatic statement of an apprenticeship Goethe says he never successfully enjoyed.

In poem 5, "Bequemes Wandern," once more a path is the symbolic setting. It is a path of ease—broad, well-marked, effortless. Even in the darkest hour it is negotiable and leads without undue exertion to the intended goal. The pilgrim's progress is assured: "Da kann der Waller jede Stunde loben." Goethe asserts that he did not trek this kind of path all too frequently, but certainly more than once it characterized the ease of his journey: "Wir sagen nicht, wir hätten's oft gesehn, / Dergleichen Wege doch gelang's zu gehn."

A second recollection is linked to the setting. It is the restlessness of youth that Goethe recalls, a drive that makes itself felt at any hour and allows even the most difficult mountain path to be ascended with ease. Clouds seem to mark the end of the trail to those who watch from below. But Goethe reprimands them and their limited vision:

> Man schelt' es nicht, denn wohl genießt sie rein,
> Auch über Wolken, heitern Sonnenschein.

Sunshine greets the effort at the peak. The poem marks the high point of the cycle.

The two paths are both images of achievement, the first assured by the broadly laid path, the second by the burning restlessness Goethe links with youth. In poem 6, "Gehinderter Verkehr," an explicit contrast is prepared. Mountain peaks are replaced by guarded coastlines, broad paths by narrowed impasses. Unlike the previous images of enclosure (the home, the secret asylum), the guarded fortifications along the shore line are signs of dominion and oppression. They are an obstacle to travel (and by extension, to life itself), not a welcome retreat. (By contrast, in both stanzas of poem 5 reference is made in temporal terms to the complete absence of any hindrance.) Here, the obsession with security and power transforms the day and night of easy achievement into a day and night of burdensome difficulty: "Sei's wie es sei, und immer Hinderniß./So Tag und Nacht den Reisenden zur Last." The setting recalls, with a jarring return to earth from the enthusiasm of the sunlit peaks, that not every path is one of easy ascent. While the descent from the heights is a familiar turn at the conclusion of Goethe's smaller cycles of 1821 (cf. the "Nimbus"stanza of "Howards Ehrengedächtnis" and poem 15 of *Wilhelm Tischbeins Idyllen*), it is not Goethe's final word. He concludes the poem and the cycle with the admission: "Es ist vielleicht zu düster aufgefaßt." He thus recalls the problem of the critics in poem 5 who perceived only "Nebeldunst" at the end of the trail. Sunshine remains a possibility even here. Furthermore, a life that has been characterized by a plurality of paths, by an alternation between experiences of enclosure and attractions of the wider world, cannot dwell too long or too exclusively on the apparent obstacles that do exist. In each of the previous poems Goethe has employed the generalized "we" to locate himself within the setting. It is absent in the final poem. He is an observer, and like the implied observers in poem 5 he sees a landscape that is darkened, clouded over, and without promise. Unlike them, however, he has knowledge of the sunshine that can await a traveler beyond the clouds. Even if he no longer has the energy to scale the peaks as the youth in poem 5, the dismal prognosis of poem 6 need not be the final word.

In the opening poems Goethe asserts that the leaves eventually wither and fall—time passes and a particular scene fades. The cycle of poems is a sign of how new leaves can replace the old, and how the past that has been lost can be recovered. The passing of time and the recovery of one's own past are concerns that do not cease to be significant for Goethe with the completion of the cycles of 1821, however. In Goethe's last lyric cycle, the *Chinesisch-deutsche Jahres- und Tageszeiten*, the passing of time and the poet's recovery of what has gone before, are central to the cycle's design.

Chinesisch-deutsche
Jahres- und Tageszeiten

On 12 May 1827 Goethe retreated to his garden house on the Ilm simply to pass a pleasant hour, "eine freundliche Stunde zu verweilen" (WA IV, 42, 189), as he later wrote to Zelter, and lingered there in productive isolation until 8 June. During the summer weeks that followed he returned almost daily to the small house on the edge of the Ilm meadow that had been his home fifty years earlier when he had first arrived in Weimar. The days were filled with activity: "diese Tage her [bin ich] immer thätig und ich hoffe andern wie mir erfreulich. Der zweite Theil der Wanderjahre ist abgeschlossen; . . . Nun aber soll das Bekenntnis im Stillen zu Dir gelangen, daß ich . . . mich wieder an Faust begeben habe" (WA IV, 42, 189–90). There are more letters saying that the isolation afforded by the retreat from the center of Weimar life was necessary for the completion of pressing and long unfinished tasks: "Um nur einigermaßen was mir obliegt zu beseitigen, mußte ich mich in meinen untern Garten flüchten" (WA IV, 42, 182–83). He also wrote:

Ich bin in meinen Garten im Thale gezogen und genieße schon gute Frucht von dieser Absonderung. Es liegen so manche Dinge die ich selbst werthachten muß, weil sie sich aus einer Zeit herschreiben die nicht wiederkommt, lange Jahre vor mir da, und bedürfen eigentlich nur einer gewissen genialen Redaction. Vollständige Pläne, schematisch aufgestellt, einzelnes ausgearbeitet! (WA IV, 42, 197–98)

The most pressing of these tasks was, as Goethe indicated in his letter to Zelter, the uncompleted *Faust* manuscript. But *Faust* was not Goethe's exclusive preoccupation during these weeks. A number of short lyric poems were written at the same time that reflect the composure and well-being of the poet in his garden setting. On 15 May, three days after arriving in the "Frühlingsumgebung" that Goethe found so incomparable,[1] he recorded in his *Tagebuch*: "Einiges an den chinesischen Jahreszeiten" (WA III, 11, 57). The poems are not mentioned again until 1 August: "Chinesische Jahreszeiten supplirt" (WA III, 11, 92). Their existence is revealed for the first time in a letter of 24

October. Goethe, referring to unpublished manuscripts he held, wrote to Zelter that he had "kleiner Gedichte mancherley, drunter eine Sammlung mit der Rubrik: Chinesische Jahreszeiten" (WA IV, 43, 122–23).

The fourteen poems of the *Chinesisch-deutsche Jahres- und Tageszeiten*, the title under which they were published in the *Berliner Musenalmanach für 1830*, are not the product of an intensive and rigorously schematic plan. Rather, they are related to the more pressing revisions and completions scheduled for the summer in the same way as the early poems of the *Römische Elegien* complemented the rigorous attention demanded by the *Tasso* manuscript and as the writing of the *Sonette* complemented the concentration demanded by *Pandora*.

The poems do not mark Goethe's first response to the poetry of China. Earlier in the same year, after reading Peter Perring Thoms's translation of *Hua Ts'ien Ki (Chinese Courtship)*, a novel of the Ming dynasty, he had freely translated selected poems from the work *Bai Me Sin Yung (The Songs of a Hundred Beautiful Women)* which was appended to Thoms's volume. These poems were published in 1827 in the sixth volume of *Kunst und Alterthum* (Heft 1) under the title "Chinesisches."[2]

Goethe had also read several other Chinese works in English and French translation.[3] As a consequence, much has been written about the specifically Chinese component of the *Chinesisch-deutsche Jahres- und Tageszeiten*. Earlier attempts to trace specific motifs from these works in Goethe's poems have, however, been largely discredited.[4] The current view is that there was merely a general compatibility of literary temperament, a congruence of perception and expression between the Chinese literature Goethe enjoyed and his own reflective moments in this summer of isolated retreat.[5] To be sure, a few motifs have been identified as "Chinese," although most of them have the double identity "chinesisch-deutsch" that the title of the cycle sug-

Despite their high reputation in the eighteenth century, the novels and short stories in question have been judged uniformly undistinguished by recent scholars.[7] Goethe himself did not consider them exceptional works.[8] The poetry that is scattered in the prose texts (Thoms's translation of *Hua Ts'ien Ki* is written entirely in verse) is equally undistinguished.[9] Goethe had no knowledge of the excellence of truly great Chinese verse.

In the preface to *Chinese Courtship*, Thoms comments on the verse form used in the novel he translated: "The style of the original in Chinese, is called Mŭh-yu. It consists of four lines to a verse, and seven characters or words in each line; but the poem affords specimens of several kinds of metre, as may be noticed by the number of characters in a column."[10] Thoms reflects this verse in his translation by the use of four-lined stanzas. Although he makes additional observations on meter and rhyme, Thoms's comments are limited to a formal description of the single stanza. There is nothing in his remarks to suggest the cyclical composition of Goethe's collection.

The Chinese poetry that Goethe had read was not arranged in cycles. The idea of writing a cycle of Chinese poetry was his own, and the poems he completed in the summer of 1827 were unlike any poetry written previously, either Chinese or European. Zelter, Goethe's closest friend and critic in the last decades of his life, recognized their uniqueness and greeted the *Chinesisch-deutsche Jahres- und Tageszeiten* with great enthusiasm when he first received the manuscript in the summer of 1829: "Sie sind unschätzbar, diese Blätter! ganz was Neues, unerhört und gleich ganz verständlich."[11] A few weeks later he commented once more on their sudden and unprecedented appearance: "Die 'Chinesischen Jahreszeiten' ziehn wie ein neuer Komet und werden auch so gedeutet."[12]

Few of Zelter's contemporaries took note of the new literary phenomenon, however, and even fewer paused to chart its unique course. Furthermore, there are only scattered references to the cycle in the critical studies on Goethe that followed in the nineteenth century. There are several reasons for the critics' neglect of the poems. First, the poems were strangely out of place in the *Berliner Musenalmanach für 1830*, which contained an abundance of late Romantic verse.[13] Second, the mere fact that here was a cycle of poems did not command special attention. Lyric cycles were, by 1829, no longer infrequent. Critics have correctly noted that much of Goethe's later writing is organized in sequences that display a "cyclical tendency."[14] In the shadow of the *West-östlicher Divan* the fourteen short poems of the *Chinesisch-deutsche Jahres- und Tageszeiten* looked anything but exceptional. Third, things Chinese, Chinese literature among them, had been all the rage in Europe since the time of Voltaire; hence Goethe's Chinese poems were wrongly considered to continue an established Western tradition, and their novelty was not appreciated.[15] Finally, since the *Chinesisch-deutsche Jahres- und Tageszeiten* were completed after publication of the poetry volumes of the *Ausgabe letzter Hand* (Band 1–Band 4, 1827), they did not appear in Goethe's collected works until after his death—and then in the widely heterogeneous assortment of poetry gathered by Eckermann and Riemer into the *Nachlaß* volumes. Like much of his late poetry, the poems of the cycle were not appreciated for the unique style Goethe had developed in his post-*Divan* years, but rather were commonly judged according to a standard of lyricism derived from his earlier works. Viehoff is representative as he declares the poems to be faulty and redeemed only to the extent that they recall the nature poetry of earlier decades. He notes that the poems "uns stellenweise noch an die süßesten Töne seiner Jugendlyrik gemahnen" but concludes:

Freilich war jetzt seine Productionskraft nicht mehr jugendlich frisch und reich, und es lasteten auf ihm noch zu viele eines Abschlusses harrende sonstige Arbeiten, daher es uns nicht wundern darf, wenn die vorliegende Production etwas Lückenhaftes an sich trägt. Es ist weder der Cyklus der Jahres-, noch der der Tageszeiten vollständig durchgeführt, und das Ganze klingt epigrammatisch abrupt aus.[16]

In addition, preconceived notions of how a cycle should be structured also interfered with a more appreciative assessment of the sequence.[17]

The greater interest in Goethe's late poetry that prevailed after the turn of the century has enabled a reevaluation of the *Chinesisch-deutsche Jahres- und Tageszeiten*. Viëtor,[18] Kommerell,[19] and particularly Erich Trunz's characterization of Goethe's *Altersstil* and his attempt to set apart the short lyric poem, "das Kurzgedicht," as a distinctively Goethean genre,[20] have made the cycle less remote. But when Preisendanz published his study of the poems in 1963, he could still preface it with an observation on their relative neglect: "Die Forschung hat diesen letzten Gedichtkreis Goethes verhältnismäßig vernachlässigt."[21] It is indeed curious that Helen M. Mustard (1946) omitted, without a word of explanation, the *Chinesisch-deutsche Jahres- und Tageszeiten* from her discussion of Goethe's lyric cycles. Two articles have been published since Preisendanz's interpretation and biographical comments on the poems. The first, by Yang En-Lin, is a Marxist-flavored search for Chinese motifs in the poems.[22] The second, by Friedrich Burkhardt,[23] is of particular interest for this study, as it directly addresses the problem of cyclical structure and its relevance to the interpretation of the poems.

Although Goethe's references to the composition of the *Chinesisch-deutsche Jahres- und Tageszeiten* are few, they do indicate that the cycle was not completed in a single writing. Several months passed between the first mention of the cycle on 15 May and the remark of 1 August, "Chinesische Jahreszeiten supplirt." Some revisions may even have been made as late as August, 1829, when Goethe noted in his *Tagebuch*: "Die Gedichte für Berlin abschließlich zusammengestellt" (WA III, 12, 111). The extant manuscripts are of limited usefulness. A fair copy exists of poems II, III, VI, and XII that offers minor variants to the *Musenalmanach* text.[24] Only the fifth poem is available in multiple drafts. There is no indication of the order in which the fourteen poems were written.

Goethe's comment of 1 August, "Chinesische Jahreszeiten supplirt," is of special interest. "Supplieren" is a term that Paul Böckmann has directly associated with Goethe's composition of *Faust II*: "So gebraucht Goethe den Begriff des Supplierens in zweifachem Sinn: einmal sollen die verschiedenen Motive und Situationen sich wechselseitig supplieren; zum andern aber soll auch der Leser seinerseits sie supplieren, indem er sie mit seinem eigenen Wissen verknüpft.[25] The use of the term indicates that explicit transitions are purposely omitted. The reader is enjoined to participate actively and to complete the proper association of events, images, and motifs to discover the text's meaning. Goethe's *Tagebuch* entry indicates that he himself undertook to make some of these transitions and linking bonds in the *Chinesisch-deutsche Jahres- und Tageszeiten* more explicit (as he also did in *Faust II*).

Despite his revisions, however, it is apparent to anyone who has attempted to interpret the fourteen poems of the *Chinesisch-deutsche Jahres- und Tageszeiten* as a group that their continuity is not easily described.[26] The title of the cycle suggests that a passing of seasons and a passing of hours organizes the fourteen poems in sequence. The promise to follow the seasons from spring through summer, fall, and winter is partially redeemed in the poems, but the promise to follow the passing hours of the day appears, at first, to have been forgotten. The hours do pass, but almost imperceptibly. As Burkhardt has noted, it is only in two of the poems (V, VIII) that the time of day is specifically mentioned, and both poems present an evening setting. He has concluded that the evening poems serve to indicate more clearly the seasonal transition that follows, from spring to summer (V) and from summer to autumn (VIII).[27] There are some recurrent motifs that link the poems (the peacock [IV–V], the rose [IX–XII]). Finally, the last four poems are held together by their form, the dialogue. None of these principles of organization is realized in all poems of the cycle. While there is formal consonance in the series, no two poems are structurally identical. Metrical and rhyming schemes vary. The structure of the cycle conforms to Goethe's remarks to Soret in 1831 on the organization of the trilogy: "il est nécessaire de faire les coupures sans liaisons trop senties."[28]

The *Chinesisch-deutsche Jahres- und Tageszeiten* are notably poems of Goethe's old age. They begin with an image of years of honorable service as the poet identifies himself with a Mandarin now eager to lay aside the responsibilities of his class and to pass his days in activi-

ties of leisure. Unlike many poems of waning years, however, the
first poems in Goethe's cycle do not introduce a seasonal correlate to
the poet's age.[29] Initially, the poems neither proclaim the arrival of
fall and the approach of winter nor set the Mandarin's retreat from
the northern realm in the rays of a late afternoon sun. In almost
defiant opposition to these expectations it is in the daylight of springtime that the poet-Mandarin divests himself of the Northern burdens
he has borne and elects the freshness and renewal ("am Wasser und
im Grünen") of a garden world. For the knowledgeable there is the
play on the Chinese "Peking" or "Northern city" to add to the delight
of the imagery.[30] For Goethe there is a long and negative association
of the "Norden" with graying skies and a burdened spirit, and the
move to a milder climate is made all the more inviting by these lingering images. Not only does the poet-Mandarin's new life (and here is
the unspoken link between the springtime setting and the season of
renewal) begin in the daylight of springtime, but it is suggested in the
opening poem that this season itself is a good reason for his departure
from the burdens of his Northern office. Casting these off he settles in
the garden world that is the setting for the cycle.

The poems are clearly unified by their recurrent references to this
garden world that the poet has sought out as his retreat. The garden
is set apart, as the visit and departure of the colleagues from the
northern city effectively underscore. They are intruders. Burkhardt
treats these visitors and their conversation with the Mandarin-poet
with complete seriousness. There is, however, as much irony in this
exchange as there is insight. The visitors express their disapproval of
the poet's use of his leisure time in the garden when they address
him in poem XII:

> Hingesunken alten Träumen,
> Buhlst mit Rosen, sprichst mit Bäumen
> Statt der Mädchen, statt der Weisen.
>   (XII, 1–3)

But they also reveal their misapprehension of his purposeful activity.
The garden sequence is reduced to a romantic fantasy, and deemed
foolish. As this initial attack on the poet's isolation is modified and
the visitors prepare to leave at the poet's urging (XIII) they request of
him a piece of useful wisdom to take with them on their journey:
"Hast noch was Kluges mitzuteilen?" Burkhardt considers this a sign
of respect and reconciliation and a satisfactory conclusion to the motif
introduced by the opposition of city and garden, "Gesellen" and
"Mandarin," namely, the motif of the responsible relationship of the

individual to society. In fact, Burkhardt elevates it to the fundamental theme of the entire cycle: "die Verantwortung persönlicher Lebensgestaltung vor Zeit und Gesellschaft."[31]

The problem with this interpretation of the colleagues' intrusion into the garden is that it stops short of realizing the full use Goethe makes of these critics and of their presence in the cycle. Like the lone and anxious voice in poem XI, the comments of these visitors function as a foil to the insights acquired by the poet in these days of observation and reflection that the cycle records. We will return later to poem XI for a detailed consideration. At this point it is sufficient to note that it concludes with a formulaic pronouncement that stands in marked contrast to the unsettling fear that begins the poem. This pronouncement is offered as comforting assurance to the person who confesses how alarmed he is by sophistical talk about natural laws (cf. X, 8) in a world where nothing is permanent. As poem XI stands in the sequence of poems, with multiple links to previous motifs (the rose, the process of blossoming, and the search for a law to explain these phenomena), it has the impact of profound insight. It is therefore all the more disconcerting to hear the opening words of the companions as they characterize the garden experience as a doting fantasy of an old man wooing roses and chatting with trees. The reader is compelled to ask himself, obviously finding this characterization inappropriate, just what the poet has been doing in these garden hours, and with this question begins a process of reflection on the comprehensive meaning of the cycle.

In the poem that follows the poet does not bother to comment directly on the companions' remarks. He faults their interruption of his solitude and opposes two processes, "Belehrung" and "Begeisterung." Conversation is instructive, he tells them, but inspiration is found only in solitude. It is typical of the cycle's structure that, while on the most explicit level it is the pattern of disruption and departure that links poems XIII and XIV, of far greater import is the poet's characterization of his own activity as "Begeisterung." It is an answer to the comments in poem XII, and more importantly, it recalls the lines that opened the cycle, where the poet's intention is described as "Fröhlich trinken, geistig schreiben." It also goes to the heart of the cycle's meaning, for it is through this process of "Begeisterung" and "geistig schreiben" that the poet has come to know the meaning of life in these latter days. He has acquired the insight into his own autumn to answer the confused visitor in poem XII—that is, to pass one's time in neither longing nor remorse, but instead in satisfaction and quiet joy:

> Die stille Freude wollt ihr stören?
> Laßt mich bei meinem Becher Wein;
> Mit andern kann man sich belehren,
> Begeistert wird man nur allein.
>
> (XIII)

Much of this is lost on the colleagues who are preparing for a speedy departure. Their request for "noch was Kluges" to take along with them on their return journey is a misunderstanding of the poet's purposes. It is a request for quick instruction, a usable teaching, "eine Lehre," immediately after the poet has explicitly opposed the two processes of "Belehrung" and "Begeisterung" in the previous poem. The answer that follows, therefore, and that closes the cycle is quite unexpected and yet to the point:

> Sehnsucht ins Ferne, Künftige zu beschwichtigen,
> Beschäftige dich hier und heut im Tüchtigen.
>
> (XIV, 3–4)

What the poet has learned in the garden retreat cannot be said directly. It is not knowledge that is exchangeable, debatable, packageable—it cannot be reduced to "was Kluges." Rather, it is insight into the processes of life itself. Therefore, the advice he gives to the departing visitors is functional rather than cognitive. It is advice that, if followed, can lead ultimately to the same insight for the impatient colleagues, but only in time. Some lines from *Faust II* complement the closing words of the cycle:

> Dem Tüchtigen ist diese Welt nicht stumm
> Was braucht er in die Ewigkeit zu schweifen
> Was er erkennt, läßt sich ergreifen.
>
> (11446–448)

The advice to forego senseless longing for the distant future and to become purposefully engaged in the present is advice Goethe often gave himself and others.

The point of this extended exchange that concludes the cycle is not really, as Burkhardt suggests, to provide a thematic resolution to the tension between the individual and society that is introduced by the poet-Mandarin's initial departure from the Northern provinces, but rather to raise explicitly the question of the significance of the garden sojourn. The misapprehension the visitors display is the beginning of the reader's comprehension of the experience in the garden and the meaning of the cycle. The request for "noch was Kluges" is both ironic in its function and quite appropriate, for it reveals the failure of the visitors to understand what has transpired in the garden. Yet the poet-Mandarin's response provides them with a means to achieve the same understanding of life and its processes that he has acquired in his garden solitude.

What is it that has taken place in the course of the fourteen poems? As the title of the sequence indicates, the seasons have progressed, imperceptibly the hours have passed, and the Mandarin-poet has found himself finally in the autumn that is commensurate with his advancing years, in the evening of his life. This change does not take place all at once—in the course of the cycle the poet has noted the advancing day (V), the pressing fullness of summer (VI)—but when it does occur it effects a transformation in the landscape and in the poet as well.

It is a commonplace to note that the poems of the *Chinesisch-deutsche Jahres- und Tageszeiten* are exceptionally graphic in their observation of the natural world. In them it is the plant, or animal, or landscape itself that is central to the poem and the descriptions are unusually devoid of verbal action. It is therefore all the more notable when two poems, VIII and IX, provide an exception to this rule. In both it is the single word "nun" that signals the change. "Nun im östlichen Bereiche" begins the second stanza of poem VIII, and "Nun weiß man erst, was Rosenknospe sei" continues poem IX. In the eighth poem the landscape is transformed as the moon rises and a soothing coolness is experienced by the poet. These changes are linked by the double "nun" to the autumn setting that follows and the new awareness the poem proclaims.

There are three seasons in the *Chinesisch-deutsche Jahres- und Tageszeiten* (spring I–V, summer VI–VIII, autumn IX–XIII), and accordingly Burkhardt has argued for a tripartite progression in the poem,[32] modifying Preisendanz's interpretation which turns on the central axis of poem VIII.[33] While Burkhardt is correct in noting the three-season sequence, it is imperative that the uniqueness of the final stage, the autumn of poem IX (linked to the night of VIII) not be minimized.

On the surface the poems present a varied array of sights and sounds: flowers, grazing sheep, peacocks, lovers in a secluded garden, sunshine and sunset, brightly colored tiles and rich foliage. Each is pictured in turn and with directness and simplicity creates an appealing display of the garden's wonders. These surface images are, however, somewhat distracting. Their real significance, and the significance of these garden hours, is there to be seen, but it requires a bit more discernment, a bit more time. Once the essential meaning is discovered, it joins the wonders of the garden world and the poems of the cycle in a purposeful continuity.

Zelter, when he perceived the deceptive simplicity of *Chinesisch-deutsche Jahres- und Tageszeiten*, used a metaphor from his music to describe the composition of the cycle:

Deine Gabe, welche diesen Almanach ziert, ist nicht so leicht, als sie sich anfühlt; ich, der ich die kleinen lieben Dinger täglich ansehe, nähere mich auch nur nach und nach, da ich mir Deine gute Stunde erlaure, Dich im Zimmer sitzend, vor einem Gebilde stehend, im Garten wandelnd sehe, um aus der Blume die Frucht zu erraten. Eine Reise vom Nordlande aus nach China ist auch nicht bald vollendet, da man unterwegs durch Geschrei indischer Gänse oder sonst sich aufgehalten sieht, und wer zuletzt den Generalbaß nicht befragt, geht auch leer davon.[34]

"Generalbaß," or basso continuo, refers to a technique in musical notation in which the bass line determines the harmonic structure of the piece. It is this same bass line, and not the more audible treble phrases, that sustains the continuity of the work. The treble line is part of the supporting chord structure, and the listener who hears only it and remains on the surface of the composition will fail completely to comprehend the real structure and development of the work.

As a structural metaphor for the composition of the *Chinesisch-deutsche Jahres- und Tageszeiten*, Zelter's comment is insightful. There is a continuity in the poems that is not sustained by the treble line, by the surface variety of colors and images that the individual poems present, although these images are all part of the total structure of the cycle, and provide it with its harmonic resonance.

The motif of blossoming is fundamental to this continuity and is introduced in the second poem of the cycle by a bed of early narcissus blossoming in the springtime garden. The process of blossoming, or "blühen," recurs and finds its highpoint in poem XI in the formulaic description, "das ewige Gesetz,/ Wonach die Ros' und Lilie blüht."[35] It is the expectation of bountiful blossoming that provides the image of paradise in poem III ("bunt geblümt erblühn"), and the blooming garden is the setting for the lovers in poem V. But the garden changes in poem VI, and with the encroaching summer the blossoms are replaced by thistles and nettles; the ever-thickening foliage obstructs the searching glances of the lover so that he can see no longer the roof of the beloved's house. In a world that has been "verdeckt" and "verdichtet," the poet retreats to recollection of past delights, and confesses his fidelity to these memories:

Wohin mein Auge spähend brach,
Dort ewig bleibt mein Osten.
(VI, 11–12)
Das fühl' ich noch und denke dran
Und bleib' ihr ganz zu eigen.
(VII, 7–8)

This does not mark the end, however. There is a final blossom, a late rose, and an insight that concludes poem XI and the flowering of the cycle, the insight into "das ewige Gesetz, wonach die Ros' und Lilie blüht." In the passing of time a new kind of permanence has been achieved. Fall has not brought fading glory and withering life, but a triumph within the blossoming world, a rose that is its crown and fulfillment.

We will return to these images. First we must note that a progression parallel to this seasonal sequence occurs in the transition from daylight to night. The poems move from the spring daylight of the opening poem, and the vitality and boundless pleasure that these hours promise ("Schal' auf Schale, Zug in Zügen"—bountiful drink and bountiful verse is the image that closes poem I), through the darkness of night in the middle of poem VIII, that is both nadir and turning point in the cycle, to the new light and new calm that concludes this poem in soothing moonlight.

The progression of the light is not stressed; it proceeds almost imperceptibly. It is often only implicit in the imagery. The daylight of the first poem gives way to the golden rays of the approaching evening in poem V, and the sky, previously only metaphorically visible in the images of the "Sonnenfeier" (III) has turned to blue. The sky that was to provide unlimited vistas once the clouds parted in poem III is now nearer and more tangible, a vaulting ceiling over the lovers and their garden ("Im Garten, überwölbt vom Blauen" [V]). This corresponds effectively to the generally increasing density of foliage and the narrowing of focus that the next poem, poem VI, makes explicit. In poem VIII this process of darkening sky and enclosure is central: "Dämmerung senkte sich von oben." The sun is setting, but the image that opens poem VIII turns our attention away from the retreating light and towards the encroaching darkness. The deepening sky has neared and now dominates the garden landscape. The light, still present, but increasingly pale, finally loses to the imminent triumph of the night. Time progresses within poem VIII, and its passage is marked by the fading of the light. A single star shines in line 4, but by line 8 there is not even starlight to reflect in the lake with its assurance of the abiding presence of the heavenly on earth. Instead the stanza concludes: "Schwarzvertiefte Finsternisse/ Widerspiegelnd ruht der See."

It is into this blackness that has closed the day, signaled the end, disrupted all sight, and, consequently, divided the poet from his own garden world, that the moon rises, slowly at first, foreshadowed in the landscape, and reaches the poet in his darkened isolation with its soothing light. Night has not brought the end to light and life, but a new light and a new vision, a light to which the poet attributes a magical quality as it touches his heart, the core of his being. Both the "Tageszeiten" and the "Jahreszeiten," the progression of hours and of seasons, have concluded not in darkness and death, but in a new vision of life.

A detailed discussion of each of the three stages in the cycle, which we can identify by their seasonal correlates, spring, summer, and fall, will demonstrate how this basic progression of hours (of light) and of seasons (of blossoming), which is the basso continuo in the composition, acquires its full harmonic structure.

The flowering of springtime and its daylight brightness characterize the poet's garden experience in the first stage. It is a world rife with expectation. Analogies that constantly enlarge the garden boundaries repeatedly point to the infinite that is visible in the finite world. The occasion for each of the poems is minimal: a bed of narcissus, sheep on the meadow, a peacock's call and his strutting display. The poet's perception of each enlarges its meaning, and reveals the association that ever expands this flowering and unfolding landscape. The entire first stanza of the second poem, for example, is descriptive metaphor. The narcissus are like lilies, like candles, like stars, and implicit in the description, like young maidens. The poet's whimsical familiarity with "die guten" further establishes their youth. It is a virgin garden that he beholds—white, pure, modest—but not without erotic tension: "Leuchtet aus dem Mittelherzen/ Rot gesäumt, die Glut der Neigung." There is the tension of expectation, and it is with a sense of anticipation that the poem closes.

Expectation is the motif that is central to the poem that follows. What the poet sees is sheep on the meadow. What he expectantly projects is the transformation of this white dotted field (recalling the white flowers of poem II) into a brightly colored paradise. It is in the blossoming flowers that he will behold the paradise he anticipates.[36] They are signs of the infinite, signs of the fulfillment that will come in time. The poem concludes in three successive characterizations of this future expectation: "Wunscherfüllung," "Sonnenfeier," "Wolkenteilung." Each is an image of paradise achieved in the symbolic vocabulary of Goethe's late poetry. What Goethe has accomplished in this poem and continues in the poems that follow is the creation of an extensive network of signs of expectation, the expectation that spring holds, that marks the new day (represented in the parting of the morning mists and the clearing skies), and that is the sign of youth.

The floral paradise is not realized in any of the poems that follow, at least not directly. Rather it is the peacock with his brightly colored tail, his "himmlische Gefieder," that continues the unfolding of the garden. The peacock is introduced by his call, which the poet humorously compares with the cry of Indian geese, birds with a voice so disruptive that the very mention of them jars the meter of the poem into a sudden and anomalous dactyl. The peacock's cry is quite as unlovely as that of the geese, but it is bearable because it reminds the poet of his "heavenly feathers." The virginal modesty of the narcissus is replaced by the strutting display of the male bird that is part of its courtship ritual, its tail expanded to challenge the sun in her golden glory. This display is analogous to another courtship in the poem, an analogy made explicit in the final lines of the first draft of the poem which read: "Und da sie uns Verliebte sieht/ Wird sie was ähnliches erschauen." [37] The lines were made less personal in a later revision, and the analogy became implicit rather than explicit: "Ein Liebespaar, wo sie's ersieht,/ Glaubt sie das Herrlichste zu schauen." The use of the superlative marks the flowering of this love as the high point of the unfolding and blossoming that has characterized the springtime garden.

Summer marks a change. Spring had brought pleasure not only to the cuckoo and the nightingale, as poem VI begins, but also to the poet. The desire to arrest the progression of seasons, to pass a life in eternal springtime, is acknowledged but not honored. Summer is presented as aggressive and unsparing: "Doch drängt der Sommer schon überall/ Mit Disteln und mit Nesseln." It is not the thistles and nettles alone that trouble—unpleasant weeds in the expected paradise—but the obscurity and enclosure that the growth brings. It is a paradox, for the summer with its continued growth has become the antithesis of the opening and flowering of the springtime garden. Summer is a closing in, a cessation of former activity, and a time of recollection of the better spring days. Hopeful thoughts of the future are replaced by recollection of the past in poems VI and VII. The revision of poem V to remove any personal reference makes the object of the "Liebesblick" in VI uncertain. In VII it becomes clear that it is a personal recollection that the poet cherishes in these summer months, a past experience that has been made ever present to him in memory: "Das fühl' ich noch und denke dran/ Und bleib' ihr ganz zu eigen." It is also linked by the closing line of VI, "Dort ewig bleibt mein Osten," to all that has passed before—the day's beginning, the lovers, the flowering garden, all that the summer growth now obscures.

Spring does not return, day does not break again, but the autumn and the night which has fallen do not mark the end. The East that is the poet's comfort in poem VII, that carries the association of sunrise and renewal,[38] yields a new light. Goethe had noted in his reading of Chinese prose the central figure of the moon.[39] But the image of the moon with its fullness and clarity had already been made Goethe's own much earlier. In the *West-östlicher Divan* it is used in expression of the fullness of Hatem's and Suleika's love ("Die Sonne kommt," "Vollmondnacht"). In the 1818 poem "Um Mitternacht" it acquires a symbolic independence:

> Bis dann zuletzt des vollen Mondes Helle
> So klar und deutlich mir ins Finstere drang.
> (WA I, 3, 47)

It is of interest that Goethe, in the winter of 1827, explicitly contrasts these two earlier works:

Ich habe, sagte er, diesen Abend die Bemerkung gemacht, daß diese Lieder des Divans gar kein Verhältnis mehr zu mir haben. Sowohl was darin orientalisch als was darin leidenschaftlich ist, hat aufgehört in mir fortzuleben; es ist wie eine abgestreifte Schlangenhaut am Wege liegen geblieben. Dagegen das Lied: *Um Mitternacht* hat sein Verhältnis zu mir nicht verloren, es ist von mir noch ein lebendiger Teil und lebt mit mir fort.[40]

In poem IX the single rose is able to restore the entire garden to fullness. How this happens is not explained. But we are told that seeks out the poet. He is the recipient of its balm. It is the soothing coolness of the moon that fills the new moment and the poet himself.

The repeated "nun" at the beginning of poem IX confirms that a new stage has begun in the garden experience. If the first was marked by visions of blossoming and unfolding life, the second by narrowing sight and recollection, this third stage is one of symbolic perception. In the individual bud, the single rose, the meaning of the whole is made visible. It is made visible for the first time—in the fullness of summer the single flower was obscured. Goethe does not say explicitly that only age understands what youth is, that only at the end can one appreciate the beginning and its promise. Rather, he writes of the rose, the single rose that he sees blossoming in his autumn garden.

In poems IX the single rose is able to restore the entire garden to fullness. How this happens is not explained. But we are told that now, in the passing of the rose season, the true meaning of the bud-ding of the first flower is revealed. Fall has arrived, spring is gone, but a single flower is adequate to restore the whole.

I have called this stage symbolic perception because it is linked so clearly with Goethe's discussion of the symbol and symbolic language in the *Maximen und Reflexionen*: "Das ist die wahre Symbolik, wo das Besondere das Allgemeinere repräsentiert, nicht als Traum und Schatten, sondern als lebendig-augenblickliche Offenbarung des Unerforschlichen."[41] The contemplation of the single flower brings insight into the processes of all of nature, an insight that cannot be acquired by scientific inquiry. It is the unresearchable that is revealed. Knowledge is imparted—"Nun *weiß* man erst, was Rosenknospe sei"—but it is a special knowledge and one explicitly linked to the autumn, to age, to observation and insight in this flowering world.

Why the rose? Poem X is the answer. It is the most beautiful flower, the final superlative in a sequence of high praise that has gradually crescendoed in the cycle:

IV.   himmlisches Gefieder (Pfau)
V.   das Herrlichste (Liebespaar)
VI.   zu schönstem Raub (Liebesblick)
VII. schöner als der schönste Tag (Liebesbegegnung)
X.   Allerschönste (Rose)

In poem X Goethe proclaims the rose an "allgemeines Zeugnis," recalling his definition of the true symbol as the representation of the general by the specific. But it is not simply that the rose is a symbol of the plants and flowers in the poet's garden. The rose is a symbol of the very process that creates, orders, and sustains the garden. In the rose the laws of nature are made visible. The rose is not only the most beautiful of flowers, but also has an almost infinite number of varieties.[42] Viewing the many different kinds of roses and recognizing that they are not different plants, but varieties of one and the same plant—that is what Goethe called grasping a law of nature: "Zum Schönen wird erfordert ein Gesetz, das in die Erscheinung tritt. Beispiel von der Rose. In den Blüten tritt das vegetabilische Gesetz in seine höchste Erscheinung, und die Rose wäre nun wieder der Gipfel dieser Erscheinung."[43] The single rose in the autumn garden is not only the visible realization of the law that orders the garden, it is its crowning event. The catalog of names with which the poet addresses the flower, "Allerschönste," "Königin," "allgemeines Zeugnis," "wundersam Ereignis," culminates finally in the ultimate tautology, "du bist es," the complete identification of "Erscheinung" and "Idee," "du bist kein bloßer Schein."

For this reason Keller calls the rose the symbol of the symbol:

"Indem sich in ihr Schauen und Glauben einen, bildet sie ab, was nicht bildbar ist, und seinem Wesen nach nicht Bild werden kann."[44] The rose is a "wundersam Ereignis" according to poem X. When the possible is one with the impossible, when "das Mögliche und Unmögliche eins werden," then the "Wunderbare des Wunders" is revealed. As Keller has noted, this Wilhelm Meister learns in the gallery,[45] and this Goethe proclaims as the essence of the rose in the *West-östlicher Divan*:

> Unmöglich scheint immer die Rose
> Unbegreiflich die Nachtigall.[46]
> (WA I, 6, 148)

What is the purpose of the sequence? The ideas and images are familiar. Certainly Goethe did not simply repeat, as an exercise in versification, in these poems his concept of the symbol. Goethe introduces the troubled inquirer of poem XI to make his purpose clear: "Mich ängstigt das Verfängliche/ Im widrigen Geschwätz." The fear of the insidious nature of so much human discourse has become for this man a trap. It is his failure to recognize any basis for natural law in a world in flux that has occasioned his anxiety, his entanglement in "das bängliche/ Das graugestrickte Netz." Laws, the speaker implies, can be found in a stable world, not in a world where everything is in constant flux—where, for example, a star which we on earth now see, may have disappeared long ago (XI, 4). What is said to be a law of nature is merely a man-made theory.[47] The poet's response is brief: "Getrost! Das Unvergängliche/ Es ist das ewige Gesetz,/ Wonach die Ros' und Lilie blüht." How does he arrive at this insight? He has seen it in the rose: "Das Schöne ist eine Manifestation geheimer Naturgesetze, die uns ohne dessen Erscheinung ewig wären verborgen geblieben."[48] He has seen it in the garden. The phrase "Wonach die Ros' und Lilie blüht" is a formula (grammatically the plural verb "blühen" would be required), and while it does not deny the revealing presence of the last rose, it encompasses all the flowers of the garden, all the events that have marked the passing of days and hours. "Das ewige Gesetz" has been visible in the narcissus, the peacock, in the expectation of flowering fields, and in the memory of past love. It has been visible "im Abglanz, im Beispiel, Symbol, in einzelnen und verwandten Erscheinungen" (WA II, 12, 74).

In the fall, in the rose, the poet has achieved the final insight. "Das Höchste ist das Anschauen des Verschiedenen als identisch,"[49] Goethe wrote in the *Maximen und Reflexionen*. The differences are not denied, but in the rose, in the identity of "Schauen" and "Glauben," the participation of the entire garden world in one single process is recognized. Goethe described "die Idee" as "das, was immer zur Erscheinung kommt und daher als Gesetz aller Erscheinungen uns entgegentritt."[50] There is a permanence in the change of seasons, in the blossoming and fading of the flowers, in the alternation of night and day, and in the meeting and separation of lovers.[51] It is a permanence not achieved by living in an eternal spring, or dwelling in peaceful recollection, but in the perception of the true meaning of change itself, a perception that comes at the end, in the fall, in the coolness of the moonlit night.

In a draft for a letter to Zelter Goethe reveals this perception as his own: "Ich könnte noch viel sagen, wie die letzten Sendungen mich beschäftigen, auch im Einzelnen ist es wohl heiter und artig, aber zuletzt erscheint es mir: es seyen Rosen, die abfallen, aber nicht ohne Nachkommenschaft und Keime. Je älter ich werde, je mehr vertrau ich auf das Gesetz, wonach die Rose und Lilie blüht" (WA IV, 46, 350). He explicitly links his faith in the "Gesetz wonach die Ros' und Lilie blüht" with advancing age.

Goethe deliberately contrasts the perception of the rose and the knowledge it brings with the process of scientific inquiry. After proclaiming the identity of "Schauen" and "Glauben" in this single flower, an identity that marks the culmination of man's knowledge,[52] he adds one more couplet to complete the poem:

> Doch Forschung strebt und ringt, ermüdend nie,
> Nach dem Gesetz, dem Grund Warum und Wie.
>
> (X)

He does not begin with an "und," but with the emphatic assertion "doch." In spite of this "nevertheless," scientific inquiry has not tired in its struggle to articulate the law, the reason how and why.

There is no explicit link made between this concluding pronouncement in poem X and the anxiety that is expressed by the visitor in poem XI. It is significant, however, that it is specifically the unreliability of human discourse that distresses the man. Twice in poem X the rose is proclaimed an event that banishes this discord: "unwidersprechlich" and "Streitsucht verbannend." The knowledge that the rose brings exists on another plane and should have muted the endless scientific debates—yet it didn't.

The anxiety expressed in poem XI successfully underscores the power of the insight the autumn has brought to the poet. It is not nature alone but all of human experience that stands revealed in the fullness of the rose. "Das graugestrickte Netz" is here the antithesis of the flowering garden. Gray is characterized by Goethe in the *Far-benlehre* as "Unfarbe" (WA II, 5¹, 144–45)[53] and is used in the *Rö-mische Elegien* (VII, 2, 4) to mark the absence of both color and form: "Da mich ein graulicher Tag hinten im Norden umfing,/ . . . Farb- und gestaltlos die Welt . . ." (WA I, 1, 242). Where the poet delights in the beauty of varied and colorful sights, the man in poem XI sees only fleeting images from the constriction of his gray entanglement. In the *Zahme Xenien* a relative of this anxious man speaks, a man of "Sorgen":

> Wenn wir in die schöne Welt hinein blicken
> Da schwebt ein Spinnenweben = Grau.
>   (WA I, 3, 352)

More directly the gray net, the web, the enmeshment and entangle- ment is the opposite of the "Schleier," the transparent gauze that both conceals and reveals the "Idee," the immutable that is ever present in the changing world. In the *Chinesisch-deutsche Jahres- und Tageszeiten* the image of the "Schleier" is only used once (III), but analogies abound in the blossoming of the garden world.

It is at this point in the cycle, after the abstract formulation of the insight the poet has gained in his many seasons, in his days and hours in his garden, that the uninvited visitors arrive on the scene with their promise of rescue. The function of the final poems has already been discussed. In closing, it is useful to note once more the characterization of the poet-Mandarin's garden activity as "Begeiste- rung" and his initial intention as he retreated to the garden to engage in "geistig schreiben." This is in explicit contrast to "Belehrung" and imparts, as we have seen, a knowledge that is not drawn out of endless debates and argument, but rather observation and insight.[54] In the *Chinesisch-deutsche Jahres- und Tageszeiten* the gaining of this knowledge has been celebrated.

In his *Noten und Abhandlungen zum West-östlichen Divan* Goethe de- scribed the essence of Oriental poetry (admittedly with specific refer- ence to Persian verse) as the predominance of "Geist," and he asserted that this unifying principle is grasped only with age:

Der höchste Charakter orientalischer Dichtkunst ist, was wir Deutsche Geist nennen, das Vorwaltende des oberen Leitenden; hier sind alle übrigen Eigen- schaften vereinigt, ohne daß irgend eine, das eigenthümliche Recht behaup- tend, hervorträte. Der Geist gehört vorzüglich dem Alter, oder alternden Weltepoche. Übersicht des Weltwesens, Ironie . . . finden wir in allen Dich- tern des Orients. (WA I, 7, 76)

It is this "Übersicht des Weltwesens," this overview of the seasons and the hours in their changing patterns, that is achieved in the cycle. It belonged very much to the Orient as Goethe conceived of it and was also very much his own in these later years. The double name he chose for the cycle is apt. The poems are both "Chinesisch" and "Deutsch."

VII

Conclusion

The word "Cyklus" entered the German language at the turn of the nineteenth century. It does not appear in Adelung[1] (neither in the 1774 nor 1811 edition), for example, but it is included in the *Ergänzung* of 1813.[2] There it is introduced strictly as a time expression, however, without any literary meaning.[3] Grimm states that "Cyklus" can be found since the eighteenth century in German, and he traces the development of the word from its primary meaning of "periodic succession in time" (with specific reference to the sun and moon cycles) to a more generalized application, as a reference to any series, including, finally, both the literary and visual arts.[4]

A second and quite restrictive use of the word "Cyklus" must also be noted. As classical scholars began publishing in the vernacular, they introduced into German a variety of technical terms from Greek and Latin. *Kyklos* had been, at least since the post-Alexandrian era, such a *terminus technicus*.[5] It described the body of legends which had formed the subject of the ancient Greek epic poems, constituting a sort of legendary history of the world from earliest times.[6] In Latin the term *cyclus epicus* was used. A number of lesser epics completing the story of the Trojan War and a series of Theban heroic lays are among the fragments of the *cyclus epicus*. Nothing is known with certainty about their authors. Pindar and the tragedians used the *cyclus epicus*, it is known, and, primarily for this reason, it has remained of interest to classical scholars.

The term *cyclus epicus* was introduced into the vernacular by Goethe's contemporaries. They selected various German equivalents:

Herder: jenen mythischen oder *epischen Cyclus*[7]

Fr. Schlegel: die Sänger dieser historischen Periode des *kyklischen Epos*[8]

Creuzer: *die kyklischen Gedichte*[9]

Göttingische
Anzeigen: die Bruckstücke des *epischen Cyclus*[10]

Welcker: Denn in meinen Vorlesungen habe ich zwar die *epischen Gedichte* aufgezählt, einen so frühen und so weiten und verschiedenartigen *Kyklos* . . .[11]

148

In the discussions of the *cyclus epicus* the terms "Cyklus" and "cyklisch" gained greater currency. Even scholars such as Welcker, who argued that the Latin term *cyclus* ought to be understood specifically to mean the heroic lays of ancient Greece (and ought not be extended to include other collections of mythology, such as Ovid's *Metamorphoses*, as some had asserted)[12] used the German terms "Cyklus" and "cyklisch" with increasing flexibility. For example, in his attempt to clarify the peculiar unity of the poems of the *cyclus epicus*, Welcker posited in more general terms a "cyclischer Bildungstrieb" and drew structural analogies to interlocking rings and interwoven threads.[13] He also attempted to clarify the double function of the larger poems of the epic cycle, declaring them simultaneously "abgerundete Ganze und . . . cyclische Glieder."[14]

It is evident that "Cyklus" in the earlier decades of the nineteenth century was a word whose meaning was less and less prescribed by either of its original, and rather limited, usages. No longer used only to designate a periodic succession in time nor simply as a German equivalent of the *cyclus epicus*, "Cyklus" could claim no single literary definition. Goethe's recorded uses of the word "Cyklus" illustrate well the range of its meaning, and they frustrate any attempt to describe a more definite pattern. Goethe, like his contemporaries, used the word "Cyklus" as a synonym for "Suite," "Reihenfolge," and "Kreis"—he also recognized a literary usage for the term—but he apparently attached no specific meaning to it.[15] "Cyklus" was clearly not a term that he favored.

Goethe does demonstrate a curious tendency to use the word "Cyklus" in reference to works composed in three parts, works that might also be called trilogies. He perceived *Wallenstein* "als einen Cyklus von Stücken" (WA I, 40, 4). He described the reliefs on a grave that depict the artistry of a young dancer as "cyclisch": "Die drei Bilder muß ich als cyclisch, als eine Trilogie ansehen" (WA IV, 22, 360). The original draft of the letter did not include the words "cyclisch, als." They were added in the margin as an appositive to "Trilogie."[16] Finally, there is Goethe's reference, reported by Eckermann, to the "Paria" poems and once more the equation of "Trilogie" and "Cyklus": "Auch mein 'Paria' ist ein vollkommene Trilogie, und zwar habe ich diesen Cyclus sogleich mit Intention als Trilogie gedacht und behandelt."[17]

The only other reference by Goethe to his poetry as a "Cyklus" is a single reference to his "Bei Allerhöchster Anwesenheit Ihro Majestät der Kaiserin Mutter Maria' Feodorowna in Weimar Maskenzug. 18. Dez. 1818." Goethe in writing to Zelter about the newly completed piece states: "und recht merkwürdig ist es, daß kein Sonett in diesen Cyklus passen wollte; auch dein Gefühl wird schwerlich einen Punct angeben, wo es stehen könnte" (WA IV, 31, 160).

The poems that are most generally acknowledged as cycles today and that have been the subject of this study were not called cycles during Goethe's lifetime. It has not been my intention to dispute their present designation as lyric cycles, but rather to demonstrate that both the term "lyric cycle" and the poems it describes are better understood when the variety of lyric traditions and diversity of poetic structures they represent are recognized.

Goethe's lyric cycles must inevitably prove somewhat of an irritation to those attempting to trace a history of the cycle. I have argued that the lyric cycle, as it emerged as an explicit poetic structural device in the early nineteenth century, could claim the ancestry of no single literary tradition. The Latin love elegy, Petrarch's *Canzoniere*, the idea of a "Roman in Liedern," that took its origins, in part, from the epistolary novel, the folk song, and the structure of Greek classical drama all played a role in the composition of the poems. The list is by no means exhaustive. Studies of the *West-östlicher Divan*, for example, and inquiries into other lyric collections less commonly designated cycles would introduce even more varied examples and would reinforce the claim that no single mode of poetic organization, no single literary tradition, informed the emergence of the lyric cycle as a standard poetic structural device.

Goethe's cycles range from three to over two hundred poems. The largest we have examined in this study has been the twenty poems of the *Römische Elegien*. Goethe chose at times to include all the poems related to a single cycle in the final composition (*Sonette*). At other times he arranged selected poems (*Römische Elegien, West-östlicher Divan*). Not all of the cycles can claim the same success as a poetic composition. It is diversity that characterizes Goethe's lyric cycles.

The question of the impact Goethe's lyric cycles had on his contemporaries and the extent to which his poems gave direction to the emerging definition of the lyric cycle as a standard poetic structural device in the nineteenth century can only be posed in terms of the individual cycle. For various reasons, however, the results are uniformly negative. The *Römische Elegien*, as we have noted, were, as a cycle, a unique response to the poetry of the Latin love elegists. Few followed Goethe's lead. The distich was rarely used in lyric cycles of the nineteenth century. When Goethe wrote his *Sonette*, sonnet sequences were already numerous. His poems, unpublished until 1815, did not have a marked influence on the writing of his contemporaries. For the poets who wrote in the later decades of the nineteenth century, it was not Goethe's *Sonette*, but rather Platen's *Sonette aus Venedig*, that set the course of the sonnet cycle. Trilogies have not generally been regarded as lyric cycles, and Goethe's equation of the words "Trilogie" and "Cyklus" has not found imitators. Indeed, one should note that for all the varied and structurally distinctive texts that have been united under the common designation "lyric cycle," few, if any, are composed of only three poems. In its own right, the lyric trilogy has not developed as a standard poetic structural device. Only the "Müllerin" ballads, quite apart from Goethe's description of them as a trilogy, can claim a small role in the later development of the lyric cycle. Even this claim is uncertain, however, because the significance of the "Müllerin" ballads for the popular song cycle by Wilhelm Müller, "Die schöne Müllerin," is debated. The *Chinesisch-deutsche Jahres- und Tageszeiten* were misunderstood in Goethe's lifetime and forgotten in the course of the nineteenth century. Rilke's appreciation of the cycle was exceptional. Well into the twentieth century the poems were neglected. Like the *Chinesisch-deutsche Jahres- und Tageszeiten*, the *West-östlicher Divan* was misunderstood. Critics compared the poems unfavorably with the poetry of Goethe's earlier years: "Als der Divan 1819 erschien, hat man ihn wenig beachtet, kaum verstanden. Das 19. Jahrhundert hatte für seine Geistigkeit und Stilform wenig Sinn und sah in ihr ein bedauerliches Absinken im Vergleich zu der Lyrik der Jugend und der klassischen Zeit."[18] According to Trunz, it was not until 1900 that a new appreciation of the *Divan* was expressed.[19]

One must conclude from these examples that Goethe's lyric cycles had little significance for the development of the lyric cycle as a standard poetic structural device in the nineteenth century. It has only been in the twentieth century, with the attempt to trace the cycle from classical times to its culmination in the works of Stefan George that Goethe's cycles have been joined together and accorded a new historical role. With great eloquence Gundolf inaugurated the new description: "das ganze Altertum von Alkäus und Pindar, bis zu den römischen Elegikern, Dante und Petrarca, dann Shakespeare in seinen Sonetten, in Deutschland wieder der klassisch, das heißt geduldig und augenhaft gewordene Goethe, und in unseren Tagen Stefan George."[20] He has drawn an impressive genealogy. But there is a problem here, one that does not reside solely in Gundolf's attempt to appropriate the lyric cycle to the formal domain of the classical sensibility. According to Gundolf, such a procedure is beyond the aesthetic potential of the undisciplined romantics: "andeutende, ahnungsvolle, musikalische, romantische Lyrik kann nicht zyklisch sein . . . weil sie nicht sondert und ordnet."[21] Not only is "lyric cycle," the family name he gives the works of these blue bloods of western literature, in reality a nineteenth-century patronymic, but also, if we are to accept Gundolf's value judgment, one popularized by the black sheep of the family—the romantics.[22] Furthermore, as the central argument of this study has shown, the lyric cycle simply does not possess the strong unbroken family ties that Gundolf suggests. Attempts to define the essence of the lyric cycle, most notably Joachim Müller's essay, "Das zyklische Prinzip in der Lyrik,"[23] also reveal an orientation centered on the works of George: "Darüber hinaus aber sehe ich in Georges Gedichtkreisen eine letzte Erfüllung des Wesens des zyklischen schlechthin."[24]

It has been the purpose of this study to challenge concepts of the lyric cycle that encourage such a reductive description of its history and its structures. Goethe's lyric cycles, examples of poetic excellence and marked diversity, have rightly been accorded new appreciation in the twentieth century. At the same time, however, in their diversity and excellence, they suggest that the history of the lyric cycle can only be written when fixed notions of the lyric cycle and its structure have been abandoned and a new inquiry into the specific genesis and composition of each cyclical group begun. This study has attempted such a beginning.

Notes

I. Introduction

1. While it is apparent that poems were arranged in sequence prior to 1800 (the most notable examples in German literature are Baroque sonnet sequences by Weckherlin, Gryphius, and Greiffenberg), these sequences were not called cycles. There is no direct relationship between these seventeenth century arrangements and the writings of Goethe and his contemporaries. The term "lyric cycle" is the invention of the nineteenth century.

2. While the *Venetianische Epigramme*, unlike Goethe's other epigrammatic cycles, do include a few poems which might be considered "lyric" rather than "epigrammatic" (criteria of tone as well as verse form are employed in making the rather elusive distinction), the cycle as a whole is marked by critical observation and brevity. The 103 poems are arranged topically and fully three-fourths of them are four lines or less. I have followed Wolfgang Preisendanz's lead in *Die Spruchform in der Lyrik des alten Goethe und ihre Vorgeschichte seit Opitz*, Heidelberger Forschungen (Heidelberg: Carl Winter Universitätsverlag, 1952), and have identified the *Venetianische Epigramme* with Goethe's epigrammatic sequences, including the 1782 epigrams collected under the rubric "Antiker Form sich nähernd," *Vier Jahreszeiten*, and the *Xenien*.

3. Carl Becker, "Das Buch Suleika als Zyklus," in *Varia Variorum. Festgabe für Karl Reinhardt* (Münster: Böhlau Verlag, 1952), pp. 240, 244.

4. Hans-Egon Hass, "Über die strukturelle Einheit des West-östlichen Divan," *Stil- und Formprobleme in der Literatur, Vorträge des VII. Kongresses der internationalen Vereinigung für moderne Sprachen und Literaturen in Heidelberg*, ed. Paul Böckmann (Heidelberg, 1959), pp. 312–13. Although his conceptual framework is adapted and developed by Ingeborg Hillmann in her dissertation on the thematic structure of the *Divan* poems, Hillmann successfully avoids using organic metaphor to characterize the cycle. Ingeborg Hillmann, *Dichtung als Gegenstand der Dichtung. Untersuchungen zum Problem der Einheit des "West-östlichen Divan"*, Bonner Arbeiten zur deutschen Literatur, 10 (Bonn: H. Bouvier u. Co. Verlag, 1965), p. 21.

5. Hass, "Über die strukturelle Einheit des West-östlichen Divan," p. 312.

6. Helen Mustard, *The Lyric Cycle in German Literature*, Columbia University German Studies, 17 (New York: King's Crown Press, 1946), pp. 61–77.

7. Elisabeth Reitmeyer, *Studien zum Problem der Gedichtsammlung mit eingehender Untersuchung der Gedichtsammlungen Goethes und Tiecks*, Sprache und Dichtung, 57 (Bern: Paul Haupt, 1935).

8. An additional book has appeared since the completion of this study which addresses the organization of the *Divan* as well as the *Römische Elegien* and the *Sonette*. Marianne Wünsch, *Der Strukturwandel in der Lyrik Goethes. Die systemimmanente Relation der Kategorien "Literatur" und "Realität": Probleme und Lösungen*, Studien zur Poetik und Geschichte der Literatur, 37 (Stuttgart: W. Kohlhammer Verlag, 1975), is concerned with the postulated relationship of a literary text to the reality outside of itself insofar as this relationship functions within the text as a structural component. She raises related issues such as the unity of the text and its self-defined relationship to its reader. Goethe's earlier "Erlebnis" poetry is used to establish the structural paradigm. The

153

three cycles are considered three successive transformations that attempt to resolve the same structural problems present within the "Erlebnis-Postulat" of Goethe's earlier poetry. "Nicht Werkstrukturen, sondern zu lösende Probleme sind konstant" (p. 183). The study is provocative as an investigation of the problem of structural innovation, both in its integration of a wide range of poetic material and in its stimulating theoretical approach. That it is also necessarily abstract is admitted by the author. Detailed analyses of texts are made only in an exemplary manner and, in general, precise identification of structural transformations replaces interpretation as the monograph's goal.

II. The *Römische Elegien*

1. WA IV, 9, 46; WA IV, 9, 57; WA IV, 9, 102–3; WA IV, 9, 112; WA IV, 9, 117; WA IV, 9, 120; WA IV, 9, 146.

2. WA IV, 9, 163; WA IV, 9, 198; WA IV, 9, 239; WA IV, 9, 227.

3. WA IV, 9, 198; WA IV, 9, 199.

4. Jacob Grimm and Wilhelm Grimm, "Zyklus," *Deutsches Wörterbuch* (Leipzig: S. Hirzel, 1954), XXXII, 1452.

5. Heinrich Viehoff, *Goethe's Gedichte erläutert und auf ihre Veranlassungen, Quellen und Vorbilder zurückgeführt* (Düsseldorf: Verlag der Bötticher'schen Buchhandlung, 1846), p. 112. See also Johann Wilhelm Schaefer, "Ueber Goethe's römische Elegieen und venetianische Epigramme," *Deutsches Museum*, 1 (1851), 289, and Johann August Lehmann, *Goethe's Liebe und Liebesgedichte* (Berlin: Allgemeine deutsche Verlags-Anstalt, 1852), p. 246.

6. Friedrich Gundolf, *Goethe* (Berlin: Georg Bondi, 1916), p. 440.

7. Not included in the *Römische Elegien*.

8. WA IV, 9, 115; WA IV, 9, 120; WA IV, 9, 162–63.

9. See WA IV, 12, 104–5.

10. The following dates are penciled on the Reinschrift, H[50], of the *Römische Elegien*, although it is not clear whether these refer to the composition, revision, or fair copy of the manuscript: Elegy VI: 5 February 1790; Elegy XVI and Elegy XVII: 24 December 1789. Additionally, Max Hecker (*Nachwort und Erläuterungen zur Faksimile-Ausgabe der Handschrift von Goethe's 'Römische Elegien'* [Leipzig: Insel Verlag, 1920], p.22), notes the date 8 February 1790 for Elegy VII. This date is not visible on the facsimile. Goethe's reference to Elegy XV in a letter to Knebel (WA IV, 9, 120) is only marginally useful as the letter is undated and its placement disputed. Hecker places the letter in October, 1788. I am inclined to regard the *Weimar Ausgabe* placement of 17 May 1789 as more probable. Cf. Hecker, pp. 3, 22; WA IV, 9, 351. The elegy mentioned in Goethe's letter of 6 April 1789 to Karl August (WA I, 53, 4–6) is generally considered to be the original Elegy XVI, "Zwey gefährliche Schlangen," eventually excluded from the collection. A number of poems had been completed by 6 April 1789 (cf. WA IV, 9, 103).

11. Hans Gerhard Gräf, *Goethe über seine Dichtungen* (Frankfurt: Rütten und Loening, 1912), III, 2, 496.

12. By contrast, the Neo-Latin poet Johannes Secundus (1511–36) continued the tradition of Latin love poetry by writing several books of elegiac verse as well as the well-known collection *Basia*. Goethe expresses his enthusiasm for Secundus in a poem written in 1776, "An den Geist Johannes Secundus," which he revised as "Liebesbedürfnis" for the 1789 *Schriften*. Once more, a single poem is the chosen response. Goethe's use of the Neo-Latin tradition in the *Römische Elegien* is argued by Georg Ellinger, "Goethe und Johannes Secundus," *Goethe Jahrbuch*, 13 (1892), 199–201. Stuart Atkins provides a more cautious evaluation of the relationship of Secundus to the *Römische Elegien*, and at the same time convincingly describes Goethe's life-long interest in Renaissance poetry and his debt to its traditions. Stuart Atkins, "Goethe und die Renaissancelyrik," in *Goethe und die Tradition*, ed. Hans Reiss, Wissenschaftliche Paperbacks, Literaturwissenschaft, 19 (Frankfurt am Main: Athenäum Verlag, 1972), 102–29.

13. Quoted in Regine Otto, "Karl Ludwig von Knebel. Entwürfe zu einer Monographie," Diss. Jena, 1967, p. 166. The letter (24 July 1798, to Göschen) is in the collection of the Goethe und Schiller Archiv der Nationalen Forschungs- und Gedenkstätten der klassischen deutschen Literatur in Weimar, Knebel, VII, 5, 10.

14. Heinrich Düntzer and Ferdinand Gottfried von Herder, eds., *Von und An Herder* (Leipzig: Dyk'sche Buchhandlung, 1862), III, 130.

15. Karl Ludwig von Knebel, *Elegieen von Properz* (Leipzig: Göschen, 1798), p. 30.

16. Wilhelm Adolf Boguslaw Hertzberg, *Sextus Aurelius Propertius. Elegien im Versmaß der Urschrift. Übersetzt und durch Anmerkungen erläutert* (Stuttgart: J. B. Wetzler'sche Buchhandlung, 1838), p. 8. His argument is questionable.

17. Ibid., p. 84.

18. Friedrich Gottlieb Barth, *Vorlesungen über einige Elegien des Properz nebst einer prosaischen Uebersetzung der Königinn aller Elegien* (Dresden: Gröllische Buchhandlung, 1775), Vorrede.

19. Ferdinand Bronner, "Goethes römische Elegien und ihre Quellen," *Neue Jahrbücher für Philologie und Pädagogik*, 148 (1893), 314.

20. Friedrich Beißner, *Geschichte der deutschen Elegie*, Grundriß der germanischen Philologie, 14 (Berlin: Walter de Gruyter & Co., 1941), p. 127. The edition, *Alb. Tibullus. Nebst einer Probe aus dem Properz und den Kriegsliedern des Tyrtäus* (Zürich: Orell, Geßner, Füßli und Comp., 1783) was prepared by Karl Friedrich Reinhard, a friend of Goethe's, and published anonymously. A copy of the translation was in Goethe's library.

21. *Des Sextus Aurelius Propertius Werke*, trans. Johann Heinrich Voß (Braunschweig: Friedrich Vieweg, 1830). Cf. Franz Ludwig Anton Schweiger, *Handbuch der classischen Biographie. Zweiten Theiles zweite Abtheilung. Lateinische Schriftsteller*, M-V (Leipzig: F. Fleischer, 1834), p. 833.

22. In October of 1788 Knebel presented Goethe with a Latin edition of the elegists: *Catullus, Tibullus, Propertius ad fidem optimorum librorum denuo accurate recensiti adiectum est pervigilium veneris* (Göttingen: A. Vandenhoeck, 1762). See also Lieselotte Blumenthal, "Schillers und Goethes Anteil an Knebels Properz-Übertragung," *Jahrbuch der deutschen Schillergesellschaft*, 3 (1959), 71–93, and Gertrud Herwig-Hager, "Goethes Properz-Begegnung. 'Der Besuch' und Properz I, 3," in *Synusia. Festgabe für Wolfgang Schadewaldt*, ed. Helmut Flashar and Konrad Gaiser (Pfullingen: Verlag Gunther Neske, 1965), pp. 429–53.

23. In addition to the passages in the two elegies that were finally removed from the collection, Schiller also questioned parts of Elegy V. Goethe decided not to alter the poem. See WA IV, 10, 260.

24. Schiller especially hoped to retain the second Elegy. He viewed the loss of the sixteenth with greater indifference. Friedrich Schiller, *Werke. Nationalausgabe* (Weimar: Hermann Böhlaus Nachfolger, 1958), XXVII, 185.

25. Portions of these poems were considered too offensive even for the first volume of the *Weimar Ausgabe*. They were withheld and first published after the death of Herzogin Sophia. Cf. WA I, 1, 412–24 and WA I, 53, 3–7 and 451–52.

26. Charlotte von Stein to Lotte Schiller (7 November 1794) in *Charlotte von Schiller und ihre Freunde*, ed. Ludwig von Urlichs and Emilie von Gleichen (Stuttgart: J. G. Cotta'scher Verlag, 1862), II, 298. Goethe proceeded to publish one elegy, XIII, "Amor bleibet ein Schalk," as a single poem with the title "Elegie, Rom 1789" in the *Deutsche Monatsschrift*, July 1791, pp. 185–88.

27. The title *Römische Elegien* was first used in the 1806 edition of the *Werke*. In the *Horen* the poems are simply called *Elegien*. The H[50] manuscript, originally entitled *Erotica Romana*, was corrected to read *Elegien Rom 1788*. Cf. WA I, 1, 411.

28. Max Hecker, *Faksimile-Ausgabe der Handschrift von Goethes 'Römische Elegien'* (Leipzig: Insel Verlag, 1920) is a facsimile of this manuscript. It is also available in Albert Leitzmann, *Goethes Römische Elegien nach der ältesten Reinschrift* (Bonn: A. Marcus und E. Weber's Verlag, 1912).

29. These two elegies were found after Goethe's death together with the two poems (2 and 16) removed from the collection. Priapus's message of fertility is carried in very explicit metaphors of male potency and again raised questions of good taste. Thematically the poems are inappropriate. Among the *Venetianische Epigramme* are a number of related poems that would fit nicely into the *Römische Elegien*, except that they too strain the fictional boundaries of the Roman love story. The epigrams reflect Goethe's delight with the swelling of his mistress's body. (Christiane was carrying her first child in these months.) See Harry Gerald Haile, "Prudery in the Publication History of Goethe's Roman Elegies," *German Quarterly*, 49 (1976), 287–94 for a defense of the Priapus poems in the cycle.

30. Heinrich Justus Heller, "Antike Quellen von Goethes elegischen Dichtungen," *Neue Jahrbücher für Philologie und Pädagogik*, 88 (1863), 300–12, 351–71, 401–26, 451–71, 493–519. A response from Heinrich Düntzer appeared in vol. 90 of the same journal (1864), pp. 180–201 and a counter from Heller appeared in vol. 92 (1865), pp. 397–418, 466–74, 508–24, 564–75. See also Ferdinand Bronner, "Goethes römische Elegien und ihre Quellen," *Neue Jahrbücher für Philologie und Pädagogik*, 148 (1893), 38–50, 102–12, 145–50, 247–65, 305–16, 367–71, 440–69, 525–41, 572–88. Elisabeth Eggerking attempted to summarize and close the argument in her dissertation, *Goethes Römische Elegien* (Bonn: Carl Georgi Universitäts-Buchdruckerei, 1913).

31. Hecker, 1113.

32. Werner Keller, *Goethes dichterische Bildlichkeit. Eine Grundlegung* (München: Wilhelm Fink Verlag, 1972), p. 24.

33. Myra-Richards Jessen, *Goethe als Kritiker der Lyrik. Beiträge zu seiner Ästhetik und seiner Theorie*, Diss. Bryn Mawr, 1932 (Tübingen: privately published, 1932), offers a systematic discussion of Goethe's poetic terminology. More general are: Wolfgang Schadewaldt, "Goethes Begriff der Realität," *Goethe. Jahrbuch der Goethe-Gesellschaft* (Weimar), 18 (1956), 44–88. Matthijs Jolles, *Goethes Kunstanschauung* (Bern: Francke Verlag, 1957). Naoji Kimura, *Goethes Wortgebrauch zur Dichtungstheorie im Briefwechsel mit Schiller und den Gesprächen mit Eckermann* (München: Max Hueber Verlag, 1965).

34. Keller, *Goethes dichterische Bildlichkeit*, p. 28.

35. Quoted in Walther Killy, "Mythologie und Lakonismus in der ersten, dritten und vierten Römischen Elegie," *Gymnasium*, 71 (1964), 135.

36. Cf. "Willkommen und Abschied," lines 15–16; "An den Mond, erste Fassung," lines 9–10; *Urfaust* 462, 916. Propertius I, 9 (17–18); I, 10 (10): I, 13 (26); II, 34 (44): III, 6 (39); III, 17 (9).

37. The passage is not unrelated to the climactic confrontation between Thoas and Iphigenie in the fifth act of Goethe's play *Iphigenie* (1779–85), where he also employs the metaphors of fire and water to record the interaction of the principal characters.

38. Silvia the Vestal . . . went in the morning to fetch water to wash the holy things. . . . Mars saw her (this sight) and he desired and he possessed that which he desired. . . . Sleep left her; she lay pregnant. Now indeed within her womb there was the founder of the city of the Romans.

39. Ovid, *Amores* I, 4, 17–20.

40. Cf. I, 13–14; IV, 31–32; VII, 25–26; XIII, 52; XVI, 9–10; XVII, 7–8; XIX, 69–70. See also Barbara Herrnstein Smith, *Poetic Closure. A Study of How Poems End* (Chicago: University of Chicago Press, 1968).

41. Killy, "Mythologie und Lakonismus," p. 146.

42. Ibid., p. 140.

43. Ibid., p. 138.

44. Ibid., p. 139.

45. Ibid., p. 141.

46. Cf. Gerhard Kaiser, "Wandrer und Idylle: ein Zugang zur zyklischen Ordnung der 'Römische Elegien,'" *Archiv für das Studium der neueren Sprachen und Literaturen*, 202 (1965), 1–27.

47. Cf. Rückert's "Maiengruß an die Neugenesene"; Droste-Hülshoff's "Der Weiher," "Die Elemente," "Der Säntis."

48. Kaiser, "Wandrer und Idylle."

49. Ibid., p. 15.

50. Cf. Dominik Jost, *Deutsche Klassik*. *Goethes "Römische Elegien"* (Pullach bei München: Verlag Dokumentation, 1974). Jost, p. 77, also argues that symmetry is fundamental to the cycle's structure. With little elaboration he asserts "axial-symmetrische Entsprechung, spiegelverkehrt nach der Mitte zu . . . ; tiefe Pause in der Mitte."

51. *Der Briefwechsel zwischen Goethe und Knebel*, ed. Gottschalk Eduard Guhrauer (Leipzig: F. A. Brockhaus, 1851), pp. 193–94.

52. Leitzmann, *Goethes Römische Elegien*, provides useful documentation of the public and private response to the *Römische Elegien* in his selection of letters and critical reviews.

53. Friedrich Schiller, "Die sentimentalischen Dichter," *Die Horen* I, no. 12 (1795), 44. Cf. Friedrich Schiller, *Werke*. *Nationalausgabe* (Weimar: Hermann Böhlaus Nachfolger, 1962), XX, 465.

54. Friedrich Schlegel, "Elegien aus dem Griechischen," *Athenäum* 1 (1798), 108 (rpt. Darmstadt: Wissenschaftliche Buchgesellschaft, 1960).

55. August Wilhelm Schlegel, "Rezension der Horen," *Jenaische Allgemeine Literaturzeitung*, 4 (1796). Cf. A. W. Schlegel, *Sämmtliche Werke*, ed. Eduard Böcking (Leipzig: Weidmann'sche Buchhandlung, 1846), X, 62.

56. A. W. Schlegel, *Sämmtliche Werke*, X, 64.

57. A. W. Schlegel, *Geschichte der klassischen Literatur*, Kritische Schriften und Briefe III, ed. Edgar Lohner (Stuttgart: W. Kohlhammer Verlag, 1964), p. 243. Cf. A. W. Schlegel, *Vorlesungen über schöne Litteratur und Kunst*, ed. Jakob Minor, Deutsche Litteraturdenkmäler des 18. und 19. Jahrhunderts, 17–19 (Heilbronn: Verlag von Gebr. Henninger, 1884), II, 290.

58. Friedrich Schlegel, "Rezension von Goethes Werken 1808," *Heidelbergische Jahrbücher der Literatur*, I, 158. Cf. F. Schlegel, *Kritische Ausgabe*, III (München: Verlag Ferdinand Schöningh, 1975), 123.

59. F. Schlegel, "Rezension von Goethes Werken 1808," p. 122. The comparison is made to "Alexis und Dora" and to "Der neue Pausias und sein Blumenmädchen," which Schlegel considered the best of the distich poems.

60. Bernhard Wyß, *Heinrich Keller. Der Züricher Bildhauer und Dichter* (Frauenfeld: J. Hubers Buchdruckerei, 1871), p. 17.

61. Ibid., p. 65.

62. Ibid., p. 20.

63. Ibid., p. 65.

64. Ibid., p. 18.

65. Cf. Addendum to a letter of 25 December 1797, *Schillers Briefwechsel mit Körner* (Leipzig: Verlag von Veit & Comp., 1859), IV, 106.

66. The poem was sent to Wilhelm von Humboldt on 10 July 1797. Cf. *Humboldts Briefe an Karl Gustav von Brinkmann*, ed. Albert Leitzmann (Leipzig: K. W. Hiersemann, 1939), p. 101.

67. Cf. Blumenthal, "Schiller und Goethes Anteil an Knebels Properz-Übertragung," p.76.

III. The *Sonette*

1. Unlike "Sammlung," which was used without explicit structural reference, the terms "Blumenlese" and "Blumenstrauß" were used specifically to designate poetic anthologies. For example, August Wilhelm Schlegel's collection of Italian, Spanish, and Portuguese verse in German translation, which he published in 1804, is entitled *Blumensträuße italiänischer, spanischer und portugiesischer Poesie*. The *Musenalmanache* and *Taschenbücher* were frequently referred to as either "Blumenstrauß" or "Blumenlese,"

as were collections of songs. "Blumenkranz" is a variant. The following titles are representative: *Allgemeine Blumenlese der Deutschen* (Zürich, 1784); *Carolinens Blumenkranz zur Bildung des Herzens* (Berlin, 1796); Heinrich Christian Schnorr, *Musikalisches Blumensträußchen*, 3 vols. (1795); F. H. Himmel, *Blumenstrauß, meinen Gönnern und Freunden gewidmet bey meinem Abschiede aus Berlin* (1797).

2. A. W. Schlegel, rev. of *Petrarca. Ein Denkmal edler Liebe und Humanität*, by Friedrich Butenschön, *Jenaische Allgemeine Literaturzeitung* (1796). Cf. A. W. Schlegel, *Sämmtliche Werke* ed. Eduard Böcking (Leipzig: Weidmann'sche Buchhandlung, 1846), X, 202–3.

3. A. W. Schlegel, *Geschichte der romantischen Literatur*, Kritische Schriften und Briefe IV, ed. Edgar Lohner (Stuttgart: W. Kohlhammer Verlag, 1962), p. 183. Cf. A. W. Schlegel, *Vorlesungen über schöne Litteratur und Kunst*, ed. Jakob Minor, Deutsche Litteraturdenkmäler des 18. und 19. Jahrhunderts, 17–19 (Heilbronn: Verlag von Gebr. Henninger, 1884), III, 203–4. Schlegel is the first to establish a theoretical model for a collection of lyric poems as an aesthetic whole. Cf. Helen Mustard, *The Lyric Cycle in German Literature*, Columbia University German Studies, 17 (New York: King's Crown Press, 1946), pp. 36–37. It is uncertain whether Goethe was acquainted at this time with the critical opinions Schlegel advanced in his 1803 lectures. He does not mention them in correspondence or recorded conversation. It can be assumed he knew the 1796 review in the *Jenaische Allgemeine Literaturzeitung*. Cf. Minor III, 203–4.

4. Walter Mönch, *Das Sonett. Gestalt und Geschichte* (Heidelberg: F. H. Kerle Verlag, 1955), p. 30.

5. Ibid., p. 59.

6. Ibid., pp. 30–31. In the "corona dei sonetti" as defined by Crescimbeni (1663–1728) the final sonnet, the "sonetto magistrale," supplies the first and last lines for the other fourteen. The first and second lines of the final sonnet determine the opening and concluding lines of the first poem, the second and third lines determine the second, and so on. The form has a number of variants.

7. Petrarch (1304–74) never chose a title for his collection of poems, but referred to them simply as *Rerum vulgarium fragmenta*. They are most frequently called by the generic names *Canzoniere* or *Rime*. Goethe may have thought of Petrarch when he used the phrase "Fragmenten Art erotischer Späße" in reference to the *Römische Elegien*. Both Petrarch and Goethe seem to use "fragments" to designate poems written separately and later collected, roughly "miscellaneous" or "loosely strung together."

8. Mönch, *Das Sonett*, p. 71.

9. Cf. Martha Foote Crow, *Elizabethan Sonnet-Cycles* (London: Kegan Paul, Trench Trübner & Co., 1896) and Denys Bray, *Shakespeare's Sonnet-Sequence* (London: The Richards Press, 1938).

10. Sonnet cycles were written by Weckherlin, Gryphius and Greiffenberg. Mustard, *The Lyric Cycle*, p. 8, states that the cycle was not as popular in the Baroque period as Welti suggests. Cf. Heinrich Welti, *Geschichte des Sonettes in der deutschen Dichtung* (Leipzig: Verlag von Veig & Comp., 1884).

11. Welti, *Geschichte des Sonettes*, p. 137. Sulzer notes in his article on the sonnet: "Bey uns ist es völlig in Abgang gekommen; aber in Italien scheint man noch darein verliebt zu sein." Johann George Sulzer, *Allgemeine Theorie der Schönen Künste* (Leipzig: M. G. Weidmann, 1771), p. 1095.

12. Mustard, *The Lyric Cycle*, p. 26. Cf. Theodor Feigel, *Vom Wesen der Anakreontik und ihrem Verlauf im Halberstädtischen Dichterkreis mit besonderer Berücksichtigung Klamer Schmidts*, Diss. Marburg, 1909 (Cassel: Rich. Trömner, 1909). According to Johanna Schneider in "Johann Nicholaus Meinhards Werk über die italiänischen Dichter und seine Spuren in der deutschen Literatur," Diss. Marburg, 1911, p. 52ff., among the poems written in imitation of Petrarch there is only one sonnet to be found before 1776.

13. Friedrich von Blankenburg, *Litterarische Zusätze zu Johann George Sulzers allgemeiner Theorie der schönen Künste, in einzelnen, nach alphabetischer Ordnung der Kunstwörter auf einander folgenden Artikeln abgehandelt* (Leipzig: Weidmann'sche Buchhandlung, 1798), III, 198.

14. Ludwig August Unzer, "Tcheou. Ein chinesisches Sonett," *Göttinger Musenalmanach*, 1773, p. 124. Klamer Schmidt's *Elegien an meine Minna* (1773) includes one sonnet, p. 70, and Friedrich Schmitt's *Gedichte* (Nürnberg, 1779) has nine. In the *Teutscher Merkur* 4, no. 2 and no. 3 (1776), twelve sonnets were published anonymously (most probably all by Klamer Schmidt). Daniel Schiebeler, "Das Sonett," *Auserlesene Gedichte* (Hamburg, 1773), p. 163. Johann Nikolaus Götz, "Über das neue Jagdschloß zu**," *Vermischte Gedichte* (Mannheim, 1785), p. 155.

15. Jörg-Ulrich Fechner, *Das deutsche Sonett. Dichtungen, Gattungspoetik, Dokumente* (München: Wilhelm Fink Verlag, 1969), p. 27.

16. Friedrich Rassmann, *Sonette der Deutschen* (Braunschweig: Schulbuchhandlung, 1817), p. iii. Fechner, *Das deutsche Sonett*, p. 27, has described the sonnet as the distich of the romantic movement.

17. Cf. Hans-Jürgen Schlütter, *Goethes Sonette. Anregung, Entstehung, Intention*, Goethezeit, 1 (Bad Homburg, v. d. H.: Verlag Gehlen, 1969), pp. 13–32.

18. "Goethe und die Romantik. Briefe mit Erläuterungen I," ed. Carl Schüddekopf and Oskar Walzel, *Schriften der Goethe Gesellschaft*, 13 (1898), p. 54. Goethe and August Wilhelm Schlegel maintained an active correspondence in these years and exchanged occasional visits.

19. Although the word "Cyklus" was not yet current, it was used by Friedrich Schlegel in a letter to his brother in reference to the three sonnets entitled *Hymnen* in the *Musenalmanach*: "Du erinnerst Dich noch der Sonette an Apollo und Diana Ephesiaca. Ich habe eines an die Isis hinzugenommen, andere an Cybele und sie sind unterwegs, bis es ein kleiner Zyklus ist; der steht Dir dann auch zu Diensten." *Friedrich Schlegels Briefe an seinen Bruder August Wilhelm*, ed. Oskar Walzel (Berlin: Speyer & Peters, 1890), p. 457. This is, however, an isolated example.

20. *Der Thalsohn*: Werner had completed a two-part drama, *Die Söhne des Tals*, in 1803.

21. Paul Hankamer, *Spiel der Mächte. Ein Kapitel aus Goethes Leben und Goethes Welt* (Tübingen: Rainer Wunderlich Verlag, 1947), pp. 51–52.

22. Zelter, I, 195. Years later Zelter expressed greater misgivings about his ability to set sonnets to music. In a letter to Goethe with reference to the "Maskenzug. Bey Allerhöchster Anwesenheit Ihro Majestät der Kaiserin Mutter Maria Feodorowna in Weimar" he states: "Deine Festgedichte gehen spazieren von mir zu Langermann und von da zurück. Ein Sonett habe ich allerdings am wenigsten vermißt, weil ich ihm trotz meiner Bemühungen noch niemals habe eine musikalische Form abgewinnen können, die natürlich wäre." Zelter II, 13.

23. Beethoven's "An die ferne Geliebte," Op. 98 (1816) is the first song cycle of note; text by Alois Jeitteles, *Gedichte in Selam*, 1815. See Leslie Orrey, "The Songs," in *The Beethoven Reader*, ed. Denis Arnold and Nigel Fortune (New York: W. W. Norton & Co., 1971), pp. 411–39. Schubert's cycles are based on texts by Wilhelm Müller: *Die schöne Müllerin* (1820) and *Die Winterreise* (1823).

24. Entitled "Kunst und Natur," the sonnet is part of the collection *Gesänge für die Liedertafel*. The other two sonnets are: "Jedes Ding in jeder Stunde" (Paul Gerhardt), Nr. II. 4. in *Sämtliche Lieder, Balladen und Romanzen*, Kunst- und Industrie-Comtoir, 1800–1813; "Ach könnt' ich vergessen sie" Sonett aus dem 13. Jahrhundert (Herder), Nr. 3. in *Neue Liedersammlung* (Zürich, 1821). For a complete listing of Zelter's compositions see Georg Richard Kruse, *Zelter*, Musiker-Biographien 34, Reclams Universal Bibliothek NR. 5815 (Leipzig: P. Reclam, 1915).

25. The Roman numerals indicate the place of the sonnet in the cycle of seventeen as it appeared in 1827 in the *Werke*. This is the standard text for the poems. For the Zelter cycle I have used the order indicated in H[31], WA I, 2, 300. The notes in the apparatus are contradictory, and the entry for Sonett VI, p.301, indicates a different arrangement for the poems. H[31] is no longer extant.

26. All three have been championed as the beloved celebrated in the *Sonette*. Bettina, whose letters provided motifs for a number of the poems, is perhaps her own best

promoter. She rearranged the correspondence in *Goethes Briefwechsel mit einem Kinde* to establish herself as the referent of the sonnets. Cf. Bettina von Arnim, *Bettinas Leben und Briefwechsel mit Goethe, auf Grund ihres handschriftlichen Nachlasses*, ed. Reinhold Steig, rev. Fritz Bergemann (Leipzig: Insel Verlag, 1927). Silvie von Ziegesar has been suggested by Hans M. Wolff, *Goethe in den Wahlverwandtschaften (1802 bis 1809)* (Bern: Francke, 1952), as the inspiration for the poems. Kuno Fischer, *Goethes Sonetten-Kranz*, Goethe Schriften, 4 (Heidelberg: Carl Winter's Universitätsbuchhandlung, 1895), interprets all the sonnets as testament to Goethe's love for Minna, refusing to accommodate even the most explicit evidence of Bettina's correspondence. Various combinations have also been advanced, but Minna Herzlieb prevails. The biographical controversy is not germane to this study. For additional references see Trunz, HA 1, 632–36, and Schlütter, *Goethes Sonette*, pp. 131–35.

27. Hankamer, *Spiel der Mächte*.

28. Walther Killy, *Wandlungen des lyrischen Bildes* (Göttingen: Vandenhoeck & Ruprecht, 1956), pp. 17–22.

29. Hankamer, *Spiel der Mächte*, p. 53.

30. Ibid., p. 57.

31. In "Mahomets-Gesang" (1772/73), a celebration of prophetic leadership under the metaphor of a growing stream, this same fusion is used.

32. Hankamer, *Spiel der Mächte*, p. 56.

33. Goethe published Sonnets I-XV in the 1815 edition of the *Werke*. In a draft for the *Tag- und Jahreshefte*, written in 1823, Goethe remarked: "Noch einige [Sonette] sind im Hinterhalte; sie bleiben zurück, weil sie die nächsten Zustände nur allzudeutlich bezeichneten" (WA I, 36, 392). Sonnets XVI and XVII were first published in 1827 in the *Ausgabe letzter Hand*.

34. Emil Staiger, *Goethe*, II (Zürich: Atlantis Verlag, 1959), 446.

35. Cf. Bettina von Arnim, *Bettinas Leben und Briefwechsel mit Goethe*, pp. 38–39, p. 191. See also Schlütter, *Goethes Sonette*, pp. 86–87.

36. Goethe was absorbed in the spring of 1808 with an articulation of the differences between masculine and feminine love, with particular reference to Werner's sonnets and his own. (Cf. Goethe's *Tagebuch* and Riemer's *Tagebuch*, entries 13 and 15 June.) Whether Goethe purposefully limits the experience of renunciation to the masculine sphere and has intentionally portrayed the woman as the one who will eternally long for the fulfillment that only a man can bring, or whether this is only a secondary implication, is unclear. Schlütter summarizes the conclusion Goethe reached: "Die Liebe des Mannes ist enthusiastisch, begeistert, schwärmerisch, die weibliche dienstfertig, gefällig. Darin liegt, daß die eine sich aktiv, geistig, schöpferisch zeigt, die andere aufnehmend, willig, abhängig." Schlütter, *Goethes Sonette*, p. 105.

37. Hankamer, *Spiel der Mächte*, p.68.

38. Cf. Schlütter, *Goethes Sonette*, pp. 90–96.

39. In Friedrich Johannes Frommann, *Das Frommannsche Haus und seine Freunde* (Jena: Fr. Frommann, 1870), p. 120.

40. Welti, *Geschichte des Sonettes*, p. 195. Petrarch begins the celebration of his beloved's name in the fifth poem of the *Canzoniere*: "Cosi LAUdare e REverire insegna." Frequently he evokes her name in a pun on the word "aura" or "air," as in the sequence 194, 196, 197, 198, "L'aura gentil," "L'aura senera," "L'aura celeste," "L'aura soave." He also played upon the similarity between the name Laura and the Latin and Italian words for laurel, the symbol of a poet's fame.

41. Zelter I, 216.

42. Studies that are centered on biographical questions include: Friedrich Johannes Frommann, *Das Frommannsche Haus und seine Freunde*; Kuno Fischer, *Goethes Sonettenkranz*; Hans M. Wolff, *Goethe in der Periode der Wahlverwandtschaften*.

43. For example, Henry Hatfield, *Goethe, A Critical Introduction* (Cambridge: Harvard

University Press, 1964) omits the sonnets. Barker Fairley, *Goethe as Revealed in His Poetry* (New York: Ungar, 1963) slights them.

44. Friedrich Gundolf, *Goethe* (Berlin: Georg Bondi, 1916), p. 577.

45. Ibid., p. 578.

46. Ibid., p. 578.

47. Staiger, *Goethe*, II, 444.

48. Schlütter, *Goethes Sonette*, p. 10.

49. Ibid., p. 10.

50. Hankamer, *Spiel der Mächte*, p. 72.

51. One need not assent completely to Schlütter's division of the sonnets into two distinct groups, the Jena sonnets and the Weimar sonnets (the latter having been written after Goethe's return to Weimar on 16 December 1807) to conclude that some of the *Sonette* were written and read to the company in Jena (cf. Goethe's letters, *Tagebuch*, and the dated manuscripts), while others remained to be composed later in Weimar (cf. letters, WA IV, 19, 479 f.). Schlütter's speculative attempt to chart the composition of the cycle by means of stylistic devices is not immediately relevant to this discussion.

52. Elisabeth Reitmeyer, *Studien zum Problem der Gedichtsammlung mit eingehender Untersuchung der Gedichtsammlungen Goethes und Tiecks*, Sprache und Dichtung, 57 (Bern: Paul Haupt, 1935), p. 88.

53. Ibid., p. 91.

54. Mustard, *The Lyric Cycle*, p. 65.

55. Ibid., p. 63.

56. Joachim Müller, *Goethes Sonette–Lyrische Epoche und motivische Kontinuität*, Abhandlungen der sächsischen Akademie der Wissenschaften zu Leipzig (Philologisch-historische Klasse) 58, 3 (Berlin: Akademie Verlag, 1966), pp. 17–21.

57. Ibid., p. 7.

58. Ibid., p. 36.

59. Goethe's role in the "Sonettenkrieg" that raged about him for years was minimal. Although publicly he ignored its skirmishes, "Das Sonett" (1800) was regarded as ammunition for the anti-sonnet forces. The *Sonette*, more favorable to the cause, appeared after the major battles had been fought. See Welti, *Geschichte des Sonettes*, pp. 199–216.

60. Ibid., p. 228.

61. Ibid., p. 226.

IV. The Trilogies

1. Frédéric Soret, *Conversations avec Goethe*, ed. A. Robinet de Cléry (Paris: Editions Montaigne, 1931), p. 137.

2. Jacob Grimm and Wilhelm Grimm, "Trilogie," *Deutsches Wörterbuch* (Leipzig: S. Hirzel, 1954), XXII, 540. For an account of the trilogy in nineteenth century German drama see Horst Steinmetz, *Trilogie. Entstehung und Struktur einer Großform des deutschen Dramas nach 1800*, Probleme der Dichtung, 11 (Heidelberg: Carl Winter Verlag, 1968). Goethe also intended to write dramatic trilogies for the modern stage, a plan he never realized. *Die natürliche Tochter* and *Pandora* were both conceived as part of such trilogies.

3. Frédéric Soret (1795–1865) was employed as a tutor in the Weimar court from 1822 to 1832 and enjoyed a close relationship with Goethe. Their conversations are recorded by Soret in *Conversations avec Goethe*. The correspondence between Goethe and Soret and a German translation of the conversations is available in *Zehn Jahre bei Goethe. Erinnerungen an Weimars klassische Zeit 1822–32*, ed. Heinrich Hubert Houben (Leipzig: F. A. Brockhaus, 1929).

4. The poems are: "L'invocation du Berger. 1ere Nuit" (*Création* no. 1, pp. 2–4), "Le jeune homme et l'étoile" (*Chaos* Jg. II, no. 12, pp. 46–47), "L'étoile filante. 3ieme Nuit" (*Création* no. 0, pp. 2–4), "Minuit" (*Chaos* Jg. II, Nr. 13, Beilage pp. 1–4). *Chaos* edited by

Ottilie von Goethe, appeared from 1829 to 1832. *Création* was the French supplement, edited by Soret. The English supplement, *Creation*, was edited by Goff. See Ilse-Marie Barth, *Literarisches Weimar. Kultur/Literatur/Sozialstruktur im 16.–20. Jahrhundert*, Sammlung Metzler, 93 (Stuttgart: Metzler, 1971), pp. 98–99.

5. The discussion of the trilogies is found in part III of Eckermann's *Gespräche*. The entries are little more than a reworking of Soret's journals. The central conversation of 1 December is largely adapted from Soret's entry of 7 December 1831. Cf. Julius Petersen, *Die Entstehung der Eckermannschen Gespräche*, 2d ed., Deutsche Forschungen, 2 (Frankfurt am Main: Verlag Moritz Diesterweg, 1925), pp. 18, 68–75, 89–90, 134, 143, 151.

6. Fragments in the notes and papers that were collected for *Die Reise in die Schweiz* give evidence that several other dialogue poems were begun, but never completed, at the same time Goethe was writing the "Müllerin" ballads. See WA I, 34², 122 and 128.

7. See WA IV, 12, 302.

8. See WA IV, 12, 330; WA IV, 12, 355.

9. See WA IV, 13, 194.

10. The text is reprinted in Albert Leitzmann, *Die Quellen von Schillers und Goethes Balladen*, Kleine Texte für theologische und philologische Vorlesungen und Übungen, 73 (Bonn: A. Marcus und E. Weber's Verlag, 1911), pp. 39–40. Frau von Stein did translate the poem into German. This text is reprinted in Heinrich Düntzer, *Goethes lyrische Gedichte*, 2d ed. (Leipzig: E. Wartig, 1874), pp. 379–81.

11. It should be noted that Goethe was not the only poet to discover in Paisiello's libretto the idea for a sequence of poems. Wilhelm Müller's cycle *Die schöne Müllerin* is indebted to the opera as well. Luise E. Peake's recent dissertation ("A Preliminary Inquiry into the Beginnings of the Romantic Song Cycle and the Nature of an Art Form," Columbia, 1968) inquires into the development of the song cycle, explores the composition of Müller's poems, and raises a number of issues directly related to the argument of this monograph. The relationship of Goethe's ballads to Müller's cycle has never been completely resolved. Bruno Hake ("Wilhelm Müller. Sein Leben und Dichten" [Kapitel IV: Die schöne Müllerin], Diss. Berlin, 1908, p.11) denies that Goethe's "Balladenfolge" played any role in the writing of the poems. He does note, however, that Arnim planned at one point to rework Goethe's ballads into a *Liederspiel*, and this necessarily raises the issue of Müller's awareness of these plans. Cf. Arnim's letter to Brentano, 27 February 1805, in Reinhold Steig, *Achim von Arnim und Clemens Brentano* (Stuttgart: J. G. Cotta'sche Buchhandlung, 1894), p. 135. Philip Allen ("Wilhelm Müller and the German Volkslied," *The Journal of Germanic Philology*, 2 [1899], 315) also argues that Müller's debt to Goethe has been overstated in the past. James Tate Hatfield's introduction to his critical edition of Müller's *Gedichte*, Deutsche Literaturdenkmäler, 137 (Berlin: B. Behr, 1906), p. 451, is responsible for the repeated assertion that the poems are directly related.

12. Heinrich Viehoff, *Goethes Gedichte erläutert und auf ihre Veranlassungen, Quellen und Vorbilder zurückgeführt*, 3rd ed. (Stuttgart; Carl Conradi, 1876), II, 244.

13. Hermann Baumgart, *Goethes lyrische Dichtung in ihrer Entwicklung und Bedeutung* (Heidelberg: Carl Winter, 1933), II, 39. Düntzer, *Goethe's lyrische Gedichte*, p. 371, also insists that a new lad is present in each poem and, therefore, the unity of the sequence is marginal.

14. Max Kommerell, *Gedanken über Gedichte* (Frankfurt am Main: Vittorio Klostermann, 1943), p. 378. No critical consensus concerning an appropriate interpretation of all four poems has emerged. Furthermore, although Goethe's fondness for the poems apparently remained strong throughout his lifetime, few critics have found them to be of real interest. Trunz did not include them in his selection for the *Hamburger Ausgabe*.

15. Karl August Kütner, *Charaktere teutscher Dichter und Prosaisten. Von Kaiser Karl dem Großen, bis aufs Jahr 1780* (Berlin: C. F. Voss und Sohn, 1781), pp. 533–35, quoted in August Langen, *Dialogisches Spiel. Formen und Wandlungen des Wechselgesangs in der*

deutschen Dichtung (1600–1900) (Heidelberg: Carl Winter Universitätsverlag, 1966), p. 114.

16. See Langen, *Dialogisches Spiel*, for a discussion of these poems in the tradition of the poetic dialogue, pp. 112–15.

17. The poet is most probably Ernst Wratislaw Wilhelm von Wobeser. Cf. Helen Mustard, *The Lyric Cycle in German Literature*, Columbia University German Studies, 17 (New York: King's Crown Press, 1946), p. 23.

18. *Teutscher Merkur*, 46 (1784), 32–33.

19. *Schillers Briefe*, ed. Fritz Jonas (Stuttgart: Deutsche Verlags-Anstalt), IV, 556.

20. Soret, *Conversations avec Goethe*, p. 137.

21. Soret, *Zehn Jahre bei Goethe*, p. 600.

22. There is a second report of Goethe's comments made by Eckermann in his memoir dated 1 December. Using Soret's memoirs and letters and rewriting these materials for Part III of his *Gespräche*, Eckermann revised Goethe's description of the "Müllerin" trilogy and made of it a paradigm for all lyric trilogies: "Diese Form, erwiederte Goethe, ist bei den Modernen überall selten. Es kommt darauf an, daß man einen Stoff finde, der sich naturgemäß in drei Partieen behandeln lasse, so daß in der ersten eine Art Exposition, in der zweiten eine Art Catastrophe, und in der dritten eine versöhnende Ausgleichung statt finde. In meinen Gedichten vom 'Junggesellen und der Müllerin' finden sich diese Erfordernisse beisammen, wiewohl ich damals, als ich sie schrieb, keineswegs daran dachte eine Trilogie zu machen." Soret, *Zehn Jahre bei Goethe*, p. 604. (Eckermann, p. 578.) This was not Goethe's intent.

23. Soret, *Conversations avec Goethe*, p. 140.

24. Soret, *Zehn Jahre bei Goethe*, p. 601.

25. Ibid.

26. Soret, *Conversations avec Goethe*, p. 140.

27. Christoph August Tiedge, *Das Echo oder Alexis und Ida. Ein Ciclus von Liedern* (Halle: Rengersche Buchhandlung, 1812), p. lv.

28. August Wilhelm Schlegel, *Geschichte der romantischen Literatur*, Kritische Schriften und Briefe, IV, ed. Edgar Lohner (Stuttgart: W. Kohlhammer Verlag, 1965), 182. [A. W. Schlegel, *Vorlesungen über schöne Litteratur und Kunst*, ed. Jakob Minor, Deutsche Litteraturdenkmäler des 18. und 19. Jahrhunderts, 17–19 (Heilbronn: Verlag von Gebr. Henninger, 1884), III, 203–4.] Schlegel's text from which I quote consists of lecture notes—some written out, some mere jottings and disconnected sentences.

29. Ibid., p. 183. (Minor III, 204.)

30. Ibid., p. 183. (Minor III, 205.)

31. Heinrich Viehoff, *Goethe's Gedichte erläutert und auf ihre Veranlassungen, Quellen und Vorbilder zurückgeführt* (Düsseldorf: Verlag der Bötticher'schen Buchhandlung, 1846), p. 112.

32. Johann August Lehmann, *Goethe's Liebe und Liebesgedichte* (Berlin: Allgemeine deutsche Verlags-Anstalt, 1852), p. 245–47.

33. Soret, *Conversations avec Goethe*, p. 138.

34. Soret, *Zehn Jahre bei Goethe*, p. 600.

35. Ibid., p. 604. (Eckermann, p. 578.)

36. Cf. HA 1, 676.

37. WA IV, 27, 302. Cf. Eckermann (10 November 1823), p. 53.

38. Soret, *Zehn Jahre bei Goethe*, p. 604. (Eckermann, p. 578.)

39. Eckermann (10 November 1823), p. 53.

40. This discussion of the "Trilogie der Leidenschaft" is restricted to questions of structural design. Recent interpretations of the poems include two studies by Valters Nollendorfs, "Goethe's 'Elegie.' A Nonbiographical Approach," *Germanic Review*, 40 (1965), 75–86, and "Time and Experience in Goethe's *Trilogie der Leidenschaft*," in *Husbanding the Golden Grain. Studies in Honor of Henry W. Nordmeyer*, ed. Luanne Frank and Emery George (Ann Arbor: The University of Michigan Press, 1973), pp. 223–37.

41. WA IV, 38, 11. Cf. HA 1, 705–6.

42. Soret, *Zehn Jahre bei Goethe*, p. 604. (Eckermann, p. 578.)

43. Soret, *Zehn Jahre bei Goethe*, p. 604. [Emphasis mine.]

44. Ibid., p. 604. [Emphasis mine.]

45. Ibid., p. 604. [Emphasis mine.]

46. Cf. WA IV, 23, 185–87; WA IV, 26, 312–13; quoted in HA 1, 702.

47. Mustard, *The Lyric Cycle*, p. 77.

48. Elizabeth Wilkinson, *Goethes Trilogie der Leidenschaft als Beitrag zur Frage der Katharsis*, Reihe der Vorträge und Schriften, 18 (Frankfurt am Main: Freies Deutsches Hochstift, 1957), p. 8.

49. Ibid., pp. 10–11.

50. Soret, *Conversations avec Goethe*, pp. 137–38.

51. Soret, *Zehn Jahre bei Goethe*, pp. 604–5. (Eckermann, p. 579.)

V. The Smaller Cycles of 1821

1. When the first lines that Goethe wrote in honor of Howard (lines 23–52 of the poem "Howards Ehrengedächtnis") were not understood and a letter from England requested clarification of their meaning, Goethe added the opening lines to the poem: "Nachdem ich aufmerksam geworden daß dem bewußten, Howards Ehrengedächtniß gewidmeten Gedicht wirklich etwas abgehe, um gerundet und verständlich zu seyn, entschloß ich mich, drey Strophen als Einleitung zu schreiben, wodurch zwar jenem Mangel wohl abgeholfen seyn möchte, doch füge um meine Absicht deutlich zu erklären, noch einige Bemerkungen hinzu" (WA IV, 50, 47). Goethe describes the writing of *Zu meinen Handzeichnungen* in related terms, and makes explicit reference to the third cycle we are considering, *Wilhelm Tischbeins Idyllen:* "Im Gefühl übrigens, daß diese Skizzen, selbst wie sie gegenwärtig vorgelegt werden, ihre Unzulänglichkeit nicht ganz überwinden können, habe ich ihnen kleine Gedichte hinzugefügt. . . . Ein Gleiches haben wir schon oben bei flüchtigen Zeichnungen eines Freundes gethan" (WA I, 49¹, 333).

2. See Gisbert Kranz, *Das Bildgedicht in Europa. Zur Theorie und Geschichte einer literarischen Gattung* (Paderborn: Ferdinand Schöningh, 1973) for a history of poetry written about the visual arts, and an index of poets and artists whose works have been linked.

3. "Zugleich vermelde daß ich so eben beschäftigt bin, meine sämmtlichen poetischen, literarischen und wissenschaftlichen Arbeiten, sowohl gedruckte als ungedruckte, übersichtlich aufzustellen, . . . damit der weitläufige und in manchem Sinne bedenkliche Nachlaß in's Klare komme" (WA IV, 36, 20–21). Cf. Dieter Welz, *Selbstsymbolik des alten Goethe*, Deutsche Studien, 17 (Meisenheim am Glan: Verlag Anton Hain, 1972), pp. 4–22.

4. " . . . ich habe auch hiezu, um die Poesie nicht zu Prose herabzuziehen . . . gewöhnlich geschwiegen" (WA I, 41¹, 329–30). See also WA IV, 12, 104–5.

5. Goethe wrote "Über die Entstehung der zweiundzwanzig Blätter meiner Handzeichnungen," (WA I, 49¹, 237–43) in June of 1821.

6. Erich Trunz designates the three poems a trilogy in the *Hamburger Ausgabe:* "Trilogie zu Howards Wolkenlehre," HA I, 349–51. See also Peter Eichhorn, *Idee und Erfahrung im Spätwerk Goethes*, Symposion, 35 (Freiburg: Verlag Karl Alber, 1971), p. 279 and Marianne Wünsch, *Der Strukturwandel in der Lyrik Goethes. Die systemimmanente Relation der Kategorien "Literatur" und "Realität": Probleme und Lösungen*, Studien zur Poetik und Geschichte der Literatur, 37 (Stuttgart: W. Kohlhammer Verlag, 1975), p. 281.

7. The dating of "Atmosphäre" is difficult. Although it may have been written in March of 1821, together with the opening lines of the "Ehrengedächtnis" [cf. *Goethe über seine Dichtungen*, Hans Gerhard Gräf ed. (Frankfurt: Rütten und Leoning, 1912), III, 2, 363], Goethe's comment on the "Einleitung" he has written is a specific reference to the first 22 lines of "Howards Ehrengedächtnis." Cf. WA III, 8, 32; WA IV, 50, 47.

8. Two informative essays on the Howard poems and Goethe's scientific investigations are Max Hans Schulze, "Goethe und die Meteorologie," *Wissenschaftliche Annalen*, 6 (1957), 101–16, and Albrecht Schöne, "Über Goethes Wolkenlehre," *Jahrbuch der Akademie der Wissenschaften in Göttingen* (1968), 26–48. See also Kurt Badt, "Goethes Wolkengedichte im Zusammenhang mit den Wolkenstudien Constables und anderer Zeitgenössischen Maler," *PEGS*, 20 (1951), 21–52, and Badt, *Wolkenbilder und Wolkengedichte der Romantik* (Berlin: Walter de Gruyter & Co., 1960). Badt's primary interest, however, is the relationship of Goethe's poems and meteorological studies to contemporary landscape painting.

9. Howard's original essay, entitled "On the Modifications of Clouds, and on the Principles of their Production, Suspension, and Destruction," was published in 1803.

10. Werner Keller, "Die antwortenden Gegenbilder. Eine Studie zu Goethes Wolkendichtung," *Jahrbuch des Freien Deutschen Hochstifts* (1968), 191–236.

11. "Die cirröse Wolkenform ist fortan Goethes sublimstes Sinnenbild für eine Geistigkeit, die aus dem Irdischen hinwegdrängt. Sie ist sein Aszensionssymbol, das offenbare Zeichen des Steigerunggesetzes, das einem Topos gleich in der Altersdichtung gehandhabt wird." Keller, "Die antwortenden Gegenbilder," p. 223. See also Schöne, "Über Goethes Wolkenlehre," pp. 31–32; Badt, "Goethes Wolkengedichte," p. 32; Keller, *Goethes dichterische Bildlichkeit*, pp. 25, 118, 153, 248, 289.

12. Hecker, 201.

13. Hecker, 1002.

14. Badt, *Wolkenbilder*, p. 25, links the progression of beasts with the conversation between Hamlet and Polonius, *Hamlet* (act 3, scene 2); Keller, "Die antwortenden Gegenbilder," p. 219, refers to *Antony and Cleopatra* (act 4, scene 14).

15. The opening recalls a similar confusion that is the occasion for one of Goethe's first nature poems, "Die Metamorphose der Pflanzen": "Dich verwirret, Geliebte, die tausendfältige Mischung, / Dieses Blumengewühls über den Garten umher." The patronizing tone of the earlier poem is gone, however, replaced by candor, for the confusion expressed is as much Goethe's own experience as it is the bewilderment of naïveté.

16. Hecker, 384.

17. Regine Otto, in the notes to volume 1 of the *Berliner Ausgabe* (Berlin: Aufbau-Verlag, 1965), I, 940, suggests that the reordering was a printing error. Elisabeth Reitmeyer, *Studien zum Problem der Gedichtsammlung mit eingehender Untersuchung der Gedichtsammlungen Goethes und Tiecks*, Sprache und Dichtung, 57 (Bern: Paul Haupt, 1935), pp. 118, 257, defends the sequence as published in the *Ausgabe letzter Hand*.

18. Erich Trunz is the notable exception. He has published an extensive essay on the cycle, critical notes, the correspondence between Goethe and Tischbein (1821–22), journal entries, and reproductions of the oil paintings and sketches thematically related to the original drawings, which are now lost. Trunz also provides bibliographical references to related works on Tischbein and the Goethe-Tischbein encounter in Rome. Erich Trunz, "Wilhelm Tischbeins Idyllen," in Erich Trunz, *Studien zu Goethes Alterswerken*, Goethezeit, 2 (Frankfurt: Athenäum Verlag, 1971), pp. 7–23; "Die 'Idyllen' in Goethes und Tischbeins Briefwechsel und Tagebüchern," ibid., pp. 24–34; "Über Goethes Verse und Prosa zu Tischbeins Idyllen," ibid., pp. 35–74. The cycle is also discussed in Eva Bosshardt, *Goethes späte Landschaftslyrik*, Diss. Zürich, 1962 (Zürich: Verlag Lüssi & Co., 1962), pp. 65–109; in Emil Staiger, *Goethe*, III (Zürich: Atlantis Verlag, 1959), pp. 220–28; in Max Kommerell, *Gedanken über Gedichte* (Frankfurt am Main: Vittorio Klostermann, 1943), pp. 114–17

19. Cf. WA I, 49[1], 333.

20. Trunz, "Über Goethes Verse und Prosa zu Tischbeins Idyllen," pp. 35–38.

21. Ibid., p. 41.

22. Cf. Trunz, "Über Goethes Verse und Prosa zu Tischbeins Idyllen," p. 54.

23. Trunz, "Über Goethes Verse und Prosa zu Tischbeins Idyllen," p. 47.

24. The setting is a favored backdrop for eighteenth-century idylls. Cf. the Goethe

family portrait painted in 1763 by Johann Konrad Seekatz; "Der Wanderer" (WA I, 2, 170–77).

25. "Idyl(l)," *Princeton Encyclopedia of Poetry and Poetics*, ed. Alex Preminger, enlarged ed. (Princeton: Princeton University Press, 1974), p. 362.

26. For additional references to "Gott-Natur" see Trunz, HA I, 679.

27. Bosshardt, *Goethes späte Landschaftslyrik*, p. 80.

28. Goethe repeatedly expressed the innermost principle of creative nature in the metaphor of weaving. Cf. Keller, *Goethes dichterische Bildlichkeit*, pp. 193–206.

29. Bosshardt notes that the second couplet in poem 20 is a slight reworking of some lines Tischbein himself wrote at the bottom of an earlier sketch: "Sind die Striche nicht alle deutlich zu lesen, / So sind sie doch der erste Gedanke gewesen." Bosshardt, *Goethes späte Landschaftslyrik*, 97.

30. It is not surprising that Trunz published only part of the cycle in the *Hamburger Ausgabe*: poems 1, 2, 3, 4, 8, 9, 15. See HA 1, 374–76.

31. Reproductions of the six etchings are available in Ludwig Münz, *Goethes Zeichnungen und Radierungen* (Wien: Österreichische Staatsdruckerei, 1949), plates 158–63. They are also reprinted in the appendix to Bosshardt, *Goethes späte Landschaftslyrik*, plates 1–6. The original sketches are not all extant. In the *Corpus der Goethe Zeichnungen*, ed. Gerhard Femmel (Leipzig: Veb. E. A. Seemann Buch- und Kunstverlag, 1958–73) the sketches for 4, 5, and 6 (vol. IVa, no. 47; vol. VIa, no. 125; vol. IVa, no. 46) and sketches related to 2 and 3 (vol. IVa, nos. 267 and 268; vol. IVa, no. 264) are reproduced. The original sketch for 1 is unknown. The sketches for 4 and 5 are also available in the appendix to Bosshardt, plates 4a and 5a.

32. WA III, 8, 68; WA III, 8, 73.

33. The *Kunst und Altertum* text is available in WA I, 49[1], 331–36. The poems were placed under the rubric "Kunst" in the *Ausgabe letzter Hand*. WA I, 3, 131–34.

34. Bosshardt, in *Goethes späte Landschaftslyrik*, disagrees and states that the poems and the pictures are virtually incomprehensible apart from one another: "Die Gedichte sind ohne die zugehörigen Bilder kaum, diese nicht ohne jene zu verstehen" (p. 45).

35. WA IV, 35, 124; WA III, 8, 127.

36. Willoughby has traced this same opposition, expressed in the metaphors of the wanderer and the hut, through Goethe's works. Leonard Willoughby, "The Image of the Wanderer and the Hut in Goethe's Poetry," *Études Germaniques*, 6 (1951), 207–19.

37. Ibid., p. 211.

38. In the *Corpus der Goethe Zeichnungen*, IVa, p. 22, the setting is not identified. The sketch is dated around 1810. Bosshardt, *Goethes späte Landschaftslyrik* considers the determination of the biographical occasion for each picture and poem to be a primary interpretive task: "Die Frage nach den biographischen Hintergründen und Gegebenheiten drängt sich zudem bei jedem dieser Gedichte und bei jeder Zeichnung unumgänglich auf" (p. 45). She is, however, able to make few definitive identifications. She attempts to link "Geheimster Wohnsitz" with the Allstedt castle, but admits that the identification is most problematic. See pp. 52–58.

VI. *Chinesisch-deutsche Jahres- und Tageszeiten*

1. Cf. WA IV, 42, 189.

2. WA I, 41[2], 272–75. Cf. also WA I, 42[1], 230–34; WA I, 5[1], 50–51; WA I, 5[2], 245–46.

3. For a complete listing and description of these works see Christine Wagner-Dittmar, "Goethe und die chinesische Literatur," in *Studien zu Goethes Alterswerken*, ed. Erich Trunz, Goethezeit, 2 (Frankfurt am Main: Athenäum Verlag, 1971), pp. 152–65. See also Hideo Fukuda, "Über Goethes letzten Gedichtzyklus 'Chinesische-deutsche Jahresund Tageszeiten,'" *Doitsu Bungaku* (Die deutsche Literatur) 22 (1955), 54–56.

4. Most prominent among these studies is Woldemar Freiherr von Biedermann, "Chinesisch-deutsche Jahres- und Tageszeiten," *Goethe-Forschungen*, Neue Folge

(Leipzig: F. W. V. Biedermann, 1886), pp. 426–46. A much later work, Elizabeth Selden, "China in German Poetry from 1773–1833," *University of California Publications in Modern Philology*, 25 (1942), 141–316, attempts to locate source material for Goethe's poems in *Chinese Courtship* (pp. 195–207). See also Wagner-Dittmar, "Goethe und die chinesische Literatur," pp. 122–26, for a survey of the critical literature.

5. Erich Trunz, "Goethes späte Lyrik," *DVJS* 23 (1949), 324. Fukuda, "Über Goethes letzten Gedichtzyklus," p. 58. Wagner-Dittmar, "Goethe und die chinesische Literatur," pp. 125–26.

6. Fukuda, "Über Goethes letzten Gedichtzyklus." Yang En-Lin, "Goethes 'Chinesisch-deutsche Jahres- und Tageszeiten,'" *Goethe Jahrbuch* 89 (1972), 154–88.

7. Fukuda, "Über Goethe letzten Gedichtzyklus," p. 56; Wagner-Dittmar, "Goethe und die chinesische Literatur," pp. 152–88.

8. Eckermann (31 January 1827), p. 173.

9. Representative are the comments made by Wagner-Dittmar, "Goethe und die chinesische Literatur." In reference to the poems in *Iu Kiao Li ou les deux cousines*, tr. Jean-Pierre-Abel Rémusat, she states: "Sie machen einen sehr blaßen und farblosen Eindruck, ohne den Zauber und die Atmosphäre, die die chinesischen Gedichte sonst auszeichnen" (p. 160). The poems in *Hua Ts'ien Ki (Chinese Courtship)* do not fare any better: "Es sind durchaus konventionell zu nennende Verse über das Spiel der Weidenzweige auf der Wasserfläche des Fischteichs" (p. 162).

10. Peter Perring Thoms, trans., *Chinese Courtship* (London: Parbury, Allen, and Kingsbury, 1824), p. vii.

11. Zelter, III, 184.

12. Zelter, III, 189.

13. Trunz, HA 1, 714.

14. Cf. Trunz, HA 8, 605. Erhard Bahr, *Die Ironie im Spätwerk Goethes " . . . diese sehr ernsten Scherze . . . "*. *Studien zum 'West-östlichen Divan,' zu den 'Wanderjahren' und zu 'Faust II'* (Berlin: Erich Schmidt Verlag, 1972), p. 98.

15. Cf. Wagner-Dittmar, "Goethe und die chinesische Literatur," pp. 125, 137.

16. Heinrich Viehoff, *Goethes Gedichte erläutert auf ihre Veranlassungen, Quellen und Vorbilder zurückgeführt*, 3rd ed. (Stuttgart: Carl Conradi, 1876), II, 386.

17. A notable exception to this general neglect is Rilke's high interest in the poems: "Läßt sich irgendwo nachsehen und können Sie mirs kurz andeuten, welche Stelle jene 'Deutsch-Chinesischen Jahrzeiten' (woher der Title?) in Goethes (offenbar spätester?) Produktion einnehmen? Es kommen die verschiedensten Elemente darin zusammen, will mir scheinen, die bedeutendste lyrische Ergreifung, wie sie seine mächtigsten Zeilen besitzen, und daneben, ja mitten drin, ein Spielend-Dekoratives . . ." Rainer Marie Rilke, *Briefe*, ed. Ruth Sieber-Rilke and Karl Altheim (Wiesbaden: Insel Verlag, 1950), I, 479. Cf. Trunz, HA 1, 717.

18. Karl Viëtor, "Goethes Altersgedichte," *Euphorion* 33 (1932), 105–52. Revised in Karl Viëtor, *Geist und Form* (Bern: Francke, 1952), pp. 144–93.

19. Max Kommerell, *Gedanken über Gedichte* (Frankfurt am Main: Vittorio Klostermann, 1943).

20. Erich Trunz, "Goethes späte Lyrik," 409–32. "Alterslyrik" and "Altersstil" in *Goethe Handbuch. Goethe, seine Welt und Zeit in Werk und Wirkung*, ed. Alfred Zastrau, 2d rev. ed. (Stuttgart: J. B. Metzlersche Verlagsbuchhandlung, 1961), I, 169–78 and 178–88. "Goethes lyrische Kurzgedichte," *Goethe*, 26 (1964), 1–37.

21. Wolfgang Preisendanz, "Goethes 'Chinesisch-deutsche Jahres- und Tageszeiten,'" *Jahrbuch der deutschen Schiller Gesellschaft*, 8 (1964), 137–52.

22. Yang En-Lin, "Goethes 'Chinesisch-deutsche Jahres- und Tageszeiten.'"

23. Friedrich Burkhardt, "Goethes 'Chinesisch-deutsche Jahres- und Tageszeiten,'" *Jahrbuch der deutschen Schiller Gesellschaft*, 13 (1969), 180–95.

24. Trunz (HA I, 715) prefers two variants (the first taken from a manuscript, the second from the *Musenalmanach* printing) to the *Nachlaß* text: (III, 5) "lichte Schleier"

for "leichte Schleier" and (VIII, 9) "Nun im östlichen Bereiche" to "Nun am östlichen Bereiche." Preisendanz supports both of these emendations with a detailed argument. Preisendanz, "Goethes 'Chinesisch-deutsche Jahres- und Tageszeiten,'" p. 150.

25. Paul Böckmann, "Die zyklische Einheit der Faustdichtung," *Formensprache. Studien zur Literarästhetik und Dichtungsinterpretation* (Hamburg: Hoffmann und Campe Verlag, 1966), p. 199.

26. Most critics do not attempt a comprehensive interpretation of the cycle, but are content to discuss each poem in turn, noting obvious links. Burkhardt is a notable exception.

27. Burkhardt, "Goethes 'Chinesisch-deutsche Jahres- und Tageszeiten,'" p. 181.

28. Frédéric Soret, *Conversations avec Goethe*, ed. A. Robinet de Cléry (Paris: Editions Montaigne, 1931), p. 137.

29. Cf. Faust II, V (Palast); Eichendorff, "Winterlied"; Friedrich Rückert, "Herbsthauch"; Johannes Schlaf, "Spätherbst."

30. Trunz, HA 1, 715.

31. Burkhardt, "Goethes 'Chinesisch-deutsche Jahres- und Tageszeiten,'" p. 184. According to Burkhardt, it is in poems II–XI, the poems that record the seasonal changes from spring to fall in the private garden world, that the motif of time is developed, and in poems I and XII–XIV the motif of society. The key to Burkhardt's understanding of the cycle and his final linking of these two motifs is the concept of "Steigerung." It is the triumph in the garden world of timelessness over time that the cycle records. Timelessness proves itself most timely ("das Zeitlose [erweist sich] als das wirklich Zeitgemäße", p. 194) and the rupture between the poet and society that began the cycle is replaced in the end by a new and highter unity. Accordingly, Burkhardt suggests the figure of a spiral to describe the cycle's organization (pp. 191–94).

32. Ibid., p. 181.

33. Preisendanz, "Goethes 'Chinesisch-deutsche Jahres- und Tageszeiten,'" p. 139.

34. Zelter, III, 203.

35. See Hans-Egon Hass, "West-östlicher Divan: Im Gegenwärtigen Vergangnes," in *Die deutsche Lyrik I. Form und Geschichte*, ed. Benno von Wiese (Düsseldorf: August Bagel Verlag, 1962), pp. 290–317, for a discussion of the formula "Ros' und Lilie." Cf. Burkhardt, "Goethes 'Chinesisch-deutsche Jahres- und Tageszeiten,'" p. 187.

36. The image is familiar. Cf. *Tasso* (I, 1; I, 4; II, 1), Faust 4690–94. See Peter Schmidt, *Goethes Farbensymbolik. Untersuchungen zu Verwendung und Bedeutung der Farben in den Dichtungen und Schriften Goethes*, Philologische Studien und Quellen, 26 (Berlin: Erich Schmidt Verlag, 1965), p. 135.

37. The text of lines 7–8 underwent multiple revisions. See WA I, 52, 78.

38. Trunz makes reference to *Faust* 9224. More central are the opening lines of *Faust II*, "Anmutige Gegend." See also Preisendanz, "Goethes 'Chinesisch-deutsche Jahres- und Tageszeiten,'" p. 143.

39. Eckermann (31 January 1827), p. 172.

40. Eckermann (14 January 1827), p. 152.

41. Hecker, 314.

42. See Heinrich Henel, "Goethe und die Naturwissenschaft," *JEGP*, 48 (1949), 520.

43. Hecker, 1345. Cf. Werner Keller, *Goethes dichterische Bildlichkeit. Eine Grundlegung* (München: Wilhelm Fink Verlag, 1972), pp. 224–29.

44. Keller, *Goethes dichterische Bildlichkeit*, p. 227.

45. Ibid., p. 227.

46. Cf. also "Glaube ist Liebe zum Unsichtbaren, Vertrauen aufs Unmögliche, Unwahrscheinliche." Hecker, 815.

47. Trunz, HA 1, 715 explains that "graues Netz" means a theory. He adduces *Faust* 2038.

48. Hecker, 183.

49. Hecker, 1137.

50. Hecker, 1136. Cf. Keller, *Goethes dichterische Bildlichkeit*, p. 228.

51. Goethe's own love of Ulrike von Levetzow that Preisendanz asserts the poems express is significant only within this organizing framework of the passing seasons and hours. The lovers alone are no more the essence of the cycle than the single peacock or the narcissus blossoms. Cf. Preisendanz, "Goethes 'Chinesisch-deutsche Jahres- und Tageszeiten,'" pp. 147–52.

52. "Denn das Einfache verbirgt sich im Mannigfaltigen, und da ists, wo bei mir der Glaube eintritt, der nicht der Anfang, sondern das Ende alles Wissens ist" (WA II, 5, 1). Cf. Karl Viëtor, "Goethes Altersgedichte," in *Geist und Form*, p. 182.

53. WA II, 5¹, 144–45. Cf. Schmidt, *Goethes Farbensymbolik*, pp. 157–58.

54. Goethe obtained his basic insights through intuition, the contemplation of specific objects or events which acquired symbolic (i.e., universal) significance for him. But he also tried hard to express these insights in discursive language and demonstrate their validity as scientific laws. His *Metamorphose* and his *Farbenlehre* are the outstanding examples. Cf. Goethe's description in the *Farbenlehre* of the "höhere Regeln und Gesetze, die sich aber nicht durch Worte und Hypothesen dem Verstande, sondern gleichfalls durch Phänomene dem Anschauen offenbaren" (WA II, 1, 72).

VII. Conclusion

1. Johann Christoph Adelung, *Versuch eines vollständigen grammatisch-kritischen Wörterbuchs der hochdeutschen Mundart mit beständiger Vergleichung der übrigen Mundarten, besonders aber der oberdeutschen* (Leipzig: Bernhard Christoph Breitkopf und Sohn, 1774). Johann Christoph Adelung, Dietrich Wilhelm Soltau, and Franz Schönberger, *Grammatisch-kritisches Wörterbuch der Hochdeutschen Mundart* (Wien: B. Ph. Bauer, 1811).

2. Joachim Heinrich Campe, *Wörterbuch zur Erklärung und Verdeutschung der unserer Sprache aufgedrungen fremden Ausdrücke. Ein Ergänzungsband zu Adelung's und Campe's Wörterbüchern* (Braunschweig: In der Schulbuchhandlung, 1813), p. 243.

3. Similarly Theodor Heinsius, *Volksthümliches Wörterbuch der deutschen Sprache* (Hannover: Hansche Hofbuchhandlung, 1818), p. 701, restricts the concept to the brief entry: "Zeitkreis oder Zeitbegriff."

4. Jacob Grimm and Wilhelm Grimm, "Zyklus," *Deutsches Wörterbuch* (Leipzig: S. Hirzel, 1954), XXXII, 1452.

5. "Kyklos," *Paulys Realencyclopädie der classischen Altertumswissenschaft*, ed. George Wissowa and Wilhelm Kroll, Neue Bearbeitung (Stuttgart: Alfred Druckenmüller Verlag, 1922), XI/2, 2348.

6. "Epic Cycle," *The Oxford Companion to Classical Literature*, ed. Paul Harvey (1937; rpt. Oxford: Clarendon Press, 1959), p. 161.

7. Johann Gottfried Herder, "Homer ein Günstling der Zeit," quoted in Friedrich Gottlieb Welcker, *Der epische Cyclus oder die homerischen Dichter*. 2d ed. (Bonn: Eduard Weber, 1865), p. 408. [Emphasis mine.]

8. Friedrich Schlegel, *Geschichte der Poesie der Griechen und Römer*, quoted in Welcker, *Der epische Cyclus*, p. 408. [Emphasis mine.]

9. Friedrich Creuzer, *Die historische Kunst der Griechen in ihrer Entstehung und Fortbildung, Deutsche Schriften*, III, 1 (Leipzig: Carl Wilhelm Leske, 1845), 22. [Emphasis mine.]

10. *Göttingische Anzeigen von Gelehrten Sachen* (1827), quoted in Welcker, *Der epische Cyclus*, p. vii. [Emphasis mine.]

11. Welcker, *Der epische Cyclus*, p. 410. [Emphasis mine.]

12. Ibid., p. 13.

13. Ibid., p. 312.

14. Ibid., p. 313.

15. Cf. Paul Fischer, *Goethe-Wortschatz* (Leipzig: Emil Rohmkopf, 1929), p. 905.

16. Cf. WA IV, 22, 508.

17. Eckermann (1 December 1831), p. 578.

18. HA 2, 551.

19. HA 2, 551.

20. Friedrich Gundolf, *Goethe* (Berlin: Georg Bondi, 1916), p. 442.

21. Ibid., p. 441.

22. Both Wilhelm Müller and Heine by 1823–24 designated their multi-membered lyric compositions as cycles, the first consistent repetition and application of the term to lyric poetry that I have found. Cf. *Wilhelm Müller als Kritiker und Erzähler*, ed. Heinrich Lohre (Leipzig: F. A. Brockhaus, 1927), p. 234 (20 October 1824), and Heinrich Heine, *Säkularausgabe. Werke. Briefe. Lebenszeugnisse,* ed. Fritz Eisner (Berlin: Akademie Verlag, 1970), XX, 63, 151, 153. The earliest example I have found of "Cyklus" being used explicitly in the title of a collection of poems is (Christian) Friedrich Rassmann, *Münsterischer Epigrammen-Cyklus. Ein Neujahrsgeschenk. 1809.* (Essen, 1810). This volume was in Goethe's library. We have also noted Tiedge's reference to his collection of pastoral poems as a "Ciclus" and his use of the word in the subtitle of his work. Jean Paul uses "Cyklus" as the heading for each sub-division in *Titan* (published 1800–1803), a rather eclectic and non-lyric appropriation.

23. Joachim Müller," "Das zyklische Prinzip in der Lyrik," *Germanisch-Romanische Monatsschrift,* 20 (1932), 1–20. Müller's definition is used, with modification by Wolfgang Kayser, *Das sprachliche Kunstwerk* (Bern: Francke Verlag, 1948), pp. 168–69.

24. Müller, "Das zyklische Prinzip," p. 20.

Select Bibliography

PRIMARY SOURCES

Arnim, Achim von. *Achim von Arnim und Clemens Brentano*. Ed. Reinhold Steig. Stuttgart: J. G. Cotta'sche Buchhandlung, 1894.

Arnim, Bettina von. *Bettinas Leben und Briefwechsel mit Goethe, auf Grund ihres handschriftlichen Nachlasses*. Ed. Reinhold Steig. Rev. Fritz Bergemann. Leipzig: Insel Verlag, 1927.

Blankenburg, Christian Friedrich von. *Litterarische Zusätze zu Johann George Sulzers allgemeiner Theorie der schönen Künste, in einzelnen, nach alphabetischer Ordnung der Kunstwörter auf einander folgenden Artikeln abgehandelt*. Leipzig: Weidmann'sche Buchhandlung, 1798.

Bürger, Gottfried August. *Gedichte*. Göttingen: J. C. Dietrich, 1789.

Creuzer, Georg Friedrich. *Die historische Kunst der Griechen in ihrer Entstehung und Fortbildung. Deutsche Schriften*, III. 2 vols. Leipzig: Carl Wilhelm Leske, 1845.

Eckermann, Johann Peter. *Gespräche mit Goethe in den letzten Jahren seines Lebens*. Ed. Heinrich Hubert Houben. Wiesbaden: Brockhaus, 1959.

Göckingk, Leopold Friedrich Günther von. *Lieder zweier Liebenden*. Leipzig: Weidmanns Erben & Reich, 1777.

Goethe, Johann Wolfgang von. *Corpus der Goethe Zeichnungen*. Ed. Gerhard Femmel. 7 vols. in 10. Leipzig: Veb. E. A. Seemann Buch- und Kunstverlag, 1958–73.

———. *Der Briefwechsel zwischen Goethe und Knebel*. Ed. Gottschalk Eduard Guhrauer. Leipzig: F. A. Brockhaus, 1851.

———. *Der Briefwechsel zwischen Goethe und Zelter*. Ed. Max Hecker. 4 vols. 1913–18; rpt. Bern: Herbert Lang, 1970.

———. *Der Briefwechsel zwischen Schiller und Goethe*. Ed. Emil Staiger. Frankfurt am Main: Insel Verlag, 1966.

———. *Goethe über seine Dichtungen*. Ed. Hans Gerhard Gräf. 3 parts in 9 vols. Frankfurt am Main: Rütten & Loening, 1901–14.

———. *Goethe und die Romantik. Briefe mit Erläuterungen I*. Ed. Carl Schüddekopf and Oskar Walzel. Schriften der Goethe-Gesellschaft, 13. Weimar: Verlag der Goethe-Gesellschaft, 1898.

———. *Goethes Werke*. Herausgegeben im Auftrag der Großherzogin Sophie von Sachsen, Abt. I–IV. 133 vols. in 143. Weimar: Hermann Böhlaus Nachfolger, 1887–1919.

———. *Goethes Werke*. Hamburger Ausgabe in 14 vols. Hamburg: Christian Wegner Verlag, 1948–64.

————. *Maximen und Reflexionen*. Ed. Max Hecker. Schriften der Goethe-Gesellschaft, 21. Weimar: Verlag der Goethe-Gesellschaft, 1907.

Heine, Heinrich. *Säkularausgabe. Werke. Briefe. Lebenszeugnisse.* Ed. Fritz Eisner. Berlin: Akademie Verlag. 1970– .

Herder, Johann Gottfried. *Von und an Herder*. Ed. Heinrich Düntzer and Ferdinand Gottfried Herder. 3 vols. Leipzig: Dyk'sche Buchhandlung, 1862.

Humboldt, Wilhelm von. *Humboldts Briefe an Karl Gustav von Brinkmann*. Ed. Albert Leitzmann. Leipzig: K. W. Hiersemann, 1939.

Müller, Wilhelm. *Gedichte. Vollständige kritische Ausgabe*. Ed. James Tate Hatfield. Deutsche Literaturdenkmäler, 137. Berlin: B. Behr, 1906.

————. *Wilhelm Müller als Kritiker und Erzähler*. Ed. Heinrich Lohre. Leipzig: F. A. Brockhaus, 1927.

Paisiello, Giovanni. *La Molinara ossia L'amor contrastato*. Ed. Aldo Rocchi. Firenze: Teatro Comunale, 1962.

Rassmann, Friedrich. *Münsterischer Epigrammen-Cyklus. Ein Neujahrsgeschenk. 1809*. Essen: n.p., 1810.

Schiller, Friedrich. *Werke. National Ausgabe*. Weimar: Hermann Böhlaus Nachfolger, 1943– .

————. *Schillers Briefe*. Ed. Fritz Jonas. Stuttgart: Deutsche Verlags-Anstalt, 1892–96.

————. *Schillers Briefwechsel mit Körner*. 4 vols. Leipzig: Verlag von Veit & Comp., 1859.

Schlegel, August Wilhelm. *Blumensträuße italienischer, spanischer und portugiesischer Poesie*. Berlin: Realschulbuchhandlung, 1804.

————. *Gedichte*. Tübingen: Cotta'sche Buchhandlung, 1800.

————. *Geschichte der klassischen Literatur*. Kritische Schriften und Briefe III. Ed. Edgar Lohner. Stuttgart: W. Kohlhammer Verlag, 1964.

————. *Geschichte der romantischen Literatur*. Kritische Schriften und Briefe IV. Ed. Edgar Lohner. Stuttgart: W. Kohlhammer Verlag, 1962.

————. *Sämmtliche Werke*. Ed. Eduard Böcking. 12 vols. in 6. Leipzig: Weidmann'sche Buchhandlung, 1846–47.

————. *Vorlesungen über schöne Litteratur und Kunst*. Ed. Jakob Minor. 3 vols. Deutsche Litteraturdenkmäler des 18. und 19. Jahrhunderts, 17–19. Heilbronn: Verlag von Gebr. Henninger, 1884.

Schlegel, Friedrich. *Friedrich Schlegels Briefe an seinen Bruder August Wilhelm*. Ed. Oskar Walzel. Berlin: Speyer & Peters, 1890.

————. *Kritische Ausgabe*. Ed. Ernst Behler. München: Verlag Ferdinand Schöningh, 1958– .

Schmidt, Klamer. *Phantasien nach Petrarka's Manier*. Halberstadt: Meyer, 1772.

Soret, Frédéric. *Conversations avec Goethe*. Ed. A. Robinet de Cléry. Paris: Editions Montaigne, 1931.

————. *Zehn Jahre bei Goethe. Erinnerungen an Weimars klassische Zeit. 1822–32*. Ed. and trans. Heinrich Hubert Houben. Leipzig: F. A. Brockhaus, 1929.

Sulzer, Johann George. *Allgemeine Theorie der schönen Künste*. Leipzig: M. G. Weidemann, 1771.

Tiedge, Christoph August. *Das Echo und Ida. Ein Ciclus von Liedern*. Halle: Rengersche Buchhandlung, 1812.

Welcker, Friedrich Gottlieb. *Der epische Cyclus oder die homerischen Dichter.* 2d ed. Bonn: Eduard Weber, 1865.

Werner, Zacharias. *Poetische Werke.* 15 vols. Grimma: Verlags Comptoir, 1840.

Wobeser, Ernst Wratislaw Wilhelm von. "Ein Roman in fünf Liedern von W—r." *Teutscher Merkur*, 46 (1784), 32–41.

SECONDARY SOURCES

General Works

Kayser, Wolfgang. *Das sprachliche Kunstwerk. Eine Einführung in die Literaturwissenschaft.* Bern: Francke Verlag, 1948.

———. *Geschichte der deutschen Ballade.* Berlin: Junker & Dünnhaupt Verlag, 1936.

Kettler, Hans Kühnert. *Baroque Tradition in the Literature of the German Enlightenment. 1700–1750.* Cambridge: W. Heffer & Sons Ltd., 1943.

Killy, Walther. *Wandlungen des lyrischen Bildes.* Göttingen: Vandenhoeck & Ruprecht, 1956.

Langen, August. *Dialogisches Spiel. Formen und Wandlungen des Wechselgesangs in der deutschen Dichtung (1600–1900).* Annales Universitatis Saraviensis. Reihe: Philosophische Fakultät, 5. Heidelberg: Carl Winter Universitätsverlag, 1966.

Sengle, Friedrich. *Biedermeierzeit. Deutsche Literatur im Spannungsfeld zwischen Restauration und Revolution (1815–1848).* Vols. I–II. Stuttgart: Metzler, 1971–1972.

Smith, Barbara Herrnstein. *Poetic Closure: A Study of How Poems End.* Chicago: University of Chicago Press, 1968.

Steinmetz, Horst. *Trilogie. Entstehung und Struktur einer Großform des deutschen Dramas nach 1800.* Probleme der Dichtung, 11. Heidelberg: Carl Winter Verlag, 1968.

Studies of the Lyric Cycle

Allen, Philip. "Wilhelm Müller and the German Volkslied." *The Journal of Germanic Philology*, 2 (1899), 283–322; 3 (1901), 35–91, 431–91.

Cottrell, Alan. *Wilhelm Müller's Lyrical Song-Cycles. Interpretations and Texts.* University of North Carolina Studies in the Germanic Languages and Literatures, 66. Chapel Hill: The University of North Carolina Press, 1970.

Friedländer, Max. "Die Entstehung der Müllerlieder." *Deutsche Rundschau*, 73 (1892–93), 301–7.

Hake, Bruno. "Wilhelm Müller. Sein Leben und Denken." Diss. Berlin, 1908.

Heinze, Richard. "Der Zyklus der Römeroden." *Vom Geist des Römertums. Ausgewählte Aufsätze.* Ed. Erich Burck. 3rd ed. 1938; rpt. Darmstadt: Wissenschaftliche Buchgesellschaft, 1960, pp. 190–204.

Just, Klaus Günther. "Wilhelm Müllers Liederzyklen 'Die schöne Müllerin' und 'Die Winterreise,'" *Zeitschrift für deutsche Philologie*, 83 (1964), 452–71.

Müller, Joachim. "Das zyklische Prinzip in der Lyrik." *Germanisch-Romanische Monatsschrift*, 20 (1932), 1–20.

Mustard, Helen. *The Lyric Cycle in German Literature*. Columbia University Germanic Studies, 17. New York: King's Crown Press, 1946.

Orrey, Leslie. "The Songs." *The Beethoven Reader*. Ed. Denis Arnold and Nigel Fortune. New York: W. W. Norton & Co., 1971; pp. 411–39.

Peake, Luise E. "A Preliminary Inquiry into the Beginnings of the Romantic Song Cycle and the Nature of an Art Form." Diss. Columbia, 1968.

Simons, Gabriel. "Die zyklische Kunst im Jugendwerk Stefan Georges: ihre Voraussetzungen in der Zeit und ihre allgemeinen ästhetischen Bedingungen." Diss. Köln, 1965.

Spitteler, Carl. "Über den Wert zyklischer Sammlung." *Gesammelte Werke*. Zürich: Artemis Verlag, 1947, VII, 129–32.

Goethe Literature

GENERAL

Bahr, Ehrhard. *Die Ironie im Spätwerk Goethes: ". . . diese sehr ernsten Scherze . . .". Studien zum 'West-östlichen Divan,' zu den Wanderjahren und zu Faust II*. Berlin: Erich Schmidt Verlag, 1972.

Barnes, Bertram. *Goethe's Knowledge of French Literature*. Oxford: Clarendon Press, 1937.

Barth, Ilse-Marie. *Literarisches Weimar. Kultur. Literatur. Sozialstruktur im 16.– 20. Jahrhundert*. Sammlung Metzler, 93. Stuttgart: J. B. Metzlersche Verlagsbuchhandlung, 1971.

Baumgart, Hermann. *Goethes lyrische Dichtung in ihrer Entwicklung und Bedeutung*. 3 vols. Heidelberg: Carl Winter, 1931–39.

Böckmann, Paul. "Die zyklische Einheit der Faustdichtung." *Formensprache. Studien zur Literarästhetik und Dichtungsinterpretation*. Hamburg: Hoffmann & Campe Verlag, 1966.

Düntzer, Heinrich. *Goethe's lyrische Gedichte*. 2d ed. Leipzig: E. Wartig, 1874.

Eichhorn, Peter. *Idee und Erfahrung im Spätwerk Goethes*. Symposion, 35. Freiburg: Verlag Karl Alber, 1971.

Fairley, Barker. *Goethe as Revealed in His Poetry*. New York: Ungar, 1963.

Fambach, Oscar. *Das große Jahrzehnt in der Kritik seiner Zeit. Ein Jahrhundert deutscher Literaturkritik (1750–1850)*, IV. Berlin: Akademie Verlag, 1958.

———. *Schiller und sein Kreis in der Kritik ihrer Zeit. Ein Jahrhundert deutscher Literaturkritik (1750–1850)*, II. Berlin: Akademie Verlag, 1957.

Fischer, Paul. *Goethe-Wortschatz*. Leipzig: Emil Rohmkopf Verlag, 1929.

Friedenthal, Richard. *Goethe. Sein Leben und seine Zeit*. München: R. Piper & Co. Verlag, 1963.

Fuchs, Albert. "Goethe und die französische Literatur." *Goethe Studien*. Berlin: Walter de Gruyter & Co., 1968, pp. 156–77.

Gundolf, Friedrich. *Goethe*. Berlin: Georg Bondi, 1916.

Hagen, Waltraud. *Die Drucke von Goethes Werken*. Berlin: Akademie Verlag, 1971.

Hammer, Carl, Jr. "Goethe's Silence Concerning Ronsard." *Modern Language Notes*, 75 (1960), 697–98.

Hatfield, Henry. *Goethe. A Critical Introduction.* Cambridge: Harvard University Press, 1964.

Henel, Heinrich. "Goethe und die Naturwissenschaft." *Journal of English and Germanic Philology*, 48 (1949), 507–32.

Jaszi, Andrew. *Entzweiung und Vereinigung. Goethes symbolische Weltanschauung.* Poesis und Wissenschaft, 24. Heidelberg: Lothar Stiehm Verlag, 1973.

Jessen, Myra Richard. *Goethe als Kritiker der Lyrik. Beiträge zu seiner Ästhetik und seiner Theorie.* Diss. Bryn Mawr, 1932. Tübingen: privately printed, 1932.

Jolles, Matthijs. *Goethes Kunstanschauung.* Bern: Francke Verlag, 1957.

Keller, Werner. *Goethes dichterische Bildlichkeit. Eine Grundlegung.* München: Wilhelm Fink Verlag, 1972.

Kimura, Naoji. *Goethes Wortgebrauch zur Dichtungstheorie im Briefwechsel mit Schiller und den Gesprächen mit Eckermann.* München: Max Hueber Verlag, 1965.

Kommerell, Max. *Gedanken über Gedichte.* Frankfurt am Main: Vittorio Klostermann, 1943.

Korff, Hermann August. *Goethe im Bildwandel seiner Lyrik.* 2 vols. Leipzig: Koehler & Amelang, 1958.

Kruse, Georg Richard. *Zelter.* Musiker-Biographien, 34. Reclams Universal Bibliothek, 5815. Leipzig: P. Reclam, 1915.

Lehmann, Johann August. *Goethe's Liebe und Liebesgedichte.* Berlin: Allgemeine deutsche Verlags-Anstalt, 1852.

Leitzmann, Albert. *Die Quellen von Schillers und Goethes Balladen.* Kleine Texte für theologische und philologische Vorlesungen und Übungen, 73. Bonn: A. Marcus und E. Weber's Verlag, 1911.

Leppmann, Wolfgang. *The German Image of Goethe.* Oxford: Oxford University Press, 1961.

Müller, Joachim. *Der Augenblick ist Ewigkeit. Goethestudien.* Leipzig: Koehler & Amelang, 1960.

————. "Tageszeiten, Jahreslauf, Lebensalter in Goethes Lyrik." *Neue Goethe-Studien.* Halle (Saale): Veb. Max Niemeyer Verlag, 1969, pp. 27–49.

Petersen, Julius. *Die Entstehung der Eckermannschen Gespräche und ihre Glaubwürdigkeit.* 2d ed. Deutsche Forschungen, 2. Frankfurt am Main: Verlag Moritz Diesterweg, 1925.

Preisendanz, Wolfgang. *Die Spruchform in der Lyrik des alten Goethe und ihre Vorgeschichte seit Opitz.* Heidelberger Forschungen. Heidelberg: Carl Winter Universitätsverlag, 1952.

Reiss, Hans, ed. *Goethe und die Tradition.* Wissenschaftliche Paperbacks. Literaturwissenschaft, 19. Frankfurt am Main: Athenäum Verlag, 1972.

Reitmeyer, Elisabeth. *Studien zum Problem der Gedichtsammlung mit eingehender Untersuchung der Gedichtsammlungen Goethes und Tiecks.* Sprache und Dichtung, 57. Bern: Paul Haupt, 1935.

Ruppert, Hans, ed. *Goethes Bibliothek. Katalog.* Weimar: Arion Verlag, 1958.

Schadewaldt, Wolfgang. "Goethes Begriff der Realität." *Goethe. Jahrbuch der Goethe-Gesellschaft* (Weimar), 18 (1956), 44–88.

Scherer, Wilhelm "Über die Anordnung Goethescher Schriften." *Goethe Jahrbuch*, 3 (1882), 159–73; 4 (1883), 51–78; 5 (1884), 257–87.

Schmidt, Peter. *Goethes Farbensymbolik. Untersuchungen zu Verwendung und Bedeutung der Farben in den Dichtungen und Schriften Goethes*. Philologische Studien und Quellen, 26. Berlin: Erich Schmidt Verlag, 1965.

Sengle, Friedrich. "Konvention und Ursprünglichkeit in Goethes dichterischen Werken." *Arbeiten zur deutschen Literatur. 1750–1850*. Stuttgart: J. B. Metzlersche Verlagsbuchhandlung, 1965.

Staiger, Emil. *Goethe*. 3 vols. Zürich: Atlantis Verlag, 1959.

Trunz, Erich. "Die Sammelhandschriften von Goethes Gedichten." *Zeitschrift für deutsche Literaturgeschichte*, 6 (1960), 1176–83.

———. "Goethes lyrische Kurzgedichte, 1771–1832." *Goethe. Jahrbuch der Goethegesellschaft* (Weimar), 26 (1964), 1–37.

Viehoff, Heinrich. *Goethes Gedichte erläutert und auf ihre Veranlassungen, Quellen und Vorbilder zurückgeführt*. 3 vols. Düsseldorf: Verlag der Bötticher'schen Buchhandlung, 1846, 1847, 1853.

———. *Goethes Gedichte erläutert und auf ihre Veranlassungen, Quellen und Vorbilder zurückgeführt*. 3rd ed. 3 vols. Stuttgart: Carl Conradi, 1876.

Welz, Dieter. *Selbstsymbolik des alten Goethe*. Deutsche Studien, 17. Meisenheim am Glan: Verlag Anton Hain, 1972.

Willoughby, Leonard. "The Image of the Wanderer and the Hut in Goethe's Poetry." *Études Germaniques*, 6 (1951), 207–19.

Wünsch, Marianne. *Der Strukturwandel in der Lyrik Goethes. Die systemimmanente Relation der Kategorien "Literatur" und "Realität": Probleme und Lösungen*. Studien zur Poetik und Geschichte der Literatur, 37. Stuttgart: W. Kohlhammer Verlag, 1975.

Zastrau, Alfred, ed. *Goethe Handbuch. Goethe, seine Welt und Zeit in Werk und Wirkung*. 2d rev. ed. 4 vols. Stuttgart: J. B. Metzlersche Verlagsbuchhandlung, 1961.

SPECIFIC WORKS

Included in this section are books and articles of specific importance for the indicated work. Not all are, strictly speaking, Goethe literature.

The *Römische Elegien*

Arnim, Hans von. "Entstehung und Anordnung der Römische Elegien Goethes." *Deutsche Revue*, 47 (1922), 121–36.

Atkins, Stuart. "Goethe und die Renaissancelyrik." *Goethe und die Tradition*. Ed. Hans Reiss. Wissenschaftliche Paperbacks. Literaturwissenschaft, 19. Frankfurt am Main: Athenäum Verlag, 1972, pp. 102–29.

Barth, Friedrich Gottlieb. *Vorlesungen über einige Elegien des Properz nebst einer prosaischen Uebersetzung der Königinn aller Elegien*. Dresden: Gröllische Buchhandlung, 1775.

Beißner, Friedrich. *Geschichte der deutschen Elegie*. Grundriß der germanischen Philogie, 14. Berlin: Walter de Gruyter & Co., 1941.

Beutler, Ernst. "Die Renaissance der Antholgie in Weimar." *Vom griechischen*

Epigramm im 18. Jahrhundert. Diss. Leipzig, 1905. Leipzig: R. Voigtländers Verlag, 1909. Teil 2, pp. 48–109. Rpt. in *Das Epigramm. Zur Geschichte einer inschriftlichen und literarischen Gattung*. Ed. Gerhard Pfohl. Darmstadt: Wissenschaftliche Buchgesellschaft, 1969, pp. 352–415.

Bianquis, Geneviève. *Goethe. Élégies Romaines*. Paris: Aubier. Editions Montaigne, 1955.

Bittrich, Louis. "The Modern Roman Elegy." Diss. University of North Carolina, Chapel Hill, 1967.

Blumenthal, Lieselotte. "Schillers und Goethes Anteil an Knebels Properz-Übertragung." *Jahrbuch der deutschen Schillergesellschaft*, 3 (1959), 71–93.

Bronner, Ferdinand. "Goethes Römische Elegien und ihre Quellen." *Neue Jahrbücher für Philologie und Pädagogik*, 148 (1893), 38–50, 102–12, 145–50, 247–65, 305–16, 367–71, 440–69, 525–41, 572–88.

Düntzer, Heinrich. "Goethes elegische Dichtungen in ihrem Rechte." *Neue Jahrbücher für Philologie und Pädagogik*, 90 (1864), 180–201.

Eggerking, Elisabeth. *Goethes Römische Elegien*. Diss. Bonn, 1913. Bonn: Carl Georgi Universitäts-Buchdruckerei, 1913.

Ellinger, Georg. "Goethe und Johannes Secundus." *Goethe Jahrbuch*, 13 (1892), 199–210.

Grumach, Ernst. *Goethe und die Antike*. Berlin: Walter de Gruyter & Co., 1949.

Haile, Harry Gerald. *Artist in Chrysalis. A Biographical Study of Goethe in Italy*. Urbana: University of Illinois Press, 1973.

———. "Prudery in the Publication History of Goethe's *Roman Elegies*." *The German Quarterly*, 49 (1976), 287–94.

Hallowell, Robert E. *Ronsard and the Conventional Roman Elegy*. Illinois Studies in Language and Literature, 37, no. 4. Urbana: University of Illinois Press, 1954.

Hecker, Max. *Faksimile-Ausgabe der Handschrift von Goethes 'Römische Elegien'*. 2 vols. Leipzig: Insel Verlag, 1920.

Heller, Heinrich Justus. "Die antiken Quellen von Goethes elegischen Dichtungen." *Neue Jahrbücher für Philologie und Pädagogik*, 88 (1863), 300–12, 351–71, 401–26, 451–71, 493–519.

———. "Goethes Elegieen und Epigramme und ihre Erklärer." *Neue Jahrbücher für Philologie und Pädagogik*, 92 (1865), 397–418, 466–74, 508–24, 564–75.

Herwig-Hager, Gertrud. "Goethes Properz Begegnung. 'Der Besuch' und Properz I, 3." *Synusia: Festgabe für Wolfgang Schadewaldt zum 15. März 1965*. Ed. Helmut Flashar and Konrad Gaiser. Pfullingen: Verlag Günther Neske, 1965, pp. 429–53.

Jost, Dominik. *Deutsche Klassik. Goethes "Römische Elegien."* Pullach bei München: Verlag Dokumentation, 1974.

Kaiser, Gerhard. "Wandrer und Idylle: Ein Zugang zur zyklischen Ordnung der 'Römische Elegien.'" *Archiv für das Studium der neueren Sprachen und Literaturen*, 202 (1965), 1–27.

Killy, Walther. "Mythologie und Lakonismus in der 1., 3. and 4. Römischen Elegie." *Gymnasium*, 71 (1964), 134–50.

Klinger, Friedrich. "Liebeselegien. Goethes römische Vorbilder." *Römische Geisteswelt*. 4th ed. München: Verlag Heinrich Ellermann, 1961, pp. 419–29.

Lietzmann, Albert. *Goethes Römische Elegien nach der ältesten Reinschrift*. Bonn: A. Marcus und E. Weber's Verlag, 1912.

Lind, Levi Robert, trans. *Johann Wolfgang von Goethe's Roman Elegies and Venetian Epigrams*. Lawrence: The University Press of Kansas, 1974.

Luck, Georg. "Goethes 'Römische Elegien' und die augusteische Liebeselegie." *Arcadia*, 2 (1967), 173–95.

Otto, Regine. "Karl Ludwig von Knebel. Entwürfe zu einer Monographie." Diss. Jena, 1967.

Propertius, Sextus Aurelius, et al. *Catullus, Tibullus, Propertius ad fidem optimorum librorum denuo accurate recensiti adiectum est pervigilium veneris*. Göttingen: A. Vandenhoeck, 1762.

Propertius, Sextus Aurelius. *Elegieen von Properz*. Trans. Karl Ludwig von Knebel. Leipzig: Göschen, 1798.

––––––. *Elegieen des Propertius*. Trans. Friedrich Karl von Strombeck. Braunschweig: Friedrich Vieweg, 1822.

––––––. *Des Sextus Aurelius Propertius Werke*. Trans. Johann Heinrich Voß. Braunschweig: Friedrich Vieweg, 1830.

––––––. *Elegien im Versmaß der Urschrift. Übersetzt und durch Anmerkungen erläutert*. Trans. and ed. Wilhelm Adolf Boguslaw Hertzberg. Stuttgart: J. B. Wetzler'sche Buchhandlung, 1838.

Rehm, Walther. *Europäische Romdichtung*. 2d ed. München: Max Hueber Verlag, 1960.

Requadt, Paul. *Die Bildersprache der deutschen Italiendichtung von Goethe bis Benn*. Bern: Francke Verlag, 1962.

Schaefer, Johann Wilhelm. "Ueber Goethe's römische Elegieen und venetianische Epigramme." *Deutsches Museum*, 1 (1851), 286–90.

Schiller, Friedrich. "Die sentimentalischen Dichter." *Die Horen*, I, no. 12 (1795). Rpt. Darmstadt: Wissenschaftliche Buchgesellschaft, 1959, pp. 1–55 (1379–1433).

Schlegel, Friedrich. "Elegien aus dem Griechischen." *Athenäum* I, no. 1 (1798). Rpt. Darmstadt: Wissenschaftliche Buchgesellschaft, 1960, I, 107–40.

Schroeter, Adalbert. "Beiträge zur Geschichte der neulateinischen Poesie Deutschlands und Hollands." *Palaestra*, 77 (1909), 214–21.

Schuster, Mauriz. *Tibull-Studien*. Wien: Hölder-Pickler-Tempsky A. G., 1930.

Staiger, Emil. "Goethes antike Versmaße." *Die Kunst der Interpretation. Studien zur deutschen Literaturgeschichte*. Zürich: Atlantis Verlag, 1955.

Tibullus, Albius. *Alb. Tibullus. Nebst einer Probe aus dem Properz und den Kriegsliedern des Tyrtäus. In der Versart der Urschrift übersetzt. Mit einem Anhang von eigenen Elegien*. Trans. Karl Friedrich Reinhard. Zürich: Orell, Geßner, Füßli und Comp., 1783.

Trevelyan, Humphrey. *Goethe and the Greeks*. Cambridge: University Press, 1941.

Weissenberger, Klaus. *Formen der Elegie von Goethe bis Celan*. Bern: Francke Verlag, 1969.

Wilhelm, Friedrich. *Zum Fortleben Tibulls bei deutschen Dichtern seit Mitte des 18. Jahrhunderts*. Breslau: Satura Viardrina Altera, 1921.

Wimmel, Walter. "Rom in Goethes Römische Elegien und im letzten Buch des Properz." *Antike und Abendland*, 7 (1958), 121–38.

Wyß, Bernhard. *Heinrich Keller. Der Züricher Bildhauer und Dichter*. Frauenfeld: J. Hubers Buchdruckerei, 1871.

The *Sonette*

Bray, Denys. *Shakespeare's Sonnet-Sequence*. London: The Richards Press, 1938.

Crow, Martha Foote, ed. *Elizabethan Sonnet-Cycles*. London: Kegan Paul, Trench, Trübner & Co., 1896.

Fechner, Jörg-Ulrich. *Das deutsche Sonett. Dichtungen. Gattungspoetik. Dokumente*. München: Wilhelm Fink Verlag, 1969.

Feigel, Theodor. *Vom Wesen der Anakreontik und ihrem Verlauf im Halberstädtischen Dichterkreis mit besonderer Berücksichtigung Klamer Schmidts*. Diss. Marburg, 1909. Cassel: Rich. Trömner, 1909.

Fischer, Kuno. "Goethes Sonettenkranz." *Goethe-Schriften*, 4. Heidelberg: Carl Winter's Universitätsbuchhandlung, 1895, pp. 3–112.

Frommann, Friedrich Johannes. *Das Frommannsche Haus und seine Freunde. 1792–1837*. Jena: Fr. Frommann, 1870.

Hankamer, Paul. *Spiel der Mächte. Ein Kapitel aus Goethes Leben und Goethes Welt*. Tübingen: Rainer Wunderlich Verlag, 1947.

Harris, William O. "Early Elizabethan Sonnets in Sequence." *Studies in Philology*, 68 (1971), 451–69.

Kahn, Ludwig. *Shakespeares Sonette in Deutschland*. Straßburg: Universitätsbuchdruckerei, 1934.

Mönch, Walter. *Das Sonett. Gestalt und Geschichte*. Heidelberg: F. H. Kerle Verlag, 1955.

Müller, Joachim. *Goethes Sonette–Lyrische Epoche und motivische Kontinuität*. Abhandlungen der Sächsischen Akademie der Wissenschaft zu Leipzig. Philologisch-historische Klasse, 58, 3. Berlin: Akademie Verlag, 1966.

Pacini, Lidia. *Petrarca in der deutschen Dichtungslehre vom Barock bis zur Romantik*. Italienische Studien, 1. Köln: Petrarca-Haus, 1936.

Petrarca, Francesco. *Sonnets & Songs. Italian-English Edition*. Trans. Anna Maria Armi. Intro. by Theodor Mommsen. 1946; rpt. New York: Grosset & Dunlap, 1968.

Rassmann, Friedrich. *Sonette der Deutschen*. 3 vols. Braunschweig: Schulbuchhandlung, 1817.

Schlütter, Hans-Jürgen. *Goethes Sonette. Anregung. Entstehung. Intention*. Goethezeit, 1. Bad Homburg v. d. H.: Verlag Gehlen, 1969.

Welti, Heinrich. *Geschichte des Sonettes in der deutschen Dichtung*. Leipzig: Verlag von Veig & Comp., 1884.

Wolff, Hans M. *Goethe in der Periode der Wahlverwandtschaften (1802 bis 1809)*. Bern: A. Francke, 1952.

The *West-östlicher Divan*

Becker, Carl. "Das Buch Suleika als Zyklus." *Varia Variorum. Festgabe für Karl Reinhardt*. Münster: Böhlau Verlag, 1952, pp. 225–52.

Burkhardt, Friedrich. "Über die Anordnung der Gedichte in Goethes West-östlicher Divan." Diss. Mainz, 1965.

Hass, Hans-Egon. "Über die strukturelle Einheit des West-östlichen Divans." *Stil- und Formprobleme in der Literatur. Vorträge des 7. Kongresses der internationalen Vereinigung für moderne Sprache und Literatur*. Ed. Paul Böckmann. Heidelberg: 1959, pp. 309–18.

————. "West-östlicher Divan: Im Gegenwärtigen Vergangnes." *Die deutsche Lyrik. Form und Geschichte*. Ed. Benno von Wiese. Düsseldorf: August Bagel Verlag, 1962. I, 290–317.

Helm, Karin. "Goethes Verskunst im West-östlichen Divan." Diss. Göttingen, 1955.

Henckmann, Gisela. *Gespräch und Geselligkeit in Goethes "West-östlichem Divan."* Stuttgart: Kohlhammer Verlag, 1975.

Hillmann, Ingeborg. *Dichtung als Gegenstand der Dichtung. Untersuchungen zum Problem der Einheit des 'West-östlichen Divans.'* Bonner Arbeiten zur deutschen Literatur, 10. Bonn: H. Bouvier u. Co. Verlag, 1965.

Ihekweazu, Edith. *Goethes West-östlicher Divan. Untersuchungen zur Struktur des lyrischen Zyklus*. Geistes- und Sozialwissenschaftliche Dissertationen, 14. Hamburg: Hartmut Lüdke Verlag, 1971.

Kayser, Wolfgang. "Beobachtungen zur Verskunst des West-östlichen Divans." *Kunst und Spiel. Fünf Goethe-Studien*. Kleine Vandenhoeck-Reihe. Göttingen: Vandenhoeck & Ruprecht, 1961.

Lentz, Wolfgang. *Goethes Noten und Abhandlungen zum West-östlichen Divan*. Hamburg: Verlag J. J. Augustin, 1958.

Lohner, Edgar, ed. *Interpretationen zum West-östlichen Divan Goethes*. Wege der Forschung, 288. Darmstadt: Wissenschaftliche Buchgesellschaft, 1973.

————. *Studien zum West-östlichen Divan Goethes*. Wege der Forschung, 287. Darmstadt: Wissenschaftliche Buchgesellschaft, 1971.

Maier, Hans Albert. *Goethe. West-östlicher Divan. Kommentar*. Tübingen: Max Niemeyer Verlag, 1965.

The Howard poems

Badt, Kurt. "Goethes Wolkengedichte im Zusammenhange mit den Wolkenstudien Constables und anderer zeitgenössischen Maler." *Publications of the English Goethe Society*, 20 (1951), 21–52.

————. *Wolkenbilder und Wolkengedichte der Romantik*. Berlin: Walter de Gruyter & Co., 1960.

Keller, Werner. "Die antwortenden Gegenbilder. Eine Studie zu Goethes Wolkendichtung." *Jahrbuch des Freien Deutschen Hochstifts* (1968), 191–236.

Schöne, Albrecht. "Über Goethes Wolkenlehre." *Jahrbuch der Akademie der Wissenschaften in Göttingen* (1968), 26–48.

Schulze, Max Hans. "Goethe und die Meteorologie." *Wissenschaftliche Annalen*, 6 (1957), 101–16.

Wilhelm Tischbeins Idyllen and *Zu meinen Handzeichnungen*

Bosshardt, Eva. *Goethes späte Landschaftslyrik*. Diss. Zürich, 1962. Zürich: Verlag Lüssi & Co., 1962.

Drost, Willi. *Goethe als Zeichner*. Potsdam: Akademische Verlagsgesellschaft, 1932.

Federmann, Arnold. *Goethe als bildender Künstler*. Stuttgart: Cotta'sche Buchhandlung Nachfolger, 1932.

Kranz, Gisbert. *Das Bildgedicht in Europa. Zur Theorie und Geschichte einer literarischen Gattung*. Paderborn: Ferdinand Schöningh, 1973.

Münz, Ludwig. *Goethes Zeichnungen und Radierungen*. Wien: Österreichische Staatsdruckerei, 1949.

Seligmann, Adalbert Franz. "Goethe als Zeichner." *Chronik des Wiener Goethe-Vereins*, 17 (1903), 21–29.

Trunz, Erich. "Die 'Idyllen' in Goethes und Tischbeins Briefwechsel und Tagebüchern." *Studien zu Goethes Alterswerken*. Ed. Erich Trunz. Goethezeit, 2. Frankfurt am Main: Athenäum Verlag, 1971, pp. 24–34.

————. "Über Goethes Verse und Prosa zu Tischbeins Idyllen." *Studien zu Goethes Alterswerken*. Ed. Erich Trunz. pp. 35–74.

The "Trilogie der Leidenschaft"

Nollendorfs, Valters. "Goethe's 'Elegie.' A Non-Biographical Approach." *Germanic Review*, 40 (1965), 75–86.

————. "Time and Experience in Goethe's *Trilogie der Leidenschaft*." *Husbanding the Golden Grain. Studies in Honor of Henry W. Nordmeyer*. Ed. Luanne Frank and Emery George. Ann Arbor: The University of Michigan Press, 1973, pp. 223–37.

Pfeiffer, Arthur. *Goethes Trilogie der Leidenschaft. Eine Auslegung*. Dichtungswissenschaft, 1. Saarbrücken: Saardruckerei, 1951.

Wilkinson, Elizabeth. *Goethes Trilogie der Leidenschaft als Beitrag zur Frage der Katharsis*. Reihe der Vorträge und Schriften, 18. Frankfurt am Main: Freies deutsches Hochstift, 1957.

The *Chinesisch-deutsche Jahres- und Tageszeiten*

Biedermann, Woldemar, Freiherr von. "Chinesisch-deutsche Jahres- und Tageszeiten." *Goethe-Forschungen*. Neue Folge. Leipzig: F. W. Biedermann, 1886, pp. 426–46.

Burkhardt, Friedrich. "Goethes 'Chinesisch-deutsche Jahres- und Tageszeiten.' Eine Ergänzung zur Entdeckung des biographischen Hintergrunds durch Wolfgang Preisendanz." *Jahrbuch der deutschen Schillergesellschaft*, 13 (1969), 180–95.

En-Lin, Yang. "Goethes 'Chinesisch-deutsche Jahres- und Tageszeiten.'" *Goethe Jahrbuch*, 89 (1972), 154–88.

Fukuda, Hideo. "Über Goethes letzten Gedichtzyklus 'Chinesisch-deutsche Jahres- und Tageszeiten.'" *Doitsu Bungaku*, 22 (1955), 52–62.

Preisendanz, Wolfgang. "Goethes 'Chinesisch-deutsche Jahres- und Tageszeiten.'" *Jahrbuch der deutschen Schillergesellschaft*, 8 (1964), 137–52.

Selden, Elizabeth. "China in German Poetry from 1773–1833." *University of California Publications in Modern Philology*, 25 (1942), i–x, 141–316.

Thoms, Peter Perring, trans. *Hua chien chi. Chinese Courtship, in Verse*. London: Parbury, Allen, and Kingsbury, 1824.

Tscharner, Eduard Horst von. *China in der deutschen Dichtung*. München: E. Reinhardt, 1939.

Trunz, Erich. "Alterslyrik." *Goethe Handbuch. Goethe, seine Welt und Zeit in Werk und Wirkung*. Ed. Alfred Zastrau. 2d rev. ed. Stuttgart: J. B. Metzlersche Verlagsbuchhandlung, 1961, I, 169–78.

―――. "Altersstil." *Goethe Handbuch*. Ed. Alfred Zastrau. I, 178–88.

―――. "Goethes späte Lyrik." *Deutsche Vierteljahrsschrift*, 23 (1949), 409–32.

Viëtor, Karl. "Goethes Altersgedichte." *Geist und Form. Aufsätze zur deutschen Literaturgeschichte*. Bern: Francke Verlag, 1952, pp. 144–93.

Wagner-Dittmar, Christine. "Goethe und die chinesische Literatur." *Studien zu Goethes Alterswerken*. Ed. Erich Trunz. Goethezeit, 2. Frankfurt am Main: Athenäum Verlag, 1971, pp. 122–228.

Author-Title Index

Index of Titles of Goethe's Works

UNIVERSITY OF NORTH CAROLINA
STUDIES IN THE GERMANIC LANGUAGES
AND LITERATURES

45 PHILLIP H. RHEIN. *The Urge to Live. A Comparative Study of Franz Kafka's* Der Prozess *and Albert Camus'* L'Etranger. 2nd printing. 1966. Pp. xii, 124.

50 RANDOLPH J. KLAWITER. *Stefan Zweig. A Bibliography.* 1965. Pp. xxxviii, 191.

51 JOHN T. KRUMPELMANN. *Southern Scholars in Goethe's Germany.* 1965. Pp. xii, 200.

52 MARIANA SCOTT. *The Heliand. Translated into English from the Old Saxon.* 1966. Pp. x, 206.

53 A. E. ZUCKER. *General de Kalb. Lafayette's Mentor.* Illustrated. 1966. Pp. x, 252.

54 R. M. LONGYEAR. *Schiller and Music.* 1966. Pp. x, 202.

55 CLIFFORD A. BERND. *Theodor Storm's Craft of Fiction. The Torment of a Narrator.* 2nd aug. ed. 1966. Pp. xv , 141.

56 RICHARD H. ALLEN. *An Annotated Arthur Schnitzler Bibliography.* 1966. Pp. xiv, 151.

57 EDWIN H. ZEYDEL, PERCY MATENKO, BERTHA M. MASCHE, EDS. *Letters To and From Ludwig Tieck and His Circle.* 1967. Pp. xxiv, 395.

58 *Studies in Historical Linguistics. Festschrift for George S. Lane. Eighteen Essays.* 1967. Pp. xx, 241.

59 WESLEY THOMAS AND BARBARA G. SEAGRAVE. *The Songs of the Minnesinger, Prince Wizlaw of Rügen.* Illustrated. 1967. Pp. x, 157.

60 J. W. THOMAS. *Medieval German Lyric Verse. In English Translation.* 1968. Pp. x, 252.

61 THOMAS W. BEST. *The Humanist Ulrich von Hutten. A Reappraisal of His Humor.* 1969. Pp. x, 105.

62 LIESELOTTE E. KURTH. *Die Zweite Wirklichkeit. Studien zum Roman des achtzehnten Jahrhunderts.* 1969. Pp. x, 273.

63 J. W. THOMAS. *Ulrich von Liechtenstein's Service of Ladies.* 1969. Pp. x, 229.

64 CHARLOTTE CRAIG. *Christoph Martin Wieland as the Originator of the Modern Travesty in German Literature.* 1970. Pp. xii, 147.

65 WOLFGANG W. MOELLEKEN. *Liebe und Ehe. Lehrgedichte Von dem Stricker.* 1970. Pp. xxxviii, 72.

66 ALAN P. COTTRELL. *Wilhelm Müller's Lyrical Song-Cycles. Interpretation and Texts.* 1970. Pp. x, 172.

67 SIEGFRIED MEWS, ED. *Studies in German Literature of the Nineteenth and Twentieth Centuries. Festschrift for Frederic E. Coenen.* Foreword by Werner P. Friederich. 1970. 2nd ed. 1972. Pp. xx, 251.

For other volumes in the "Studies" see page ii and following page.

Send orders to: (U.S. and Canada)
The University of North Carolina Press, P. O. Box 2288
Chapel Hill, N.C. 27514
(All other countries) Feffer and Simons, Inc., 31 Union Square, New York, N.Y. 10003

For other volumes in the "Studies" see preceding page and p. ii.

Send orders to: (U.S. and Canada)
The University of North Carolina Press, P. O. Box 2288
Chapel Hill, N.C. 27514
(All other countries) Feffer and Simmons, Inc., 31 Union Square, New York, N.Y. 10003
Volumes 1–44 and 46–49 of the "Studies" have been reprinted.
They may be ordered from:
AMS Press, Inc., 56 E. 13th Street, New York, N.Y. 10003
For a complete list of reprinted titles write to:
Editor, UNCSGL&L, 442 Dey Hall, 014A, UNC, Chapel Hill, N.C. 27514